BANKING FINANCE & ACCOUNTING

Complied and Edited by:

Alexander Fredrick

Lotus PRESS
4735/22, Prakash Deep Building
Ansari Road, Daryaganj,
New Delhi - 110002

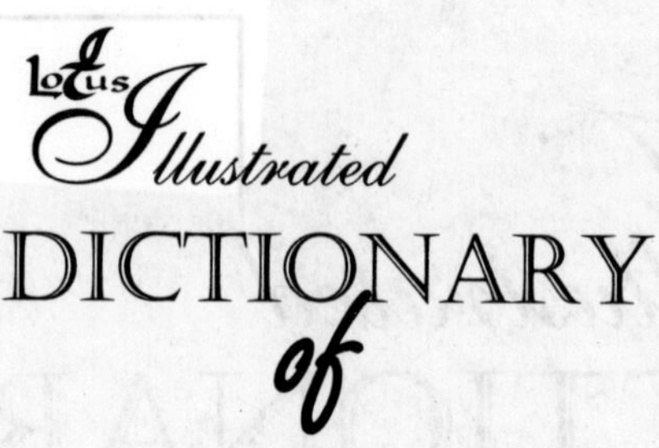

DICTIONARY of BANKING FINANCE & ACCOUNTING

ISBN 81 89093 14 2

Published by:
Lotus Press Publishers & Distributors
Unit No. 220, 2nd Floor, 4735/22,
Prakash Deep Building, Ansari Road, Darya Ganj,
New Delhi- 110002, Ph.: 32903912, 23280047, 09811838000
• E-mail : lotuspress1984@gmail.com www.lotuspress.co.in

Printed at : Bharat Offset Works, Delhi

PREFACE

The origin of banking is shrouded in mystery. But the business of lending money for interest seems to have existed for a long time. It finds mention in the Bible and in Jatak tales.

With the development of large-scale enterprise, banking too expanded in scope. Interest, which the Churches had tried to forbid, gained a respectable place in Europe. Banks in fact became so dominant that Lenin, the Russian revolutionary, thought banks could be used to plan the economy and whosever controlled the banks had the 'commanding heights' of economy in his hands.

Modern economists of neo-classical school seem to concur with this when they put the interest rate at the center of their system of economics. Whether banks should be controlled by the government or by private enterprise is likely to be a bone of contention in the days to come in our country.

Financial operations require a great deal of book - keeping. Greater the member of laws to deal with financial operations, more is the work generated for the accountant. Indian semi-socialist structure requires much accounting and control and accountants are unlikely to face an employment crunch in the near future.

With the admission of foreign banks in India, banking, finance and accounting offer more lucrative careers than ever before.

The dictionary spells out semi-technical words used by bankers. It is useful for commerce students and those involved in banking business. We think it is also very useful for the general reader who will be in a better position to understand the economy section of his daily newspaper if he has the dictionary with him.

■ **'at'/ 'for'**

used in context of general equities. Paramount terms used to differentiate an offering. Stock is offered at; stock is bid for. In an offering, the trading syntax followed is 'Quantity-at-Price'; in a bid, the syntax followed is 'Price-for-Quantity'.

■ **'back up the truck'**

in the context of general equities, 'Prepare for a very large buyer'.

■ **'bring it out'**

in the context of general equities, 'make stock available for sale to indicated buyers'.

■ **'buy them back'**

used for listed equity securities. 'Cover my short position'.

■ **'can get $xxx'**

refers to over-the-counter trading. 'I have a buyer who will pay $xxx for the stock'. Usually a standard markdown (1/8) from $xxx is applied to this price in bidding the seller for its stock. Antithesis of cost me.

■ **'cannot compete'**

in the context of general equities, cannot accommodate customers at that price level (i.e., compete with other market makers), often because there is no natural opposite side of the trade.

■ **'cannot complete'**

in the context of general equities, inability to finish an order on a principal or agency basis, given prevailing price instructions and/or market conditions.

■ **'clean your skirts'**

in the context of general equities, 'make all your obligated calls'; check with all prior obligations in a security. Often preceded by 'subject to'.

■ **'confirm me out'**

used for listed equity securities. 'Go to the floor and check with the specialist or floor broker that my previously active order has been cancelled and was not executed'. One does not have to honour any trade reported after given a 'firm out'.

■ **'cost me'**

refers to over-the-counter trading. 'The price I must pay to obtain the securities you wish to buy is [$]'. Usually, a standard markup (1/8) is then applied for resale to this buyer. Antithesis of can get.

■ **'customer picking prices'**

customer is firm on price and has set the price at which to transact.

■ **'a' shares**

ordinary shares that do not have voting rights.

■ **'10-k' and '10-q'**

financial reports that must be filed by publicly traded corporations, with the Securities and Exchange Commission (SEC). The quarterly reports are called 10Qs. The annual reports are called 10-Ks. Both must follow prescribed formats.

■ **12b-1 fee**

a type of fee charged to investors in some mutual funds. In theory, the fee is supposed to reimburse the sponsor for sales, distribution or shareholder liaison expenses. In reality, however, it is another type of administrative or management fee.

■ 20% director

a director who has actual or potential control of 20% or more of the voting shares of a company.

■ a priori

Latin phrase, meaning, from cause to effect and used generally as 'first impressions'.

■ abandonment

controlling party giving up rights to property voluntarily.

■ abandonment option

the option of terminating an investment earlier than originally planned.

■ abatement

a proportionate reduction in payments, payable or receivable.

■ ability to pay

refers to the borrower's ability to make interest and principal payments on debts. In context of municipal bonds, refers to the issuer's present and future ability to create sufficient tax revenue to fulfill its contractual obligations, accounting for municipal income and property values. In context of taxation, notions that tax rates should be determined according to income or wealth.

■ abnormal returns

the component of the return that is not due to systematic influences (market-wide influences.) In other words, abnormal returns are above those predicted by the market movement alone.

■ above par

see **par**.

■ above the line

the 'line' is in fact a figure showing net income or net profit in income statements or profit and loss accounts.

■ ABS

1. initials for Asset-Backed Security. The name for a convention used to express the rate of prepayments for an asset-backed security. ABS expresses principal prepayments as a percentage of the original number of loans or contracts in the pool of securitised loans that created the security. ABS is always expressed as a monthly rate.

■ absolute priority

rule in bankruptcy proceedings requiring senior creditors to be paid in full before junior creditors receive any payment.

■ absolute title

ownership of registered land, where the State guarantees that no one has better right to the land. Absolute leasehold title guarantees that the less or has title to grant the lease.

■ absolute trust

a trust where the Trustee has no obligation except to pass the trust assets to the beneficiaries at their request, e.g. upon reaching majority.

absorbed

used in context of general equities. Securities are 'absorbed' as long as there are corresponding orders to buy and sell. The market has reached the absorption point when further assimilation is impossible without an adjustment in price.

absorption

a term used by real estate lenders and developers, to describe the process of renting up newly built or renovated office space or apartments. The term 'absorption period' is often used to describe the period of time necessary for absorption.

abstract of title

1. a written report summarising the history of title transactions and conditions of title, that affect a given piece of land, covering the period from the present back to a date in the past.
2. A comprehensive, but cumbersome and somewhat obsolete, method of verifying the ownership and encumbrances of a parcel or parcels of real estate.
3. Details of the legal document proving an owners right to dispose off the land.
4. Such detail is usually supplied prior to completion on a mortgage and will be compared with the original documents, upon completion.

Accelerated Cost Recovery System (ACRS)

schedule of depreciation rates allowed for tax purposes.

accelerated depreciation

1. a group of methods for achieving periodic reductions in the book value of fixed assets, that make larger reductions in the early periods and progressively smaller reductions in later periods. The offsetting entry is the depreciation expense.
2. Method that records greater depreciation than straight-line depreciation, in the early years, and less depreciation than straight-line, in the later years, of an asset's holding period.

acceleration

making demand for payment in full, for a debt that has not yet matured. Usually, a remedy provided in a loan document for the lender, to use in the event of default by the borrower.

acceleration clause

a provision in a loan document stating that the entire amount of unpaid indebtedness owed to the lender may become immediately due and payable if the borrower defaults.

acceptance

a time draft that has been accepted for payment.

acceptance letter

a document issued by life insurance companies, in response to an application for cover. Deemed to be a counter offer valid for a limited period only, it details the amount of cover and the terms on which the insurer is willing to proceed. The proposer accepts the terms by payment of first premium.

■ **accessions**

goods that are physically united with other goods, in such a manner that the identity of the original goods is not lost. An example is a new motor in a piece of equipment.

■ **accommodation maker**

name used to refer to a co-maker who agrees to sign a note to induce the lender to make a loan, but who receives no direct benefit from the loan.

■ **account**

formal record that represents, in words, money or other unit of measurement, certain resources, claims to such resources, transactions or other events that result in changes to those resources and claims.

■ **account analysis**

an analysis performed to determine the profitability of each demand account to the bank. The analysis may also be used to determine the profitability of a group of demand accounts with the same owner. Account analysis is normally performed by the bank, but can be done by anyone in the depositor's organisation, provided sufficient information is available. The analysis identifies the net earnings, based on the average daily ledger balance less reserved requirements and float. The net earnings can then be compared with the various activity service charges, based on the volume of transactions and the per item price of the services.

■ **account balance**

credits minus debits at the end of a reporting period.

■ **account debtor**

an individual or business that is obligated to pay on an account, chattel paper, contract right or general intangible.

■ **account executive**

the brokerage firm employee who handles stock orders for clients. See **broker.**

■ **account payable**

amount owed to a creditor for delivered goods or completed services.

■ **account receivable**

claim against a debtor for an uncollected amount, generally from a completed transaction of sales or services rendered.

■ **account reconciliation**

the reviewing and adjusting of the balance in a personal checkbook to match your bank statement.

■ **account reconciliation services**

a cash management service. One or more of a series of bank services designed to aid a deposit customer in the reconciliation of its bank account balance. A basic account reconciliation service may simply be a listing of paid cheques in serial number order. More advanced account reconciliation services combine electronic data provided by the customer, with the bank's records, to reconcile completely the account and list all outstanding items. Many variations exist. Also called account recs, ARPs or recons.

■ account statement

in the context of banking, refers to a summary of all balances. In the context of securities, a summary of all transactions and positions (long and short) between a broker/dealer and a client.

■ accountant

person skilled in the recording

and reporting of financial transactions.

■ accountant's opinion

a signed statement from an independent public accountant after examination of a firm's records and accounts. The opinion may be unqualified or qualified.

■ accountants' report

formal document that communicates an independent account-ant's: (a) expression of limited assurance on financial statements, as a result of performing inquiry and analytic procedures, (b) results of procedures performed (Agreed-Upon Procedures Report), (c) non-expression of opinion or any form of assurance on a presentation, in the form of financial statements information that is the representation of management (Compilation Report) and (d) an opinion on an assertion made by management, in accordance with the Statements on Standards for Attestation Engagements (Attestation Report). An accountants' report does not result from the performance of an audit.

■ accounting

recording and reporting of financial transactions, including the origination of the transaction, its recognition, processing and summarisation in the financial statements.

■ accounting change

change in: (a) an accounting principle, (b) an accounting estimate or (c) the reporting entity that necessitates disclosure and explanation in published financial reports.

■ accounting earnings

earnings of a firm as reported on its income statement.

■ accounting exposure

the change in the value of a firm's foreign currency-denominated accounts due to a change in exchange rates.

■ accounting insolvency

total liabilities exceed total assets. A firm with a negative net worth is insolvent on the books.

■ accounting liquidity
the ease and quickness with which assets can be converted to cash.

■ accounting period
the period of time from one balance sheet date to the next.

■ accounts
a record of the financial data relating to a particular asset, liability, income item, expense item or net-worth item.

■ accounts payable
money owed to suppliers.

■ accounts receivable
money owed by customers.

■ accounts receivable - trade
also called trade receivables. Amounts due from the credit sales of goods or services that are not evidenced by promissory notes.

■ accounts receivable financing
a short-term financing method in which accounts receivable are collateral for cash advances.

■ accounts receivable turnover
the ratio of net credit sales to average accounts receivable, which is a measure of how quickly customers pay their bills.

■ accreting swap
an interest rate swap with an increasing notional amount.

■ accretion
1. the process of making incremental, periodic increases in the book or carrying value of an asset. For example, when a bond is purchased at a price below 100, the difference between the purchase price and the par value, the discount, is accreted. Discounts are usually accreted in roughly equal amounts that completely eliminate the discount, by the time that the bond has matured or by the call date, if applicable.
2. Increase in the value of an asset through natural physical changes, rather than the usual market forces of supply and demand, e.g. timber.

■ accretion (of a discount)
in portfolio accounting, a straight-line accumulation of capital gains on a discount bond in anticipation of receipt of par at maturity.

■ accrual
a payment incurred in one period, but not paid until the next.

■ accrual accounting
the system of accounting for income and expenditure when earned or incurred, irrespective of the actual time the money changes hands.

■ accrual basis
method of accounting that recognises revenue when earned, rather than when collected. Expenses are recognised when incurred rather than when paid.

■ accrual bond
1. bonds that pay the investor an above-market coupon rate, as long as a reference rate is between pre-set levels established at the time

the security is issued. A type of structured note. Also called range bonds.
2. A type of CMO security that does not pay the holders periodic interest in cash. Instead, periodic interest for these bonds is accrued. It is added to the principal amount due to the holder at a later date.
3. A bond on which interest accrues but is not paid to the investor during the time of accrual. The amount of accrued interest is added to the remaining principal of the bond and is paid at maturity.

■ accrued benefits

the pension benefits earned by an employee according to the years of the employee's service.

■ accrued interest

interest that has been earned but not yet paid. For example, the interest earned by a bondholder between semi-annual coupon payments or the interest earned by a lender since the last monthly interest payment was collected from the borrower.

■ accrued market discount

the rise in the market value of a discount bond as it approaches maturity (when it is redeemable at par) and not because of falling market interest rates.

■ accumulate

broker/analyst recommendation that could mean slightly different things depending on the broker/analyst. In general, it means to increase the number of shares of a particular security over the near term, but not to liquidate other parts of the portfolio to buy a security that might skyrocket. A buy recommendation, but not an urgent buy.

■ Accumulated Benefit Obligation (ABO)

the actuarial present value of the pension benefits earned to date. Measurement of the accumulated benefit obligation uses the historical compensation rates for pay-related benefit plans. The ABO must be disclosed in a footnote to the financial statements.

■ accumulated depreciation

1. the total of the periodic reductions for depreciation in fixed assets. Also called allowance for depreciation.
2. Total depreciation pertaining to an asset or group of assets from the time the assets were placed in services until the date of the financial statement or tax return.

■ accumulated dividend

a dividend that has reached its due date, but is not paid out.

■ accumulated profits tax

a tax on earnings kept in a firm to prevent the higher personal income tax rate that would obtain if profits were paid out as dividends to the owners.

■ accumulation

in the context of corporate finance, refers to profits that are added to the capital base of the company rather than paid out as dividends. See **accumulated profits tax**. In the context of investments, refers to the purchase by an institutional broker of a large number of shares over a period of time in order to avoid pushing the price of that share up. In the context of mutual funds, refers to the regular investing of a fixed amount while reinvesting dividends and capital gains.

■ **accumulation and maintenance trusts**

a trust in which any investment return or deposit interest accumulates and is used to support/educate the beneficiaries without disposal of the capital.

■ **accumulation area**

a price range within which a buyer accumulates shares of a stock.

■ **acid test**

a stern measure of a company's ability to pay its short term debts, in that stock is excluded from asset value. (liquid assets/current liabilities) Also referred to as the Quick Ratio.

■ **acid test ratio**

also called the quick ratio, the ratio of current assets minus inventories, accruals, and prepaid items to current liabilities.

■ **acorn**

a Classification Of Residential Neighbourhoods. A market research method for targeting and selecting buying indicators of particular neighbourhoods.

■ **acquired surplus**

the surplus acquired when a company is purchased in a pooling of interests combination, i.e. the net worth not considered being capital stock.

■ **acquiree**

a firm that is being acquired.

■ **acquisition**

when a firm buys another firm.

■ **acquisition cost**

the price (including the closing costs) to purchase another company or property. In the context of investments, refers to price plus brokerage commissions, of a security, or the sales charge applied to load funds.

■ **acquisition of assets**

a merger or consolidation in which an acquirer purchases the selling firm's assets.

■ **acquisition of stock**

a merger or consolidation in which an acquirer purchases the acquiree's stock.

■ **across the board**

movement or trend in the stock market that affects almost all stocks in all sectors to move in the same direction.

■ **act of god**

circumstances brought about by the forces of nature, unforeseen by reasonable foresight and not involving human influence.

■ **act of state doctrine**

this doctrine says that a nation is sovereign within its own borders, and its domestic actions may not be questioned in the courts of another nation.

■ **acting in concert**

investors working together and performing identical actions to attain the same investment goal.

■ **active**

a market in which there is frequent trading.

■ **active account**

a brokerage account in which many transactions occur. Brokerage firms may levy a fee if an account generates an inadequate level of activity.

■ **active box**

securities that are held in safekeeping and are available as collateral for securing brokers' loans or customers' margin positions.

■ **active portfolio strategy**

a strategy that uses available information and forecasting techniques to seek better performance than a buy and hold portfolio.

■ **Activities of Daily Living (ADL)**

generally used as a basis for assessing claims under a long term care contract. ADLs are considered to be basic activities essential to an active adult existence, e.g. eating, dressing, bathing, using the toilet, getting in and out of bed, walking, climbing stairs.

■ **actual market**

used in context of general equities. Firm market. Antithesis of Subject market.

■ **actuals**

the physical commodities underlying a futures contract. Cash commodity, physical asset.

■ **actuary**

a person who assesses risks and costs, in particular those relating to life assurance and investment policies, using a combination of statistical and mathematical techniques.

■ **A-D**

Advance-Decline, or measurement of the number of issues trading above their previous closing prices less the number trading below their previous closing prices over a particular period. As a technical measure of market breadth, the steepness of the A-D line indicates whether a strong bull or bear market is under way.

■ **ad hoc**

latin: 'for this particular purpose'.

■ **ad valorem**

latin: 'according to value'. For example, an ad valorem tax or duty will be calculated according to the value of whatever is being taxed, as a percentage rather than a flat rate.

■ added value

an increase in real value, resulting from changes in the makeup/content of goods or services.

■ additional bonds test

a test for ensuring that bond issuers can meet the debt service requirements of issuing any new additional bonds.

■ additional hedge

a protection against borrower fallout risk in the mortgage pipeline.

■ additional paid in capital

amounts paid for stock in excess of its par value or stated value. Also, other amounts paid by stockholders and charged to equity accounts other than capital stock.

■ adequacy of coverage

a test that measures the extent to which the value of an asset is protected from potential loss either through insurance or hedging.

■ adjustable rate

applies mainly to convertible securities. Refers to interest rate or dividend that is adjusted periodically, usually according to a standard market rate outside the control of the bank or savings institution, such as that prevailing on Treasury bonds or notes. Typically, such issues have a set floor or ceiling; called caps and collars that limits the adjustment.

■ Adjustable-Rate Mortgage (ARM)

a loan for which the interest rate (coupon rate) is adjusted periodically, to reflect changes in a previously selected index rate. ARMs may have caps and floors that limit the annual and/or the lifetime change in the coupon rate.

■ Adjustable-Rate Preferred Stock (ARPS)

publicly traded issues that may be collateralised by mortgages and MBS

■ adjusted balance method

method of calculating finance charges that uses the account balance remaining after adjusting for all transactions posted during the given billing period as its basis. Related: Average Daily Balance method, previous balance method, past due balance method.

■ adjusted basis

price from which to calculate and derive capital gains or losses upon sale of an asset. Account actions such as any stock splits that have occurred since the initial purchase must be accounted for.

■ Adjusted Debit Balance (ADB)

the account balance for a margin account that is calculated by combining the balance owed to a broker with any outstanding balance in the special miscellaneous account, and any paper profits on short accounts.

■ adjusted exercise price

the final exercise price of the option accounts for the coupon rates carried on Ginnie Mae mortgages. For example, if the standard

GNMA mortgage has a 9% yield, the price of GNMA pools with 13% mortgages in them is altered so that the investor receives the same yield.

■ Adjusted Gross Income (AGI)

gross income less allowable adjustments, is the income on which an individual is taxed by the federal government.

■ Adjusted Present Value (APV)

the net present value analysis of an asset if financed solely by equity (present value of unleveled cash flows), plus the present value of any financing decisions (levered cash flows). In other words, the various tax shields provided by the deductibility of interest and the benefits of other investment tax credits are calculated separately. This analysis is often used for highly leveraged transactions such as a leveraged buyout.

■ adjustment bond

a bond issued in exchange for outstanding bonds when a corporation facing bankruptcy is recapitulated.

■ administered rates

interest rates that the bank or other payer is contractually permitted to change at any time and by any amount. For example, the rates paid on savings accounts. All interest rates can be categorised as either fixed, administered or floating. Rates that may change at the payer's discretion are sometimes called variable rates, easily confused with floating rates, which change at contractually specified times by contractually specified amounts.

■ administrative float

float resulting from the time it takes to administratively process cheques or other related paperwork. Total elapsed time for processing cheques can range from less than a day to more than a week. Note that its basic elements are present, whether the work is done by the owner of the funds or the work is done by a bank or other lockbox vendor. Sometimes referred to as payment processing float or internal float, but since some of the sources of the float delay are not necessarily internal, the term internal float is not a completely accurate synonym.

■ administrative pricing rules

IRS rules used to allocate income on export sales to a foreign sales corporation.

■ administrative review

one of two types of real estate appraisal reviews. Administrative reviews focus primarily on the underwriting issues addressed in the appraisal. These reviews, usually performed by the loan officer, approach the appraisal from a loan underwriting point of view. Typical issues addressed in an administrative review include: How comparable are the comparable properties used in the appraisal? How reasonable are income and expense projections? Is the capitalisation rate appropriate?

■ administrator

in pension scheme terms, the person or body responsible for the management of an occupational pension scheme. Required for all exempt approved pension schemes.

■ advance

increase in the market price of stocks, bonds, commodities, or other assets.

■ advance commitment

a promise to sell an asset before the seller has lined up purchase of the asset. This seller can offset risk by purchasing a future's contract to fix the sales price approximately.

■ advance formula

a provision sometimes used in lines of credit, as a sub-limit on the maximum amount that can be borrowed. Typically, an advance formula limits the amount that can be borrowed under a line of credit to the lesser of the amount of the line or some percent of accounts receivable collateral.

■ advance funded pension plan

a pension plan in which funds are set aside in advance of the date of retirement.

■ advance refunding

in the context of municipal bonds, refers to the sale of new bonds (the refunding issue) before the first call date of old bonds (the issue to be refunded). The refunding issue usually specifies a rate lower than the issue to be refunded, and the proceeds are invested, usually in government securities, until the higher-rate bonds become callable.

■ advances

funds received for goods or services, prior to the delivery of the goods or services. Typically, the funds must be returned if the transaction is cancelled or if the recipient of the advance fails to provide the goods or services.

■ adverse opinion

an independent auditor's opinion expressing that a firm's financial statements do not reflect the company's position accurately.

■ adverse selection

a situation in which sellers have relevant information that buyers lack (or vice versa) about some aspect of product quality.

■ advertising standards authority

independent body set up by the advertising industry, which overseas a self-regulatory code of advertising standards. All advertising must be legal, decent, honest and truthful.

■ advertorial

hybrid copy consisting of an advertisement written in newspaper editorial form.

■ advisory letter

a newsletter offering financial advice to its readers.

■ affidavit

a written statement, sworn or confirmed as true before an

authorised person, which may be used in support of certain applications or as evidence in court.

■ **affiliate**

a business organisation that shares some aspect of common ownership or control with another business organisation.

■ **affiliated company**

company or other organisation related through common ownership, common control of management or owners, or through some other control mechanism, such as a long-term lease.

■ **affiliated corporation**

a corporation that is an affiliate to the parent company.

■ **affiliated person**

an individual who possesses enough influence and control in a corporation as to be able to alter the actions of the corporation.

■ **affinity card**

a card that is offered jointly by two organisations. One is a credit card issuer and the other is a professional association, special interest group or other non-bank company. For example, Citibank and American Airlines sponsor the Citibank Advantage card.

■ **affirmative covenant**

1. a provision in the lender's documents that requires the borrower to do something in the future. For example, a requirement for the borrower to provide annual audited financial statements to the bank during the term of the loan.

2. A bond covenant that specifies certain actions the firm must take.

■ **affordability index**

an index that measures the financial ability of consumers to purchase a home.

■ **affordable growth rate**

the maximum rate at which a firm's sales can grow, without straining the capacity of the firm's capital or other financial resources. This term is closely associated with a formula of the same name.

■ **after acquired clause**

a contractual clause in a mortgage agreement stating that any additional mortgageable property attained by the borrower after the mortgage is signed will be regarded as additional security for the obligation addressed in the mortgage.

■ **after-acquired property clause**

a provision in a bank's documents, the purpose of which is to extend the bank's interest in the debtor's property, to property not owned by the debtor at the time of the transaction, but subsequently acquired by the debtor.

■ **after-hours dealing or trading**

securities trading after regular trading hours on organised exchanges.

■ **aftermarket**

see **secondary market**.

■ **after-tax basis**

the comparison basis used to analyse the net after-tax returns on a corporate taxable bond and a municipal tax-free bond.

■ after-tax profit margin

the ratio of net income to net sales.

■ after-tax real rate of return

the after-tax rate of return minus the inflation rate.

■ age allowance

personal allowance against income for a person aged 65 or over. The age allowance increases for a person of 75 or more, but is reduced if income exceeds a certain level.

■ aged fail

an account between two broker/dealers that remains intact after 30 days after the settlement date. The receiving firm must adjust its capital, as it can no longer treat this account as assets.

■ agency

in context of general equities, buying or selling for the account and risk of a customer. Generally, an agent, or broker, acts as intermediary between buyer and seller, taking no financial risk personally or as a firm, and charging a commission for the service. The broker represents a customer buyer/seller to a customer seller/buyer and does not act as principal for the firm's own trading account. Antithesis of principal.

■ agency basis

a means of compensating the broker of a program trade solely on the basis of commission established through bids submitted by various brokerage firms.

■ agency cost view

the argument that specifies that the various agency costs create a complex environment in which total agency costs are at a minimum with some, but less than 100%, debt financing.

■ agency costs

the incremental costs of having an agent make decisions for a principal.

■ agency fund

fund consisting of assets, where the holder agrees to remit the assets, income from the assets or both, to a specified beneficiary in due course or at a specified time.

■ agency incentive arrangement

a means of compensating the broker of a program trade using benchmark prices for issues to be traded in determining commissions or fees.

■ agency problem

conflicts of interest among stockholders, bondholders, and managers.

■ agency theory

the analysis of principal-agent relationships, in which one person, an agent, acts on behalf of another person, a principal.

■ agent

a person who represents someone else.

■ aggregate exercise price

the exercise price multiplied by the number of shares in a put or call contract. The option premium is excluded in the aggregate exercise price. In the case of options traded on debt instruments, the aggregate exercise price is the exercise price of the underlying security multiplied by its face value.

■ aggregation

process in corporate financial planning whereby the smaller investment proposals of each of the firm's operational units are aggregated and effectively treated as a whole.

■ aggressive growth mutual fund

a mutual fund designed for maximum capital appreciation that places its money in companies with high growth rates.

■ aggressively

used in context of general equities. For a customer it means working to buy or sell one's stock, with an emphasis on execution over price. For a trader it means acting in a way that puts the firm's capital at higher risk through paying a higher price, selling cheaper, or making a larger short sale or purchase than the trader would under normal circumstances.

■ aging

a report or schedule of all outstanding accounts payable or accounts receivable, that lists all account debtors or creditors by name, shows the total amount due to each debtor and shows how much of the amount due to each debtor is due within specific time periods.

■ aging schedule

a table of accounts receivable broken down into age categories (such as 0-30 days, 30-60 days, and 60-90 days), which is used to determine if customer payments are keeping close to schedule.

■ agreement among underwriters

a contract among participating members of a syndicate that defines the members' proportionate liability, which is usually limited to and based on the participants' level of involvement. The contract outlines the payment schedule on the settlement date. Compare: Underwriting agreement.

■ ahead of itself

in context of general equities, refers to equities that are overbought or oversold on a fundamental basis.

■ ahead of you

used for listed equity securities. At the same price but entered ahead of your order/interest, usually referring to the specialist's book.

■ AIMR

The Association for Investment Management and Research (AIMR) Performance Presentation Standards Implementation Committee is charged with the responsibility to interpret, revise, and update the AIMR Performance Presentation Standards (AIMR-PPS(TM) for portfolio performance presentations.

■ air pocket stock

a stock whose price drops precipitously, often on the unexpected news of poor results.

■ alien corporation

a company incorporated under the laws of a foreign country regardless of where the company conducts its operations.

■ all equity rate

the discount rate that reflects only the business risks of a project, distinct from the effects of financing.

■ all in

an issuer's interest rate after accounting for commissions and various related expenses.

■ All Or None Order (AON)

used in context of general equities. A limited price order that is to be executed in its entirety or not at all (no partial transaction), and thus is testing the strength/conviction of the counter party. Unlike an FOK order, an AON order is not to be treated as cancelled if not executed as soon as it is represented in the trading crowd, but instead remains alive until executed or cancelled. The making of 'all or none' bids or offers in stocks is prohibited, and the making of 'all or none' bids or offers in bonds is subject to the restrictions of Rule 61. AON orders are not shown on the specialist's book because they cannot be traded in pieces. Antithesis of any-part-of order.

■ alligator spread

the term used to describe a spread in the options market that generates such a large commission that the client is unlikely to make a profit even if the markets move as the investor anticipated.

■ all-in cost

total costs, explicit and implicit.

■ allocation

the amount of premium actually used to purchase units. Under various charging structures, less than the full premium will be allocated for investment in the early years of the contract. Asset allocation is the spread of fund investments between different sectors.

■ allonge

a paper attached to negotiable instruments for signatures, when there isn't enough room on the instruments themselves for the signatures.

■ all-or-none underwriting

an arrangement whereby a security issue is cancelled if the underwriter is unable to resell the entire issue.

■ allotment

the number of securities assigned to each of the participants in an underwriting syndicate.

■ allowance

1. when taken in the context of 'tax allowance', it is a figure which reduces income which would otherwise be subject to tax.

2. Reductions to gross sales, that occur when customers are given partial credit for sold goods that the buyer is not satisfied with. An accounting term usually used together with returns.

■ allowance for doubtful accounts

a reserve for accounts receivable that may not be collectable. The allowance is always shown as a reduction from gross receivables used to calculate net receivables. An example of a contra-asset account.

■ alpha

measure of risk-adjusted performance.

■ alpha equation

regression usually run over 36-60 months of data: Return-Treasury bill= alpha + beta (S&P 500 - Treasury bill) + error. The alpha is the intercept. Note that the benchmark does not necessarily have to be the S&P 500. A mutual fund specialising in international investment might be benchmarked to a broader world market index, such as the MSCI World Index.

■ alphabet stock

categories of common stock of a corporation associated with a particular subsidiary resulting from acquisitions and restructuring. The various alphabetical categories have different voting rights and pay dividends tied to the operating performance of the particular divisions.

■ alternative mortgage instruments

variations of mortgage instruments such as adjustable-rate and variable-rate mortgages, graduated-payment mortgages, reverse-annuity mortgages, and several seldom-used variations.

■ alternative order

used in context of general equities. Order giving a broker a choice between two courses of action, either to buy or sell, never both. Execution of one course automatically eliminates the other. An example is a combination buy limit/buy stop order, where the buy limit is below the current market and the buy stop is above. If the order is for one unit of trading, when one part of the order is executed on the occurrence of one alternative, the order on the other alternative is to be treated as cancelled. If the order is for an amount of more than one unit of trading, the number of units executed determines the amount of the alternative order to be treated as cancelled.

■ amortisation

1. the process of making regular, periodic decreases in the book or carrying value of an asset. For example, when a bond is purchased at a price above 100, the difference between the purchase price and the par value, the premium, is amortised. Premiums are usually amortised in roughly equal amounts that completely eliminate the premium, by the time that the

bond has matured or by the call date, if applicable.
2. Liquidation of a loan or security by means of periodic reductions. The principal amount of loans is amortised by the periodic, usually monthly, payment of a fraction of the principal, calculated to repay the entire amount of principal due by the date of the last scheduled periodic payment. Amortisation methods differ based upon the type of loan.

■ amortisation period

for financial instruments, the time from the inception of a loan or investment instrument with scheduled principal repayments to the due date of the final contractually obligated principal repayment. For fixed assets, it is the period from the acquisition of a fixed asset to the date of the last periodic reduction (made to reflect depreciation) of the book value of that asset. (Assets may be depreciated until the book value is zero, but sometimes are only depreciated until the book value is reduced to an assumed salvage value.)

■ amortise

to write off a debt over a period of time, by putting aside regular fixed amounts. Or, to depreciate or write down the value of an asset over two or more accounting periods.

■ amortising swap

an interest rate swap with a declining notional principal.

■ amortisation factor

the pool factor implied by the scheduled amortisation assuming no prepayments.

■ amortising interest rate swap

swap in which the principal or notional amount rises (falls) as interest rates rise (decline).

■ amtel

used in context of general equities. In-house message system entered and displayed through Quotron A page.

■ analyst

employee of a brokerage or fund management house who studies companies and makes buy-and-sell recommendations on stocks of these companies. Most specialise in a specific industry.

■ analytical procedures

substantive tests of financial information, which examine relationships among data as a means of obtaining evidence. Such procedures include: (a) comparison of financial information with information of comparable prior periods, (b) comparison of financial information with anticipated results (e.g., forecasts), (c) study of relationships between elements of financial information that should conform to predictable patterns based on the entity's experience and (d) comparison of financial information with industry norms.

■ and interest

an indication that the buyer will receive accrued interest in addition to the price quoted for a bond.

■ angel

an investment-grade bond. Antithesis to fallen angel. In the context of venture capital, the first investor.

■ angels

individuals providing venture capital.

■ ankle biter

stock issued with a market capitalisation of less than $500 million.

■ announcement date

date on which particular news concerning a given company is announced to the public. Used in event studies, which researchers use to evaluate the economic impact of events of interest.

■ annual basis

the technique in statistics of taking a figure covering a period of less than one year and extrapolating it to cover a full one year period. The process is known as annualising.

■ annual effective yield

see **annual percentage yield**.

■ annual exclusion

a tax rule allowing the deduction of certain income from taxation.

■ annual fund operating expenses

for investment companies, the management fee and 'other expenses', including the expenses for maintaining shareholder records, providing shareholders with financial statements, and providing custodial and accounting services. For 12b-1 funds, selling and marketing costs are also included.

■ annual general meeting

the yearly meeting of the shareholders, called by the board of directors of a company. It is the shareholders' chance to have a say in the way their company is run.

■ annual management charge

general term for a charge levied on an investment fund, for its management and administration.

■ annual meeting

meeting of stockholder held once a year at which the managers of a company report to the stockholders on the year's results.

■ Annual Percentage Rate (APR)

1. standard measure of true interest on a loan measured over one year, reflecting the cost of paying on a monthly basis.

2. The periodic rate times the number of periods in a year. For

example, a 5% quarterly return has an A.P.R. of 20%.

Annual Percentage Yield (APY)

a precisely calculated measure of yield paid on a bank deposit account.

annual rate of return

there are many ways of calculating the annual rate of return. If the rate of return is calculated on a monthly basis, we sometimes multiply this by 12 to express an annual rate of return. This is often called the annual percentage rate (APR). The annual percentage yield (APY), includes the effect of compounding interest.

annual renewable term insurance

see **term insurance.**

annual report

report to the stockholders of a company, which includes the company's annual, audited balance sheet and related statements of earnings, stockholders' or owners' equity and cash flows, as well as other financial and business information.

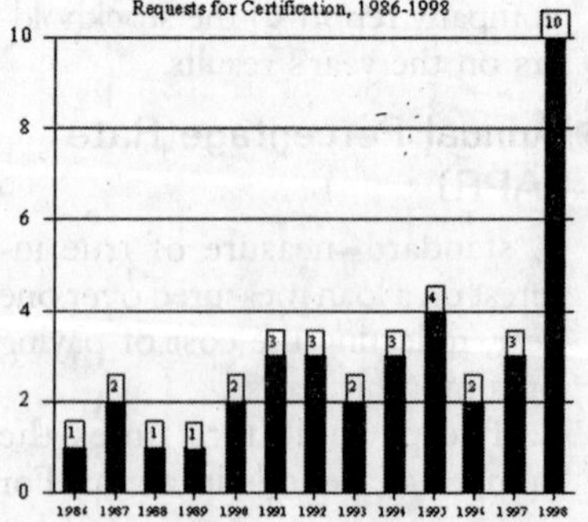

annualised gain

if stock X appreciates 1.5% in one month, the annualised gain for that stock over a twelve month period is 121.5% = 18%. Compounded over the 12 month period, the gain is (1.015)^12 -1 = 19.6%.

annualised holding-period return

the annual rate of return that when compounded times generates the same *t*-period holding return as actually occurred from period 1 to period *t*.

annualising

see **annual basis.**

annuitant

an individual who receives benefits from an annuity.

annuities

1. contracts that guarantee income, often for an individual's lifetime, in exchange for a lump sum or periodic payment. Annuity contracts have a number of standard variants, including deferred, fixed, immediate or variable.
2. to commence a series of payments from the capital that has accumulated in an annuity. The payments may be a fixed amount, for a fixed period of time, or for a lifetime.

annuity

a regular periodic payment made by an insurance company to a policyholder for a specified period of time.

■ **annuity certain**

an annuity that pays a specific amount on a monthly basis for a set amount of time.

■ **annuity deferral**

also called Income Drawdown or Income Withdrawal. The option to take income directly from a pension fund at retirement, instead of purchasing an annuity immediately.

■ **annuity due**

an annuity with *n* payments, where the first payment is made at time $t = 0$, and the last payment is made at time $t = n - 1$.

■ **annuity factor**

present value of $1 paid for each of *t* periods.

■ **annuity in arrears**

an annuity with a first payment one full period hence, rather than immediately.

■ **annuity mortgage**

more usually called a 'repayment mortgage', but sometimes referred to in these terms because of the make up of the payments, i.e. as with some annuities, a mix of capital and interest.

■ **annuity starting date**

the date when an annuitant starts receiving payments from an annuity.

■ **anticipated expenditure**

uncompleted or undelivered portion of a purchase commitment.

■ **anticipated holding period**

the period of time an individual expects to hold an asset.

■ **anticipation**

paying what is owed before it is due (usually to save interest charges).

■ **anticipatory hedge**

a hedge of a yet-to-be-acquired asset or liability.

■ **anti-dilution**

condition that may increase the computation of Earnings Per Share (EPS) or decrease loss per share, solely because of the inclusion of common stock equivalents, such as stock options, warrants, convertible debt or convertible preferred stock, nomination or selection of the independent auditors.

■ **antidilutive effect**

result of a transaction that increases earnings per common share (e.g., by decreasing the number of shares outstanding).

■ **any-interest-date**

a call provision in a municipal bond indenture that establishes the right of redemption for the issuer on any interest payment due date.

■ **any-or-all bid**

often used in risk arbitrage. Takeover bid in which the acquirer offers to pay a set price for all outstanding shares of the target company, or any part thereof; contrasts with two-tier bid.

■ any-part-of order
in context of general equities, order to buy or sell a quantity of stock in pieces if necessary. Antithesis of an all-or-none order (AON).

■ appeal
a process whereby a decision by one body may be reviewed by another, usually higher, authority.

■ appellant
someone who appeals against a decision.

■ appointed representative
term used to describe tied agents of a product provider. Although tied to selling the products of one company, they retain their own business identity, e.g. state agents and building societies.

■ appraisal
a statement or estimate of the market value of tangible personal property or real estate.

■ appraisal ratio
the signal-to-noise ratio of an analyst's forecasts. The ratio of alpha to residual standard deviation.

■ appraisal rights
a right of shareholders in a merger to demand the payment of a fair price for their shares, as determined independently.

■ appraisal surplus
the difference between the historical cost and the appraised value of fixed assets.

■ appreciation
increase in the value of an asset.

■ appropriation request
formal request for funds for capital investment project.

■ approved list
a list of equities and other investments that a financial institution or mutual fund is approved to make.

■ arbitrage
1. In theory, arbitrage is the simultaneous purchase and sale of two identical commodities or instruments, to take advantage of price variations in different markets. For example, the purchase of gold in London and the simultaneous sale of gold in New York.
2. In practice, the term is used to refer to the simultaneous purchase and sale of any two contracts or commodities with largely offsetting risks. For example, the purchase of two-year Treasuries and the sale of futures contracts for an equivalent amount.
3. In municipal finance, the specific practice of investing funds obtained at a tax-preferred low rate of interest in higher-yielding investments, until the funds are needed for the purpose intended.
4. Dealing in two or more markets (e.g. currencies, commodities) at the same time, to benefit from rate differentials, in situations where prices and returns are fixed.

■ arbitrage bonds
municipality issued bonds issued intended to gain an interest rate advantage by refunding a higher-rate bond in ahead of their call date. Lower-rate refunding issue

proceeds are invested in Treasuries until the first call date of the higher-rate issue.

■ **Arbitrage Pricing Theory (APT)**

an alternative model to the capital asset pricing model developed by Stephen Ross and based purely on arbitrage arguments. The APT implies that there are multiple risk factors that need to be taken into account when calculating risk-adjusted performance or alpha.

■ **arbitrage-free option-pricing models**

yield curve option-pricing models.

■ **arbitrageur**

an individual or broker who engages in arbitrage.

■ **arbitration**

settlement of a dispute by independent third parties, rather than by a court.

■ **are you open?**

used in context of general equities. 'Can a new customer still participate on opposing side of the trade from that which the first customer initiated?', Inquiring as to whether any portion of that trade is still available.

■ **arithmetic average (mean) rate of return**

Arithmetic Mean Return.

■ **arithmetic mean return**

an average of the sub-period returns, calculated by summing the sub-period returns and dividing by the number of sub-periods.

■ **arms index**

also known as a trading index (TRIN) (total up volume)/(total down volume). An advance/decline market indicator. Less than 1.0 indicates bearish demand, while above 1.0 is bullish. The index often is smoothed with a simple moving average.

■ **arm's length price**

the price at which a willing buyer and a willing unrelated seller would freely agree to transact.

■ **around us**

used in context of general equities.

■ **arrangement fee**

fee charged by banks or building societies for arranging loans such as overdrafts or mortgages.

■ **arrearage**

in the context of investments, refers to the amount by which interest on bonds or dividends on cumulative preferred stock is due and unpaid.

■ **arrears**

unpaid dividends or bond interest that a corporation owes its stockholders or bond holders after the payable or due date on which the dividends or interest should have been paid.

■ **articles of association**

one of the establishing documents of a limited company, which sets out the internal operation of the company, including the powers of the directors.

■ **articles of incorporation**

legal document establishing a corporation and its structure and purpose.

■ **artificial currency**

a currency substitute, e.g., special drawing rights (SDRs).

■ **ascending rate bonds**

securities with a coupon rate that increases in previously defined increments, at scheduled intervals.

■ **ascending tops**

a chart pattern that depicts that each peak in a security's price over a period of time is higher than the preceding peak. Antithesis of descending tops.

■ **asian option**

option based on the average price of the underlying assets during the life of the option.

■ **ask**

this is the quoted ask, or the lowest price an investor will accept to sell a stock. Practically speaking, this is the quoted offer at which an investor can buy shares of stock; also called the offer price.

■ **asked price**

in context of general equities, price at which a security or commodity is offered for sale on an exchange or in the OTC Market. Also called the offer or offered price.

■ **asked to bid/offer**

used in context of general equities. Usually a seller (buyer) looking to aggressively sell (buy) stock, usually asking for a capital commitment from an investment bank.

■ **assembly of financial statements**

the providing of various accounting or data-processing services by an accountant, the output of which is in the form of financial statements, ostensibly to be used solely for internal management purposes.

■ **assertion**

explicit or implicit representations by an entity's management, that are embodied in financial statement components and for which the auditor obtains and evaluates evidential matter when forming his or her opinion on the entity's financial statements.

■ **assessed valuation**

the value assigned to property by a municipality for the purpose of tax assessment. Such an assessed valuation is important to investors in municipal bonds that are backed by property taxes.

■ **assessment of risk**

risk in the context of financial planning relates to the possibility of losing money. For example, assessment of risk can be generalised for initial discussions with a client, but must be personalised for final decisions to take account of the client's subjective view of the options.

■ **asset**

1. property which has value, e.g. plant, machinery, shares, invoices. 2. Any possession that has value in an exchange.

asset activity ratios
ratios that measure how effectively the firm is managing its assets.

asset allocation decision
the decision regarding how an institution's funds should be distributed among the major classes of assets in which it may invest.

asset allocation mutual fund
a mutual fund that rotates among stocks, bonds, and money market securities to maximise return on investment and minimise risk.

asset backed investments
investments based on tangible, working capital/assets that have the potential for growth, e.g. investment in the shares of an industrial or commercial concern, rather than investment in deposits.

asset classes
categories of assets, such as stocks, bonds, real estate, and foreign securities.

asset depreciation range system
a range of depreciable lives the IRS allows for particular classes of assets.

asset for asset swap
creditors exchange the debt of one defaulting borrower for the debt of another defaulting borrower.

asset management account
account at a brokerage house, bank, or savings institution that integrates banking services and brokerage features.

asset play
a company with assets that are not believed to be accurately reflected in its stock price, making it an attractive buy or play.

asset pricing model
a model for determining the required or expected rate of return on an asset. Related: Capital asset pricing model and arbitrage pricing theory.

asset sensitive
describes an entity's position when an increase in interest rates will help the entity and a decrease in interest rates will hurt the entity. An entity is asset sensitive when the impact of the change in its assets is larger than the impact of the change in its liabilities after a change in prevailing interest rates. This occurs when either the timing or the amount of the rate changes for liabilities causes interest expense to change by more than the change in interest income.

asset stripper
someone who purchases a business with a view to selling its assets, individually, at a profit.

asset substitution
occurs when a firm invests in assets that are riskier than those that the debt holders expected.

asset substitution problem
arises when the stockholders substitute riskier assets for the firm's

existing assets and expropriate value from the debt holders.

■ **asset swap**

an interest rate swap used to alter the cash flow characteristics of an institution's assets in order to provide a better match with its liabilities.

■ **asset turnover**

measure of operational efficiency - shows how much revenue is produced per £ of assets available to the business. (sales revenue/total assets less current liabilities)

■ **asset value**

the net market value of a corporation's assets on a per-share basis, not the market value of the shares. A company is undervalued in the market when asset value exceeds market value.

■ **asset/equity ratio**

the ratio of total assets to stockholder equity.

■ **Asset/Liability Management (ALM)**

coordinated management of all of the financial risks inherent in the business conducted by a financial institution. The process of balancing the management of separate types of financial risk to achieve desired objectives, while operating within predetermined, prudent risk limits. Accomplishing that task requires coordinated management of assets, liabilities, capital and off-balance sheet positions. Therefore, in the broadest sense of the term, ALM is simply the harmonious management of cash, loans, investments, fixed assets, deposits, short-term borrowings, long-term borrowings, capital and off-balance sheet commitments.

■ **Asset-Backed Security (ABS)**

a debt security collateralised by assets. Created from the securitisation of any loans other than mortgage loans. (Securitised mortgage loans are called mortgage backed securities or collateralised mortgage obligations.) Typically, asset backed securities are created from consumer instalment or credit card loans. Securitised commercial (non-consumer) obligations are typically called collateralised debt obligations or CDOs. CDOs are sometimes defined to be a subset of ABSs.

■ **asset-based financing**

methods of financing in which lenders and equity investors look principally to the cash flow from a particular asset or set of assets for a return on, and the return of, their financing.

■ **asset-coverage test**

a bond indenture restriction that permits additional borrowing if the ratio of assets to debt does not fall below a specified minimum.

■ **assets repriced before liabilities**

a measure of the gap between the quantity of assets repricing and the quantity of liabilities repricing, within a given period of time. A simple measure of a financial institution's exposure to beneficial or adverse consequences from changes in prevailing interest rates.

■ assets requirements

a common element of a financial plan that describes projected capital spending and the proposed uses of net working capital.

■ assignee

1. the party to whom an assignment is made.
2. Someone to whom control over property is assigned.

■ assignment

transfer of any contractual agreement between two parties. One of the parties, the assignor, transfers its rights or obligations to another party, the assignee. If interests in assets of the assignor are assigned, the assignment transfers all or some of the rights of ownership to the assignee. If interests in obligations of the assignor are assigned, the assignor is totally or partially absolved from further performance.

■ assignor

someone who assigns property.

■ assimilation

the public absorption of a new issue of stocks once the stock has been completely sold by underwriter.

■ associated company

a company where another company owns between 20% and 50% of the ordinary (voting) shares.

■ associated operations

actions that are deliberately linked, one to another, to produce, by a series of steps, a particular long-term result. When used in relation to tax planning, such operations no longer escape the tax evasion net.

■ assumable

as applied to mortgage loans, assumable means that a borrower who sells his or her home may transfer the outstanding mortgage loan secured by that dwelling to the new buyers. The new buyers are said to assume the loan.

■ assumed interest rate

rate of interest used by an insurance company to calculate the payout on an annuity contract.

■ assumed name

name used by a proprietorship, partnership or corporation to conduct business that is different from the legal name of the proprietorship, partnership or corporation. Sometimes an assumed name is prefaced by the initials 't/a' for 'trading as' or 'd.b.a.' for 'doing business as'.

■ assumption

becoming responsible for the liabilities of another party.

■ assurance

often interchangeable with insurance and usually used in conjunction with life assurance.

■ asymmetric behaviour

unbalanced behaviour exhibited by financial instruments, the rates or values of which do not change in proportion to changes in market rates. For example, increases in the prime rate quickly reflect most or all of increases in prevailing interest rates, while decreases in the prime rate are slow to reflect decreases in prevailing interest rates.

■ **asymmetric information**

information that is known to some people but not to other people.

■ **asymmetric taxes**

when participants in a transaction have different net tax rates.

■ **asymmetric volatility**

phenomenon that volatility is higher in down markets than in up markets.

■ **asymmetry**

a lack of equivalence between two things, such as the unequal tax treatment of interest expense and dividend payments.

■ **at best**

a buy or sell order which means that it should be executed immediately, at the best obtainable price.

■ **at or better**

an instruction to trade at a given level or better.

■ **at par**

a price equal to nominal or face value of a security. See **Par.**

■ **at risk**

the exposure to the danger of economic loss. Frequently used in the context of claiming tax deductions. For example, a person can claim a tax deduction in a limited partnership if the taxpayer can show it is at risk of never realising a profit and of losing its initial investment.

■ **at the bell**

in context of general equities, at the opening or close of the market.

■ **at the close order**

in the context of securities, an all or none market order that is to be executed at the closing price of the security on the exchange. If the execution cannot be made under this condition, the order is to be treated as cancelled. In the context of futures and options, refers to a contract that is to be executed on some exchanges during the closing period, a period in which there is a range of prices.

■ **at the figure**

in context of general equities, at the whole integer price (excluding the fraction) closest to the side of the market (bid/ask) being discussed.

■ **at the full**

used in context of general equities.

■ **at the money**

the situation in which the current market price, the spot price, of an underlying instrument is equal to the strike or exercise price of an option to buy or sell that instrument.

■ **at the opening order**

in context of general equities, market order or limited price order that is to be executed at the opening (and corresponding price) of the stock or not at all, and any such order or portion thereof not so executed is to be treated as cancelled.

■ attestation

the signature of a witness to the signing of a will.

■ at-the-money

an option is at the money if the strike price of the option is equal to the market price of the underlying security. For example, if xyz stock is trading at 54, then the xyz 54 option is at the money.

■ attribute bias

the tendency of stocks preferred by the dividend discount model to share certain equity attributes such as low price-earnings ratios, high dividend yield, high book value ratio, or membership in a particular industry sector.

■ attrition analysis

evaluation of the reduction in the amount of an asset or liability held. For example, an analysis of the reduction in savings account balances, caused by withdrawals over time.

■ auction markets

markets in which the prevailing price is determined through the free interaction of prospective buyers and sellers, as on the floor of the stock exchange.

■ Auction Rate Preferred Stock (ARPS)

floating-rate preferred stock, whose dividend is adjusted every seven weeks through a Dutch auction.

■ audit

close examination of something, e.g. the trading books, papers and accounts of a company, or the relationship between plans and desired outcomes.

■ audit risk

the risk that the auditor may unknowingly fail to modify appropriately his or her opinion on financial statements that are materially misstated.

■ audit sampling

application of an audit procedure to less than 100% of the items, within an account balance or class of transactions, for the purpose of evaluating some characteristic of the balance or class.

■ audit trail

resolves the validity of an accounting entry by a step-by-step record by which accounting data can be traced to their source.

■ audited accounts

company accounts which have been checked and examined to determine how the figures have been achieved.

■ audited statements

the most reliable type of financial statements. The audit is based on information submitted by the client, and the CPA does not verify all of the information. Limits on the scope of the audit and on the CPA's responsibility are described in the opinion letter that accompanies the audited statements. However, the value of an audited statement is that the independent CPA is responsible for testing and verifying any numbers that seem questionable or unusual, as well as the most material financial information.

■ auditing standards

guidelines to which an auditor adheres. Auditing standards encompass the auditor's professional qualities, as well as his or her judgement in performing an audit and in preparing the auditors' report. Audits conducted by independent Certified Public Accountant (CPA), usually in accordance with Generally Accepted Auditing Standards (GAAS).

■ auditor

1. person who audits financial accounts and records kept by others.

2. Accountants employed by companies to prepare their accounts and to give a short report which is included in the annual accounts. Companies are required by the Companies Act to appoint professionally qualified auditors to prepare Statutory Accounts.

■ auditor's certificate

see **accountant's opinion**.

■ auditor's report

1. a section of an annual report that includes the auditor's opinion about the veracity of the financial statements.

2. Written communication issued by an independent Certified Public Accountant (CPA), describing the character of his or her work and the degree of responsibility taken. An auditors' report includes a statement that the audit was conducted in accordance with Generally Accepted Auditing Standards (GAAS), which require that the auditor plan and perform the audit, to obtain reasonable assurance about whether the financial statements are free of material misstatement, as well as a statement that the auditor believes the audit provides a reasonable basis for his or her opinion.

■ augmentation

an increase. For example, provision of additional employee benefits for particular individuals, where the cost, usually, is born by the employer.

■ aunt millie

an unsophisticated investor.

■ Autex

video communication network through which brokerage houses alert institutional investors of their desire to transact block business (a purchase or sale) in a given security. Indications transmit small, medium, and large sizes only, with occasional limits mentioned. Supers are messages with specific size and price included. Both 'indications' and 'supers' can be only seen by customers (institutional subscribers to Autex). Trade recaps, advertised block trades entered by the dealer/subscribers, are also displayed, but can be seen by both institutions and dealers.

■ authentication

in the context of bonds, refers to the validation of a bond certificate.

■ authorisation

in the context of financial advice, the process of qualifying to be able to sell and advise on investment products.

■ authorised capital

the total of the shares a limited company is permitted to issue to raise capital. The permitted limit will be stated in the Memorandum of Association, along with the number of shares and their nominal value.

■ authorised investment

investments in which a trustee may invest trust assets.

■ authority

a government or public agency created to perform a single function or a restricted group of related activities. Usually, such units are financed from service charges, fees and tolls, but in some instances they also have taxing powers. An authority may be completely independent of or partially dependent upon other governments for its financing or the exercise of certain powers.

■ authority bond

a bond issued by a government agency or a corporation created to manage a revenue-producing public enterprise. The difference between an authority bond and a municipal bond is that margin protections may be incorporated in the authority bond contract as well as in the legislation that enables the authority.

■ authorised shares

number of shares authorised for issuance by a firm's corporate charter.

■ autocorrelation

the correlation of a variable with itself over successive time intervals. Sometimes called serial correlation.

■ automated clearing house (ACH)

a collection of 32 regional electronic interbank networks used to process transactions electronically with a guaranteed one-day bank collection float.

■ Automated Customer Account Transfer (ACAT)

for transfers of securities from a non-equity trading account to your equity trading account with your broker.

■ Automated Order System (AOS)

investment banks, computerised order entry system that sends single order entries to DOT (Odd-Lot) or to investment banks, floor brokers on the exchange.

■ Automated Pit Trading (APT)

introduced in 1989, APT is the LIFFE screen-based trading system that replicates the open outcry method of trading on screen.

A.P.T. is used to extend the trading day for the major futures contracts as well as to provide a daytime trading environment for non-floor trading products.

■ **Automated Teller Machine (ATM)**

a computer terminal for user initiated banking transactions.

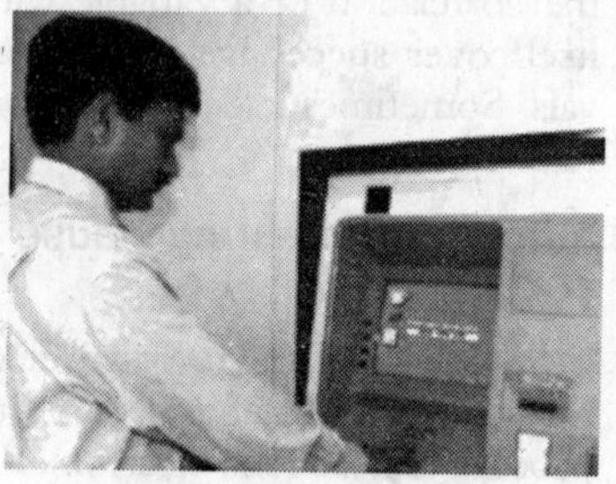

■ **automatic accrual**

a type of business agreement where the shares or business share of an individual passes automatically to the remaining shareholders or partners.

■ **automatic extension**

an automatic extension of time granted to a taxpayer to file a tax return.

■ **automatic funds transfer**

a transfer of funds from one account or investment vehicle to another using electronic or telecommunications technology.

■ **automatic investment program**

a program in which an investor can invest or withdraw funds automatically. A mutual fund, for example, automatically withdraw a pre determined specified amount from the investor's bank account on a regular basis.

■ **automatic reinvestment**

see **Constant dollar plan.**

■ **automatic stay**

The restricting of liability holders from collection efforts related to collateral seizure. Automatically imposed when a firm files for bankruptcy under Chapter 11.

■ **automatic withdrawal**

A mutual fund that gives shareholders the right to receive a fixed payment from dividends on a quarterly or monthly basis.

■ **Autoquote**

Autoquote indicative prices are generated for many of the financial options contracts traded at LIFFE using standard mathematical models as derived by Black and Scholes and Cox, Ross, Rubinstein. Autoquote calculates prices for all series by processing variables captured in real-time from other systems and trading members each time the underlying price changes. Autoquotes indicate where a series may trade, given the current level of the underlying instrument.

■ **autoregressive**

Using past data or variable of interest to predict future values of the same variable.

■ **availability**

the condition in which deposited funds are available for use by the depositor. The time lag between the date of a deposit and the date it is credited to the collected balance.

■ **availability float**

Checks deposited by a company that have not yet been cleared.

■ **availability schedule**

a schedule that determines when each bank in the cheque-clearing process will receive credit and when the depositor of cheques will be able to withdraw or invest the funds. The schedule sets a standard time period, since each cheque cannot be individually traced through the cheque-clearing process. Every major bank publishes its availability schedule based on its location and on the location of the bank on which the cheque is drawn.

■ **available balance**

the balance in an account that can be invested or withdrawn. Available balance refers to the bank ledger balances less cheques in the process of collection.

■ **available on the way in**

In context of general equities, stock is available to new customer as trade initiated by another customer is about to be consummated (on the exchange floor). Usually said to an inquiring salesperson.

■ **aval**

a guarantee.

■ **average**

the mid-point of a set of data.

■ **average**

An arithmetic mean return of selected stocks intended to represent the behaviour of the market or some component of it. One good example is the widely quoted Dow Jones Industrial Average, which adds the current prices of the 30 DJIA stocks, and divides the results by a predetermined number, the divisor.

■ **average (across-day) measures**

An estimation of price that uses the average or representative price of a large number of trades.

■ **average accounting return**

The average project earnings after taxes and depreciation divided by the average book value of the investment during its life.

■ **average age of accounts receivable**

The weighted-average age of all the firm's outstanding invoices.

■ **average clause**

where a person underinsures property, this clause in the policy allows the insurance company to pay only a proportion of the insured amount, the policyholder bearing the balance of the claim.

■ **average collection period, or days' receivables**

the ratio of accounts receivables to sales, or the total amount of credit extended per dollar of daily sales (average AR/sales 365).

■ **average cost**

in the context of investing, refers to the average cost of shares or stock bought at different prices over time.

■ **average cost of capital**

a firm's required payout to bondholders and stockholders expressed as a percentage of capital contributed to the firm. Average cost of capital is computed by dividing the total required cost of capital by the total amount of contributed capital.

■ **average daily balance**

the average daily balance is a method used to calculate finance charges. It is calculated by adding the outstanding balance on each day in the billing period and dividing that total by the number of days in the billing period. The calculation includes new purchases and payments.

■ **average down**

a strategy used by investors to reduce the average cost of shares, in which the investor purchases more shares with a fixed amount of capital as the price of the shares decrease. The investor receives more shares per dollar and decreases the average price per share.

■ **average equity**

a customer's average daily balance in a trading account at a brokerage firm.

■ **average life**

1. the time-weighed for a stream of principal cash flows.
2. Also referred to as the weighted-average life (WAL). The average number of years that each dollar of unpaid principal due on the mortgage remains outstanding. Average life is computed as the weighted-average time to the receipt of all future cash flows, using as the weights the dollar amounts of the principal paydowns.

■ **average maturity**

the average time to maturity of securities held by a mutual fund. Changes in interest rates have greater impact on funds with longer average maturity.

■ **Average Rate of Return (ARR)**

the ratio of the average cash inflow to the amount invested.

■ **average tax rate**

taxes as a fraction of income; total taxes divided by total taxable income.

■ **average up**

a strategy used by investors to lower the overall cost of shares by buying as many shares with a given amount of capital in an increasing market. Buying $1000 worth of shares at $30, $35, $40, and $45, for instance, will make the average cost of the shares $37.50.

■ **away**

a trade, quote, or market that does not originate with the dealer in question, e.g., 'the bid is 98-10 away from me.'

■ **away from the market**

in context of general equities, out of line with the inside market at this time, such as when a bid on a limit order is lower or the offer price is higher than the current market price for the security; held by the specialist for later execution unless FOK. Antithesis of in-line.

■ away from us

used in context of general equities, to characterise role of a competing broker/dealer. Trading away from us signifies that stock is bought and/or sold with institutions using other trading firms.

■ away from you

used for listed equity securities.

■ axe to grind

used in context of general equities. Involvement in a security, whether through a position, order, or inquiry.

■ back fee

the fee paid on the extension date if the buyer wishes to continue the option.

■ back months

in the context of futures and options trading, refers to the months of contracts with expiration dates farthest away.

■ back office

brokerage house clerical operations that support, but do not include, the trading of stocks and other securities. All written confirmation and settlement of trades, record keeping, and regulatory compliance happen in the back office.

■ back on the shelf

in the context of general equities, permanently cancelled order/interest in a stock by a customer.

■ back taxes

due taxes that have not been paid on time.

■ back to back

funding of one arrangement by another, e.g. annuity payments going towards regular premium payments.

■ back up

1. when bond yields rise and prices fall, the market is said to backup. 2. An investor who swaps out of one security into another of shorter current maturity is said to back up.

■ backdating

in the context of mutual funds, a feature allowing fundholders to use an earlier date on a letter of intent to invest in a mutual fund in exchange for a reduced sales charge, e.g. Giving retroactive value to purchases from the earlier date.

■ backed in

in the context of general equities, to describe result of unanticipated events that allow for a purchase at a discount or a sale at a premium.

■ back-end load

a form of sales charge imposed on investors by some mutual funds. These charges may be called back-end loads, deferred loads, deferred sales charges, contingent deferred sales charge (CDSC) or redemption fees. Regardless of the name, funds with deferred sales charges are simply one form of load funds. These funds offer investors the opportunity of paying a sales charge later, rather than paying one at the time of purchase.

■ **back-end load fund**

a mutual fund that charges investors a fee to sell (redeem) shares, often ranging from 4% to 6%. Some back-end load funds impose a full commission if the shares are redeemed within a designated length of time, such as one year. The commission decreases, the longer the investor holds the shares. The formal name for the back-end load is the contingent deferred sales charge, or C.D.S.C.

■ **backlog**

unfilled orders for goods or services. Orders for goods or services that the company has not yet delivered or rendered to its customers.

■ **back-testing**

creating a hypothetical portfolio performance history by applying current asset selection criteria to prior time periods.

■ **back-to-back financing**

an intercompany loan channeled through a bank.

■ **back-to-back loan**

a loan in which two companies in separate countries borrow each other's currency for a specific time period and repay the other's currency at an agreed-upon maturity.

■ **backup line**

a commercial paper issuer's bank line of credit covering maturing notes if, for some reason, selling new notes to cover the maturing notes is not possible.

■ **backwardation**

the fee paid by a seller of shares, for deferring the delivery of stocks and shares to the buyers.

■ **bad debt**

1. all or portion of an account, loan or note receivable, considered to be uncollectible.
2. Money owed that will not be repaid. Normally written off as a charge to the profit and loss account.

■ **bad delivery**

a delivery of securities that does not fulfill the requirements for good delivery.

■ **bad title**

title to property that does not distinctly confer ownership, usually in the context of real estate.

■ **bai-kai**

two-sided market picture, in Japanese terminology applies mainly to international equities.

■ **bailing out**

in the context of securities, refers to selling a security or commodity quickly, regardless of the price. May occur when an investor no longer wants to sustain further losses on a stock. Also refers to relieving an individual, corporation, or government entity in financial trouble.

■ bailment for hire

a safekeeping agreement between a safekeeping institution and its customer. A contract whereby a third-party bank or other financial institution, for a fee, agrees to exercise ordinary care in protecting the securities held in safekeeping for its customers.

■ balance

sum of debit entries minus the sum of credit entries in an account. If positive, the difference is called a debit balance, if negative, a credit balance.

■ balance of payments

a statistical compilation formulated by a sovereign nation of all economic transactions between residents of that nation and residents of all other nations during a stipulated period of time, usually a calendar year.

■ balance of trade

net flow of goods (exports minus imports) between two countries.

■ balance sheet

1. basic financial statement, usually accompanied by appropriate disclosures that describe the basis of accounting used in its preparation and presentation of a specified date the entity's assets, liabilities and the equity of its owners.

2. A statement of assets and liabilities, plus owners equity and reserves at a specific date.

■ balance sheet exposure

see **accounting exposure.**

■ balance sheet identity

total assets = total liabilities + total stockholders' equity

■ balanced budget

a budget in which the income equals expenditure.

■ balanced fund

an investment company that invests in stocks and bonds. The same as a balanced mutual fund.

■ balanced mutual fund

this is a fund that buys common stock, preferred stock, and bonds. The same as a balanced fund.

■ balloon interest

in the context of serial bond issues, the elevated coupon rate on bonds with late maturities.

■ balloon loan

a loan for which the final payment, larger than all of the previous, regularly scheduled payments, is due in a lump sum before the loan is fully amortised. The final payment is called a balloon payment.

■ balloon maturity

any large principal payment due at maturity for a bond or loan with or without a sinking fund requirement.

■ balloon mortgage

a mortgage loan with a balloon payment. Typically, the balloon payment is due 10 or 15 years after the loan is made.

■ balloon payment

a contractually required loan payment, almost always the final payment, that is larger than the other contractually required, periodic loan payments. Results from the fact that the required, periodic loan payments are too small to fully amortise the loan balance by the maturity date.

■ balloon rental

large final payment at the end of the lease period.

■ bancassurance

general term describing the broader financial services activities of banks and building societies, in particular their 'insurance company' activities.

■ band of investment

a method of determining a cap rate that blends the return or cash flow required by an equity investor with the return or interest rate required by the debt lender. Also called cash flow method.

■ Bank Anticipation Notes (BAN)

notes issued by states and municipalities to obtain interim financing for projects that will eventually be funded long term through the sale of a bond issue.

■ bank collection float

the time that elapses between when a check is deposited into a bank account and when the funds are available to the depositor, during which period the bank is collecting payment from the payer's bank.

■ bank discount basis

a convention used for quoting bids and offers for Treasury bills in terms of annualised yield, based on a 360-day year.

■ bank draft

a draft addressed to a bank.

■ bank float

the time between the date a cheque is deposited in a bank and the date it is charged to the drawer. Also called cheque-clearing or transit float. Not the same as float.

■ Bank for international settlements (BIS)

an international bank headquartered in Basel, Switzerland, which serves as a forum for monetary cooperation among several European central banks, the Bank of Japan, and the U.S. Federal Reserve System. Founded in 1930 to handle the German payment of World War I reparations, it now monitors and collects data on international banking activity and promulgates rules concerning international bank regulation.

■ Bank Holding Company

a company that owns or has controlling interest in two or more banks and/or other bank holding companies.

■ Bank Investment Contract (BIC)

interest guaranteed by the bank in a portfolio over a specific time frame with a specific yield.

■ **bank line**

line of credit that by a bank grants to a customer.

■ **bank services contract**

a contract with a bank outlining the responsibilities of the bank and the bank's customer.

■ **bank trust department**

bank department that deals with estates, administers trusts, and provides services such as estate planning advice to its clients.

■ **bank wire**

a computer message system linking major banks. It is used not for effecting payments, but as a mechanism to advise the receiving bank of some action that has occurred, e.g., the payment by a customer of funds into that bank's account.

■ **Banker's Acceptance (BA)**

a short term financial instrument that is the unconditional obligation of the accepting bank. Banker's acceptances, or BAs, arise from transactions involving the import, export, transit or storage of goods, including domestic as well as international transit. For investors, it is very important to realise that the underlying transaction that gives rise to a BA is almost completely irrelevant to the credit quality or the liquidity of the instrument.

■ **banker's draft**

a bill of exchange drawn on the bank, like a cheque, and presented by the bearer to the seller to purchase goods. The individual's account is then debited with the amount.

■ **bankers automated clearing services**

a computerised system facilitating the transfer of funds after clearing.

■ **bankmail**

an agreement between a company engaged in a takeover bid and a bank that the bank will not finance the bid of another acquirer.

■ **bankrupt**

person or business incapable of paying outstanding debts and whose affairs have been ordered by a court into the control of a receiver. Before someone can be declared bankrupt, they must commit an act of bankruptcy, such as entering into a situation which shows that it is unlikely that ensuing debts will be paid.

■ **bankruptcy**

inability to pay debts. In bankruptcy of a publicly owned entity, the ownership of the firm's assets is transferred from the stockholders to the bondholders.

■ **bankruptcy cost view**

the argument that expected indirect and direct bankruptcy costs offset the other benefits from leverage so that the optimal amount of leverage is less than 100% debt financing.

■ **bankruptcy risk**

the risk that a firm will be unable to meet its debt obligations. Also referred to as default or insolvency risk.

bankruptcy view

the argument that expected bankruptcy costs preclude firms from financing entirely with debt.

bank-specific liquidity risk

one of three main types of liquidity need environments. The risk that a bank might experience a funding crisis, resulting when one or more events or problems applicable just to the bank cause funds providers to lose confidence in the bank.

bar

slang for one million dollars.

bar chart

a pictorial comparison of results or measurements, illustrated by vertical bars from the height of

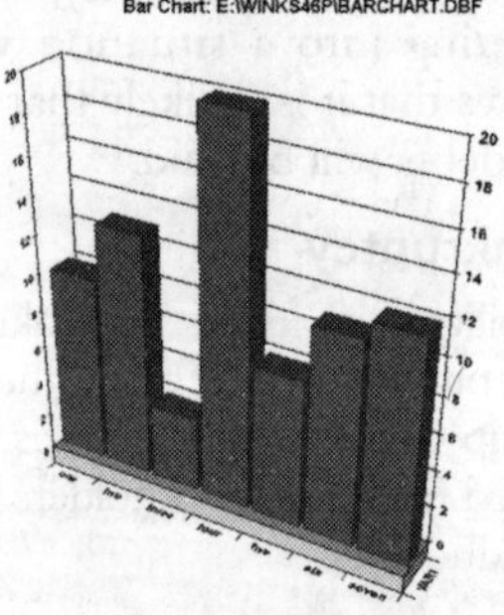

which it is possible to compare figures.

bar council

barrister's governing body, responsible for maintaining professional standards.

barbell strategy

a fixed income strategy in which the maturities of the securities included in the portfolio are concentrated at two extremes.

barefoot pilgrim

a slang term for an unsophisticated investor who has lost everything on the stock market.

bargain hunter

in the context of general equities, purchaser who is extremely selective in the price sought on a transaction.

bargain-purchase-price option

gives the lessee the option to purchase the asset at a price below fair market value when the lease expires.

barometer

economic and market data that represent an overall trend.

barrier options

option contracts with trigger points that, when crossed, automatically generate buying or selling of other options. These are exotic options.

barrister

a qualified lawyer who represents people in court and who may provide legal opinion out of court.

■ Barron's confidence index

index measuring the ratio of the average yield on 10 top-grade bonds to the average yield on 10 intermediate-grade bonds. The discrepancy between high-rated top-grade bonds and low-rated bond yields establishes a measure that is indicative of investor confidence.

■ barter

the trading/exchange of goods or services without using currency.

■ base

a technical analysis tool. A chart pattern depicting the period when the supply and demand of a certain stock are in relative equilibrium, resulting in a narrow trading range. The merging of the support level and resistance level.

■ base currency

applies mainly to international equities. Currency in which gains or losses from operating an international portfolio are measured.

■ base interest rate

related: Benchmark interest rate.

■ base market value

a group of securities, average market price at a specific time. Used for the purpose of indexing.

■ base period

a particular period of time used for comparative purposes when measuring economic data.

■ base probability of loss

the probability of not achieving a portfolio expected return. Related: Value at risk.

■ base rate

the foundation of every bank's structure of interest rates. Depositors are paid interest rates a few percentage points below the base rate, and borrowers are charged rates above the base rate.

■ basic balance

in a balance of payments, the basic balance is the net balance of the combination of the current account and the capital account.

■ basic business strategies

key strategies a firm intends to pursue in carrying out its business plan.

■ basic IRR rule

accept the project if IRR is higher than the discount rate; reject the project if it is lower than the discount rate. It is wise to also consider net present value for project evaluation.

■ basis

1. the difference between rates or prices of assets that are related but not identical. For example, the difference between the cash price and the futures price of a security. Sometimes called spread.
2. The difference between the price of a futures contract and the price of the underlying.
3. the number of days in a bond coupon period.

■ basis point

a unit of measurement for interest rates or yields that is expressed as a percentage.

■ basis price

price expressed in terms of yield to maturity or annual rate of return.

■ basis risk

the risk to a holder of financial instruments, that a change in prevailing interest rates will not affect the prices of or yields on similar instruments, in exactly equal amounts.

■ basis swap

a type of interest rate swap in which the net cash flows that the parties agree to exchange are based upon the differences between two different interest rate indexes. Banks use basis swaps to hedge basis risk, by locking in a net interest rate spread between a variable rate cost of funds tied to one index and a variable rate asset tied to a different index.

■ basket

applies to derivative products. Group of stocks that is formed with the intention of either being bought or sold all at once, usually to perform index arbitrage or a hedging program.

■ basket options

packages that involve the exchange of more than two currencies against a base currency at expiration. The basket option buyer purchases the right, but not the obligation, to receive designated currencies in exchange for a base currency, either at the prevailing foreign exchange market rate or at a prearranged rate of exchange. Multinational corporations with multicurrency cash flows frequently use basket options because it is generally cheaper to buy an option on a basket of currencies than to buy individual options on each of the currencies that make up the basket.

■ basket trades

related: Program trades.

■ bd form

an SEC required document of brokerage houses that outlines the firm's finances and officers.

■ bear

stock market jargon for a pessimist. Someone who thinks that the market is going to fall and sells shares or options in the belief that they can be bought back later at a cheaper price.

■ bear CD

a bear CD pays the holder a fraction of any fall in a given market index.

■ bear hug

often used in risk arbitrage. Hostile takeover attempt in which the acquirer offers an exceptionally large premium over the market value of the acquiree's share so as to as to squeeze (hug) the target into acceptance.

■ bear market

an investment market term meaning that the value of investments is expected to fall.

■ bear market

any market in which prices exhibit a declining trend. For a prolonged period, usually falling by 20% or more.

■ bear raid

high volume selling, in the hope of depressing prices, with a view to repurchasing at a lower price.

■ bear spread

applies to derivative products. Strategy in the options market designed to take advantage of a fall in the price of a security or commodity, usually executed by buying a combination of calls and puts on the same security at different strike prices in order to profit as the security's price falls.

■ bear trap

the predicament facing short sellers when a bear market reverses its trend and becomes bullish. The assets continue to sell in anticipation of further declines in price, and short sellers then are forced to cover at higher prices

■ bearer

the holder of an instrument.

■ bearer bill

a bill of exchange written so that the value will be paid out to the holder on presentation, e.g. cheque made out to cash.

■ bearer bond

bonds that are not registered on the books of the issuer. Such bonds are held in physical form by the owner, who receives interest payments by physically detaching coupons from the bond certificate and delivering them to the paying agent.

■ bearer bonds or stocks

securities owned by and payable to whomever holds the physical certificate. Securities without a registered owner.

■ bearer form

describes issue form of security not registered on the issuing corporation's books, and therefore payable to its bearer.

■ bearer share

security not registered on the books of the issuing corporation and thus payable to possessor of the shares. Negotiable without endorsement and transferred by delivery, thus avoiding some of the control associated with ordinary shares. Dividends are payable upon presentation of dividend coupons, which are dated or numbered. Applies mainly to international equities.

■ bearish

words used to describe investor attitude.

■ beating the gun

in the context of general equities, gaining an advantageous price in a trade through a quick response to market developments.

■ bed and breakfast

the sale of shares one day, and their repurchase the next day, done to achieve a disposal for Capital Gains Tax purposes.

■ before-tax profit margin

the ratio of net income before taxes to net sales.

beggar-thy-neighbor

an international trade policy of competitive devaluations and increased protective barriers that one country institutes to gain at the expense of its trading partners.

beggar-thy-neighbor devaluation

a devaluation that is designed to cheapen a nation's currency and thereby increase its exports at the expense of other countries. Devaluation can also reduce a nation's imports. Such devaluations often lead to trade wars.

behind

used for listed equity securities. At the same price but entered after your order/interest, such as on the specialist's book. Antithesis of ahead of you.

bell

signal on a stock exchange to indicate the open and close of trading.

bellwether industry

an industry or sector which gives a lead indicator of forthcoming changes in the economy.

below par

less than the nominal or face value of a security.

benchmark

1. a standard of comparison used for judging performance. For example, the return from a bond portfolio may be compared to the return from a benchmark instrument or portfolio. In this context, a nearly risk-free benchmark or one that closely matches the risk in the bond portfolio may be selected.
2. the process of comparing a forecast or simulation to a standard, for the purpose of evaluating the accuracy of the forecast or simulation.
3. the performance of a predetermined set of securities, used for comparison purposes. Such sets may be based on published indexes or may be customised to suit an investment strategy.

benchmark error

use of an inappropriate proxy for the true market portfolio.

benchmark interest rate

also called the base interest rate, it is the minimum interest rate investors will demand for investing in a non-Treasury security. It is also tied to the yield to maturity offered on the comparable-maturity Treasury security that was most recently issued (on-the-run).

benchmark issue

also called on-the-run or current-coupon issue or bellwether issues. In the secondary market, the benchmark issue is the most recently auctioned Treasury issues for each maturity.

benchmarking

comparing activities against agreed parameters, to assess degrees of comparative performance.

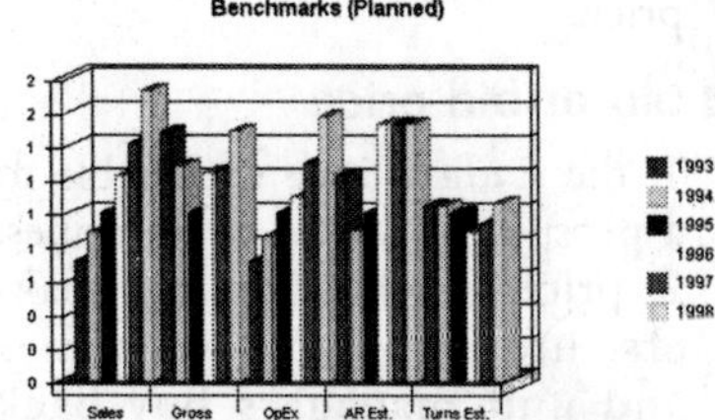

■ beneath

used for listed equity securities. 1- Behind; 2- Lower in price.

■ beneficial owner

the party that receives all of the benefits or rights of an owner of a security, even though the legal ownership of the security is recorded in the name of a broker or a bank in street name.

■ beneficial ownership

often used in risk arbitrage. Person who enjoys the benefits of ownership even though title is in another name. (Abused through the illegal use of a parking violation.)

■ beneficiary

someone who will receive the proceeds from a trust or settlement.

■ benefits in kind

refers to non-cash forms of employee benefit, such as pension scheme membership, car packages and similar.

■ best advice

a generic expression referring to the regulatory requirement for a financial adviser to offer suitable and timely advice relevant to a client's needs. Client's needs must take precedence over the adviser's remuneration.

■ best-efforts sale

a method of securities distribution/underwriting in which the securities firm agrees to sell as much of the offering as possible and return any unsold shares to the issuer. As opposed to a guaranteed or fixed-price sale, in which the underwriter agrees to sell a specific number of shares (and holds any unsold shares in its own account if necessary).

■ best-interests-of-creditors test

the requirement that a claim holder voting against a plan of reorganisation must receive at least as much as if the debtor were liquidated.

■ best's rating

a rating A.M. Best Co. assigns to insurance companies based on the company's ability to meet its obligations to its policyholders.

■ beta

a Greek letter used by mathematicians to label the degree of sensitivity to changes in one variable to changes in another. The name for correlation of the changes.

■ beta equation (security)

the market beta of a security is determined as follows: Regress excess returns of stock y on excess returns of the market. The slope coefficient is beta. Define 'n' as number of observation numbers. Beta = [(n) (sum of [xy])]-

[(sum of x) (sum of y)]/ [(n) (sum of [xx])]-[(sum of x) (sum of x)]
where:
n = # of observations (usually 36 to 60 months)
x = rate of return for the S&P 500 index
y = rate of return for the security

■ beta-adjusted gap

gap reports modified to reduce the errors caused by basis risk. The essential concept of beta-adjusted gap is that all interest rates do not change by the same amounts, but that there is an identifiable relationship, a correlation, between changes in various interest rates. Some rates are more sensitive to change than other rates. In beta-adjusted gap analysis, the volumes of assets and liabilities subject to repricing are weighted to reflect the historical sensitivity of the yields or costs of those assets and liabilities relative to some benchmark yield or cost.

■ bid

the price a potential buyer is willing to pay for a security. Sometimes also used in the context of takeovers where one corporation is bidding for (trying to buy) another corporation. In trading, we have the bid-ask spread, which is the difference between what buyers are willing to pay and what sellers are asking for in terms of price.

■ bid away

refers to over-the-counter trading. Bid from another dealer exists at the same (listed) or higher (O.T.C.) price.

■ bid or bid price

1. the trading price acceptable to a prospective buyer of securities. 2. price at which market makers, life assurance companies and unit managers buy back units from investors. Also used when unit linked policy matures or is encashed. Always less than offer price.

■ bid price

this is the quoted bid, or the highest price an investor is willing to pay to buy a security. Practically speaking, this is the available price at which an investor can sell shares of stock. Related: Ask, offer.

■ bid valuation

valuation of a unit trust on a bid value of shares held, after allowing for dealing costs. Usually indicates that the trust has more sellers than buyers.

■ bid wanted

used in the context of general equities. Announcement that a holder of securities wants to sell and will entertain bids.

■ bid/offer spread

difference between the bid price and offer price of units. Usually between 5% and 6% of the offer price of units. Used to recoup management expenses and initial costs.

■ bid-asked spread

the difference between the bid and the asked prices.

■ **bidder**

a firm or person that wants to buy a firm or security.

■ **bidding buyer**

in the context of general equities, a non-aggressive buyer who prefers to await a natural seller in the hope of paying a lower price.

■ **bidding through the market**

in the context of general equities, aggressive willingness to purchase a security at a premium to the inside market. Contrast with bidding buyer.

■ **bidding up**

moving the bid price higher.

■ **bid-to-cover ratio**

the ratio of the number of bids received in a Treasury security auction compared to the number of accepted bids.

■ **big bang**

a series of changes to the operating systems of the Stock Exchange, leading to the introduction of electronic trading.

■ **big picture**

to highlight trading interest due to the size of the trade.

■ **big producer**

a successful broker who generates a large volume of commission.

■ **big ticket**

leases on high cost assets. 'Small ticket' items would usually be items such as office equipment.

■ **big uglies**

unpopular stocks.

■ **bilateral netting**

a legally enforceable arrangement between two parties, to two or more swaps that creates a single legal obligation covering all of the individual swap contracts. This means that the size of the risk that one party is exposed to, for the default or insolvency of the counter party, is net of all of the positive and negative values of the contracts included in the bilateral netting arrangements. Parties that engage in numerous swap contracts may use bilateral netting agreements, to be able to recognise only the net sum of their obligations, rather than the gross total of the individual swap contracts.

■ **bill of exchange**

a paper document indicating that one party (the drawee) agrees to pay another party (the drawer) the sum of money noted on the bill, on demand or on a specified date, e.g. a bank note or a cheque.

■ **bill of lading**

document stating that goods have been received for shipment and which sets out the terms of delivery and receipt.

■ **billing cycle**

the number of days between statement dates.

■ **billings in excess of cost**

a liability created under a type of accrual accounting, used when firms, such as contractors, bill their customers in accounting periods for costs that they incur in subsequent accounting periods.

■ **binder**

a preliminary, temporary insurance agreement that obligates the insurance company to pay the insured if the loss insured against occurs after the binder is issued but before the insurance policy is issued.

■ **binomial option pricing model**

an option pricing model in which the underlying asset can assume one of only two possible, discrete values in the next time period for each value that it can take on in the preceding time period.

■ **bi-weekly mortgage loan**

a mortgage loan on which interest and principal payments are made every half-month (total of 26 payments) as opposed to monthly payments. This results in earlier loan retirement.

■ **black economy**

goods and services paid for by 'cash in-hand' and not recorded for tax and NI purpose.

■ **black Friday**

a precipitous drop in a financial market . The original Black Friday occurred on September 24, 1869, when prospectors attempted to corner the gold market.

■ **black market**

an illegal market.

■ **black Monday**

refers to October 19, 1987, when the Dow Jones Industrial Average fell 508 points on the heels of sharp drops the previous week. On Monday, October 27, 1997, the Dow dropped 554 points. While the point drop set a new record, the percentage decline was substantially less than in 1987.

■ **black-scholes option-pricing model**

a model for pricing call options based on arbitrage arguments. Uses the stock price, the exercise price, the risk-free interest rate, the time to expiration, and the expected standard deviation of the stock return. Developed by Fischer Black and Myron Scholes in 1973.

■ **blank cheque**

a check that is duly signed, but the amount of the check is left blank to be supplied by the drawee.

■ **blank cheque offering**

an initial public offering by a company whose business activities are undefined and therefore speculative.

■ **blanket fidelity bond**

SEC-required insurance coverage that brokerage firms are required to have in order to cover fraudulent trading by employees.

■ **blanket inventory lien**

a secured loan that gives the lender a lien against all the borrower's inventories.

blanket lien

an informal term meaning a lien on all of the debtor's current and subsequently acquired personal property assets.

blanket recommendation

a recommendation by a brokerage firm sent to all its customers advising that they buy or sell a particular stock regardless of investment objectives or portfolio size.

blind pool

a limited partnership that does not announce its intentions as to what properties will be acquired.

blind trust

a trust in which a fiduciary third party has total discretion to make investments on behalf of a beneficiary while the beneficiary is uninformed about the holdings of the trust.

blitzkrieg tender offer

in the context of a takeover, refers to a tender offer that is priced so attractively that the tender is completed quickly.

block

large quantity of stock or large dollar amount of bonds held or traded. As a rule of thumb, 10,000 shares or more of stock and $200,000 or more worth of bonds would be described as a block.

block call

in the context of general equities, conference meeting during which customer indications and orders, along with the traders' own buy/sell preferences, are conveyed to the entire organisation.

block house

brokerage firms that help to find potential buyers or sellers of large block trades.

block list

in the context of general equities, listing of stock the investment bank is looking for (wants to buy) or (wants to sell) at the beginning of the day, whether on an agency or principal basis.

block trader

a dealer who will take a position in the block trades to accommodate customer buyers and sellers of blocks.

block voting

describes a group of shareholders banding together to vote their shares in a single block.

blocked currency

a currency that is not freely convertible to other currencies due to exchange controls.

blow-off top

a steep and rapid increase in price followed by a steep and rapid drop. This is an indicator seen in charts and used in technical analysis of stock price and market trends.

blowout

the rapid sale of all shares in a new securities offering.

blue chip

a phrase taken to mean 'first class', referring to shares of a company with a good trading and dividend record or to the company itself.

■ blue list

daily financial publication featuring bonds offered for sale by dealers and banks that represent billions of dollars in par value.

■ blue-chip company

used in the context of general equities. Large and creditworthy company. Company renowned for the quality and wide acceptance of its products or services, and for its ability to make money and pay dividends. Gilt-edged security.

■ blue-sky laws

state laws covering the issue and trading of securities.

■ Bo Derek stock

high quality stock.

■ board broker

employee of the Chicago Board Options Exchange who manages away from the market orders, which cannot be executed immediately.

■ board of directors

1. individuals responsible for overseeing the affairs of an entity, including the election of its officers. The board of a corporation that issues stock is elected by stockholders.

2. Individuals elected by the shareholders of a corporation who carry out certain tasks established in the charter.

■ board order

instruction to deal only when a particular price is obtainable.

■ board resolution

a decision made by the directors of a company.

■ board room

a room at a brokerage firm where its clients can watch an electronic board displaying stock prices and transactions. Also refers to the room where Board of Directors meetings take place.

■ bogey

the return an investment manager is compared to for performance evaluation.

■ boiler room

used to describe place or operation in which unscrupulous salespeople call and try to sell people speculative, even fraudulent, securities.

■ boilerplate

standard terms and conditions.

■ bon voyage bonus

see **greenmail.**

■ bona fide

good faith.

■ bond

1. a debt security. Sometimes used only in reference to long-term debt securities. Sometimes called

a fixed-income security, even though many bonds have floating interest rates.
2. A guarantee provided by a surety or insurance company. For example, fidelity bond, indemnity bond, performance bond or payment bond.

■ **bond agreement**

a contract for privately placed debt.

■ **Bond Anticipation Note (BAN)**

a short-term note sold by a public entity that will be repaid from the proceeds of an anticipated bond issue.

■ **bond broker**

a broker on the floor of an exchange who trades bonds.

■ **bond buyer**

a daily publication featuring many essential statistics and index figures relevant to the fixed income markets.

■ **bond buyer's municipal bond index**

a municipal bond price tracking index published daily by the Bond Buyer.

■ **bond counsel**

an attorney who prepares the legal opinion concerning a municipal bond issue.

■ **bond covenant**

a contractual provision in a bond indenture. A positive covenant requires certain actions, and a negative covenant limits certain actions.

■ **bond crowd**

members of the stock exchange who transact bond orders on the floor of the exchange.

■ **bond discount**

the difference by which a bond's market price is lower than its face value. The antithesis of a bond premium, which prevails when the market price of a bond is higher than its face value.

■ **bond equivalent yield**

an annual yield, expressed as a percentage, describing the return provided to bond holders. A bond equivalent yield is double the simple interest, semi-annual yield. Since Treasury and agency notes and bonds, as well as most corporate and municipal bonds, pay interest semi-annually, the bond equivalent yield is a way to compare yields available from discount securities, such as Treasury bills and BAs with yields available from coupon securities.

■ **bond equivalent yield**

bond yield calculated on an annual percentage rate method. Differs from annual effective yield.

■ **bond indenture**

a document that sets forth the terms of a bond issue, the obligations of a bond issuer and the rights of the bond holders. The bond indenture is a contract between the company that issued the bonds and the bond trustee acting on behalf of the bond holders. Bond indentures may include a variety of provisions and thus define and create the differences in term and risk.

■ **bond indexing**

designing a bond portfolio so that its performance will match the performance of some bond index.

■ **bond mutual fund**

a mutual fund holding bonds.

■ **bond points**

a conventional unit of measure for bond prices set at $1 and equivalent to 1% of the $100 face value of the bond. A price of 80 means that the bond is selling at 80% of its face or par value.

■ **bond power**

a form used in the transfer of registered bonds from one owner to a different owner.

■ **bond premium**

see **bond discount**

■ **bond rating**

a rating based on the possibility of default by a bond issuer. The ratings range from AAA (highly unlikely to default) to D (in default).

■ **bond ratio**

the percentage of a company's capitalisation represented by bonds. The ratio is calculated by dividing the total bonds due after one year by that same figure plus all other equity.

■ **bond swap**

the simultaneous, or nearly simultaneous, purchase of one debt security with the proceeds from the sale of another debt security. The swap is done after the investor has conducted an analysis, showing that the debt security being purchased has more desirable characteristics than the debt security being sold.

■ **bond value**

with respect to convertible bonds, the value the security would have if it were not convertible. That is the market value of the bond minus the value of the conversion option.

■ **bond-equivalent basis**

the method used for computing the bond-equivalent yield.

■ **bondholder**

the firm often has stockholders and bondholders. In liquidation, the bondholders have first priority.

■ **bonding**

1. either the process of obtaining or the state of having a fidelity, indemnity, performance, payment or similar bond. In commercial construction financing, bonding usually refers to a contractor's performance bond. For employees of financial institutions, bonding usually refers to fidelity bonds. 2. refinancing short-term debt with long-term debt is sometimes called bonding out.

■ **bondpar**

a system that monitors and evaluates the performance of a fixed income portfolio, as well as the individual securities held in the portfolio. Bondpar decomposes the return into the elements beyond the manager's control—such as the interest rate environment and client-imposed duration policy constraints—and those that the management process contributes to, such as interest rate management, sector/quality allocations, and individual bond selection.

■ bonds

a generic term for life assurance policies that contain a nominal amount of life cover and a large investment content. Marketed as investments and subject to special tax treatment. Phrase also used to describe Government securities.

■ Bonds Enabling Annual Retirement Savings (BEARS)

holders of BEARS receive the face value of bonds underlying call option, which are exercised by CUBS (an acronym for Calls Underwritten by Swanbrook). If the calls are exercised by CUBS, BEARS holders receive the total of the exercise price.

■ boning

charging a lot more for an asset than its worth.

■ bonus

added to with profit policies. The amount is determined by life company's actuary and represents a distribution to, with profit policyholders of investment return achieved by fund. Payment of bonus is not guaranteed. Reversionary bonuses, normally declared annually, cannot be removed once added. Terminal bonuses added on death or maturity.

■ bonus issue

often called a 'free' or scrip issue, a bonus issue is a book-keeping transaction that transfers money from a company's reserve to its capital. Existing share prices fall, to reflect the greater number issued.

■ bonus sacrifice

a way of giving up any bonus element of earned income and diverting the sum to additional pension contributions. Treated as an additional employer contribution payment. Any notice of intention to sacrifice must be made clear before any bonus payment is announced. Tax treatment depends on specific circumstances and the local inspector.

■ book

a banker or trader's positions.

■ book cash

a firm's cash balance as reported in its financial statements. Also calledledger cash.

■ book entry

the non-physical record of ownership, custody and transfer of securities through electronic means. The system for settlement, delivery and custody of uncertificated securities.

■ book entry securities

stocks, bonds, other securities and some certificates of deposit that are purchased, sold and held with only manual or computer accounting entries rather than transfers of physical certificates to evidence the transfer. Typically, instead of a physical certificate or instrument, buyers only receive receipts or confirmations as evidence of their ownership.

■ book profit

the cumulative book income plus any gain or loss on disposition of assets.

■ book runner

the managing underwriter for a new issue. The book runner maintains the book of securities sold.

■ book to bill

in the context of general equities, high-technology industry's demand to supply ratio of orders on a firm's book to number of orders filled. Measures who the company has more orders than it can deliver (>1), equal amounts (=1), or less (<1). This monthly figure is of major interest to investors/ traders in the high-technology sector.

■ book value

1. the value at which an asset is carried and reported on the owner's balance sheet. For debt securities, the current book value may be the purchase price plus accretion (in the case of securities purchased at a discount) or the purchase price minus amortisation (in the case of securities purchased at a premium). Book value may differ, perhaps significantly, from market value.

2. Amount, net or contra account balances, that an asset or liability shows on the balance sheet of a company. Also known as carrying value.

■ book value per share

the ratio of stockholder equity to the average number of common shares. Book value per share should not be thought of as an indicator of economic worth, since it reflects accounting valuation (and not necessarily market valuation).

■ book-entry securities

system in which securities are not represented by paper certificates but are maintained in computerised records at the Fed in the names of member banks, which in turn keep computer records of the securities they own as well as those they are holding for customers. In the case of other securities where a book-entry has developed, certificates reside in a central clearinghouse or by another agent. These securities do not move from holder to holder.

■ bootstrap

term used to describe the start-up of a company with very little capital.

■ bootstrapping

creating a theoretical spot rate curve using one yield projection as the basis for the yield of the next maturity.

■ borrow

to obtain or receive money on loan with the promise or understanding that it will be repaid.

■ **borrower fallout**
in the mortgage pipeline, the risk that prospective borrowers of loans committed to be closed will elect to withdraw from the contract.

■ **bot**
shorthand for bought. Antithesis of SL, meaning sold.

■ **bottom**
refers to the base support level for market prices of any type. Also used in the context of securities to refer to the lowest market price of a security during a specific time-frame.

■ **bottom fisher**
an investor seeking stocks that have fallen to prices at or near their bottom, which he or she believes will trend up in the future.

■ **bottom-up equity management style**
a management style that de-emphasises the significance of economic and market cycles, focusing instead on the analysis of individual stocks.

■ **bought deal**
security issue in which one or two underwriters buy the entire issue.

■ **bounce**
a check returned by a bank because it is not payable, usually because of insufficient funds. Also used in the context of securities to refer to the rejection and ensuing reclamation of a security; a stock price's abrupt decline and recovery.

■ **boutique**
a small, specialised brokerage firm that offers limited services and products to a limited number of clients. Antithesis of financial supermarket.

■ **box**
term used to describe the way in which unit trust manager may hold units available for sale. Box may contain new units, units repurchased from investors or both.

■ **bracket**
a term signifying the extent of an underwriter's commitment in a new issue, e.g., major bracket or minor bracket.

■ **bracket creep**
the gradual movement into higher tax brackets when incomes increase as a result of inflation.

■ **brady bonds**
bonds issued by emerging countries under a debt reduction plan.

■ **branch**
an operation in a foreign country incorporated in the home country.

■ **breach of contract**
failure of a party to a contract to perform the necessary obligations.

■ **breach of trust**
any act or omission by a trustee, not necessarily deliberate, contrary to the terms of the trust.

■ **breadth of the market**
in the context of general equities, percentage of stocks participating

in a particular market move. Technical analysts say there was significant breadth if two-thirds of the stocks listed on an exchange move in the same direction during a trading session.

■ **break**

a rapid and sharp price decline. Related: Crash.

■ **break even analysis**

technique concerned with estimating the point at which income and expenditure are at the same level. This is termed the break-even point, at which point the business makes neither profit nor loss.

■ **break price**

used in the context of general equities. Change one's offering or bid prices to move to a more realistic, tight level where execution is more feasible. Often done to trim one's position, thus 'breaking price' from where the trades occurred (if long, 'break price' downward 1/8 a point or more).

■ **break-even analysis**

an analysis of the level of sales at which a project would make zero profit.

■ **break-even interest rate**

the maximum interest rate that a firm or property can pay from the available cash flow and still have enough cash flow, to make all required principal and interest payments.

■ **break-even lease payment**

the lease payment at which a party to a prospective lease is indifferent between entering and not entering into a lease arrangement.

■ **break-even occupancy**

the minimum occupancy level of a commercial real estate property that will generate enough cash flow to make all required principal and interest payments.

■ **break-even payment rate**

the prepayment rate of an MBS coupon that will produce the same cash flow yield (CFY) as that of a predetermined benchmark MBS coupon. Used to identify for coupons higher than the benchmark coupon the prepayment rate that will produce the same cash flow yield (CFY) as that of the benchmark coupon; and for coupons lower than the benchmark coupon the lowest prepayment rate that will do so.

■ **break-even point**

1. the price level at which income equals expense.
2. The expense level at which expense equals income.
3. The market price of a financial instrument that just equals the purchase price plus cost of carry for an investor owning that instrument.
4. The price level of a call option that equals the sum of the exercise price, plus the premium paid to acquire the option, or the price level of a put option that equals the exercise price minus the premium.

■ **break-even prepayment rate**

the specific prepayment rate (speed) at which the yield of a mortgage security is equal to the yield available from another security to which it is being compared.

■ **break-even sales**

the minimum sales level that a firm must achieve, in order to generate enough cash flow to make all required principal and interest payments.

■ **break-even tax rate**

the tax rate at which a party to a prospective transaction is indifferent between entering into and not entering into the transaction.

■ **break-even time (for convertible securities)**

the amount of time before the higher yield on the convertible bond, compared to an otherwise similar nonconvertible bond, compensates the investor for the excess cost of the convertible over the common stock. Usually calculated by using current yields rather than the coupon and dividend rates.

■ **breaking the syndicate**

terminating an agreement among underwriters, specifically the investment banking group assembled to underwrite the issue of a security.

■ **breakout**

a rise in a security's price above a resistance level (commonly its previous high price) or a drop below a level of support (commonly the former lowest price.) A breakout is taken to signify a continuing move in the same direction. Can be used by technical analysts as a buy or sell indicator.

■ **breakpoint sale**

for mutual funds, refers to the investment amount necessary to make the fund-holder eligible for a reduced sales charge.

■ **Bretton Woods agreement**

1944 agreement which established the International Monetary Fund and the World Bank.

■ **bridge financing**

interim financing of one sort or another used to solidify a position until more permanent financing is arranged.

■ **bridging loan**

a short-term loan taken out to help fund the purchase of one asset, before the sale of another asset has been finalised. Commonly seen in the property market.

■ **bridging pension**

an additional temporary pension paid from a scheme between retirement and State pension age. Usually replaced by State pension payable from State pension age.

■ **british clearers**

the large clearing banks that dominate deposit taking and short-term lending in the domestic sterling market.

■ **broad tape**

an expanded version of the ticker tape, which is displayed on a screen in the board room of a brokerage firm and shows constantly updated financial information and news.

■ **broken up**

used for listed equity securities. Prevented from executing a trade (committed to upstairs) due to exchange priority rules excluding one's order (e.g., higher bid/lower offer on floor, market order to satisfy).

■ **broker**

a party who brings buyers and sellers together. Brokers do not take ownership of the property

being traded, but rather they are compensated by commissions. Brokers are not the same as dealers, however, the same individuals and firms who act as brokers in some transactions may act as dealers in other transactions.

■ **broker fund**

generic term for an investment fund managed by a specialist financial adviser. Usually invested in the units of other investment funds/unit trusts.

■ **broker loan rate**

related: Call money rate.

■ **brokerage**

dealing fee or commission charged by a broker. May also be used as a term for a broking firm.

■ **broker-dealer**

see **dealer.**

■ **brokered cd**

a certificate of deposit issued by a bank or thrift institution bought by a brokerage firm in bulk for the purpose of reselling to brokerage customers. A broker CD features a higher interest rate, usually 1% higher, and is FDIC insured and do not usually have commissions.

■ **brokered deposits**

bank deposits solicited by a third-party broker. Usually, but not always, deposits for some amount slightly below $100,000, so that all interest as well as principal is covered by deposit insurance. Brokers are typically paid a fee by the depository bank.

■ **brokered market**

a market in which an intermediary offers search services to buyers and sellers.

■ **brought over the wall**

compelling a research analyst of an investment bank to work in the underwriting department for a corporate client, therefore allowing for the transmission of insider information. Also called 'Over the Chinese wall'.

■ **bubble theory**

security prices sometimes move wildly above their true values, or the price falls sharply until the 'bubble bursts'.

■ **buck**

slang for one million dollars.

■ **bucket shop**

an illegal brokerage firm that accepts customer orders but does not attain immediate executions. A bucket shop broker promises the customer a certain price, but waits until a price discrepancy is present and the trade is advantageous to the firm and then keeps the difference as profit. Alternatively, the broker may never fill the customer's order but keep the money.

■ **buckets**

in gap reports, the predefined time interval groups are often called buckets. The buckets can be defined to represent whatever time units a bank wants to see in its gap reports. The time intervals can be single months or years. Smaller buckets, such as one-month buckets, give more detail, which in turn can provide a more accurate measure of interest rate risk. On the other hand, smaller buckets can require a greater number of buckets to show the interest rate risk far enough into the future for prudent analysis.

■ **budget**

1. financial plan that serves as an estimate of future cost, revenues or both.
2. A budget is a financial plan that details future expected income and expenditure. Also refers to a specific sum of money set aside for a particular project. Hence, the Government's announcement each year, regarding its tax and financing plans for the future, is called the Budget.

■ **budget deficit**

the amount by which government spending exceeds government revenues.

■ **budget surplus**

the amount by which government revenues exceed government spending.

■ **build a book**

in the context of general equities, develop customer orders to gather demand/supply in order to make a bid or an offer.

■ **builder buydown loan**

a mortgage loan on newly developed property that the builder subsidises during the early years of the development. The builder uses cash to buy down the mortgage rate to a lower level than the prevailing market loan rate for some period of time. The typical buydown is 3% of the interest rate amount for the first year, 2% for the second year, and 1% for the third year (also referred to as a 3-2-1 buydown).

■ **builder's risk insurance**

insurance covering perils, resulting in loss caused by the builder's operations on the borrower's property. Usually required by property owners and by construction lenders, when a contractor is hired to make improvements in an existing building or to construct a new building.

■ **building code**

laws, usually but not always, enacted by local government units that set safety and fire protection standards. These codes affect the materials and methods used in the construction of buildings. For example, a code provision might require sprinkler systems in motel rooms.

■ **bulge**

informal term used by some lenders to describe a provision in a line of credit promissory note that allows for a temporary increase in the maximum amount that can be borrowed under the line of credit. A bulge is particularly suited to loans to firms with seasonal increases in sales.

■ **bulge bracket**

a tier of firms in an underwriting syndicate that have the highest participation level.

■ **bull**

the opposite of a bear. The optimist who believes that the market is going to rise and so buys shares now to benefit from future price rises.

■ **bull cd**

a bull CD pays its holder a specified percentage of the increase in return on a specified market index while guaranteeing a minimum rate of return.

■ **bull market**

a rising investment market. The 'opposite' of bear market.

■ **bull spread**

a spread strategy in which an investor buys an out-of-the-money put option, financing it by selling an out-of-the money call option on the same underlying security.

■ **bull-bear bond**

bond whose principal repayment is linked to the price of another security. The bonds are issued in two tranches: In the first tranche repayment increases with the price of the other security, and in the second tranche repayment decreases with the price of the other security.

■ **bullet contract**

a guaranteed investment contract purchased with a single (one-shot) premium. Related: Window contract.

■ **bullet loan**

1. a name occasionally used to describe a promissory note used for transactions that do not require any principal to be repaid until the maturity of the note. Interest is usually due periodically prior to maturity. Most often used to describe loans with time periods of at least one year.

2. A bank term loan that calls for no amortisation.

■ **bullet security**

an instrument that repays the full principal at maturity.

■ bullet strategy

a fixed income strategy in which a portfolio is constructed so that the maturities of its securities are highly concentrated at one point on the yield curve.

■ bullion coins

metal coins consisting of gold, silver, platinum, or palladium that are actively traded. Some examples include the American eagle and the Canadian maple leaf. Their price is directly connected to the underlying price of their metal.

■ bullish

words used to describe investor attitudes. Bullish refers to an optimistic outlook, while bearish means a pessimistic outlook.

■ bump-up CD

a certificate of deposit granting the owner the right to increase its yield one time for the remaining term of the CD. The power is exercised by the owner in the event of an interest rate hike.

■ bunching

describes the act of traders combining round-lot orders for execution at the same time. Bunching can also be used to combine odd-lot orders to save the odd-lot differential for customers. Also used to refer to the pattern on the ticker tape when a series of trades for a security appear consecutively.

■ bundling, unbundling

creation of securities either by combining primitive and derivative securities into one composite hybrid or by separating returns on an asset into classes.

■ burn rate

used in venture capital financing to refer to the rate at which a start-up company expends capital to finance overhead costs prior to the generation of positive cash flow.

■ burnout

depletion of a tax shelter's benefits. In the context of mortgage backed securities it refers to the percentage of the pool that has prepaid their mortgage.

■ business card

a convenient way of satisfying the compliance requirement of informing a potential client of who you are, who you work for, your business and regulatory status and your regulatory authority.

■ business combination

1. See **merger.**
2. combining of two entities. Under the purchase method of accounting, one entity is deemed to acquire another and there is a new basis of accounting for the assets and liabilities of the acquired company. In a pooling of interests, two entities merge through an exchange of common stock and there is no change in the carrying value of the assets or liabilities.

■ business cycle

repetitive cycles of economic expansion and recession.

■ business day

a day in which financial markets are open for trading.

■ **business failure**

a business that has terminated operations with a loss to creditors.

■ **business investor**

one of several types of investor identified in financial services legislation. Different levels of duty of care apply to each type of investor, to reflect their existing knowledge and experience of investment business. A business investor is not a professional investor but does regularly deal with certain investments in a business capacity. Deemed to understand the nature and risk of the type of investments they normally transact.

■ **business risk**

the risk that the cash flow of an issuer will be impaired because of adverse economic conditions, making it difficult for the issuer to meet its operating expenses.

■ **business segment reporting**

reporting the results of the separate divisions or subsidiaries of a business.

■ **busted convertible**

related: Fixed income equivalent. Mainly applies to convertible securities. Convertible bond selling essentially as a straight bond. Assuming the issuer is 'money good,' or will continue to meet credit obligations, such issues can be highly attractive since the price makes virtually no allowance for the bond's call on the common stock, although such issues usually carry high premiums.

■ **bust-up takeover**

a leveraged buyout in which the buyer sells off the assets of the target company to repay the debt that financed the takeover.

■ **butterfly**

in the context of equities, a firm with two divisions may split into two companies and issue original shareholders two shares (one in each of the new companies) for every old share they have.

■ **butterfly shift**

a nonparallel shift in the yield curve involving the height of the curve.

■ **butterfly spread**

applies to derivative products. Complex option strategy that involves selling two calls and buying two calls on the same or different markets, with several maturity dates. One of the options has a higher exercise price and the other has a lower exercise price than the other two options. The payoff diagram resembles the shape of a butterfly.

■ **buy**

to purchase an asset; taking a long position.

■ buy and sell agreement

both partnerships and director/shareholder controlled companies need agreements to help ensure a satisfactory disposal of shares in certain circumstances. The 'buy and sell' route is one such, where it is written into a wider agreement that in the event of death or retirement, one party will sell the business share and another buy. A fixed agreement rather than an option.

■ buy at best

instruction to buy until the required quantity is reached.

■ buy in

to cover, offset, or close out a short position. Related: Evening up, liquidation.

■ buy limit order

a conditional trading order that indicates a security may be purchased only at the designated price or lower. Related: Sell limit order.

■ buy minus order

in the context of general equities, rare market or limit order to buy a stated amount of a stock, provided that the price to be obtained is not higher than the last sale if the last sale is a minus or zero-minus tick, and is not higher than the last sale minus the minimum fractional change in the stock if the last sale is a plus or zero-plus tick. (If limit, then the buy cannot occur above the limit, regardless of tick.)

■ buy on close

buying at the end of the trading session at a price within the closing range.

■ buy on margin

borrowing to buy additional shares, using the shares themselves as collateral.

■ buy on opening

buying at the beginning of a trading session at a price within the opening range.

■ buy on the bad news

buying stock shortly after a price drop resulting from bad news from the company. Investors believe that the price has hit bottom and will trend upward.

■ buy order

an order to a broker to purchase a specific quantity of a security.

■ buy stop order

a buy order not to be executed until the market price rises to the stop price. Once the security has broken through that price, the order is then treated as a market order. Also known as a suspended market order.

■ buy the book

an order, typically from a large institutional investor to a broker to purchase all the shares available at the market from the specialist and other brokers and dealers at the current offer price. The book refers to the record a specialist kept before the advent of computers.

■ buy/sellback

a form of secured, short-term investment, in which a security is purchased with a simultaneous agreement to sell it back to the seller at a future date. The purchase and sales agreements are simultaneous but the settlement dates for the transactions are not. The purchase is a cash transaction, while the return sale is a forward transaction since it occurs at a future date.

■ buy-and-hold strategy

a passive investment strategy with no active buying and selling of stocks from the time the portfolio is created until the end of the investment horizon.

■ buy-and-write strategy

an options strategy that calls for the purchase of stocks and the writing of covered call options on them.

■ buyback

the covering of a short position by purchasing a long contract, usually resulting from the short sale of a commodity. Also used in the context of bonds. The purchase of corporate bonds by the issuing company at a discount in the open market. Also used in the context of corporate finance. When a firm elects to repurchase some of the shares trading in the market.

■ buydown

a lump sum payment made to a creditor by a borrower or a third party, to reduce the amount of some or all of the borrower's periodic payments to repay the indebtedness.

■ buyer in the ordinary course of business

a purchaser who buys inventory from a seller who is in the business of selling that type of inventory.

■ buyers guide

information given to a client by a Financial Adviser, showing the adviser's status and obligations to the client.

■ buyer's market

market in which the supply exceeds the demand, creating lower prices. Antithesis of seller's market.

■ buyers/sellers on balance

used for listed equity securities. Indicates that at a given time (usually before the opening of a stock/market or at expiration time), there are more buyers/sellers in the marketplace, usually with market orders.

■ buying climax

a rapid rise in the price of a stock resulting from heavy buying, which usually creates the market condition for a rapid fall in the price.

■ buying power

the amount of money available to buy securities, determined by adding the total cash held in brokerage accounts and the amount that could be spent if securities were margined to the limit.

■ buying the index

purchasing the stocks in the S&P 500 in the same proportion as the index to achieve the same return.

■ **buyout**

purchase of a controlling interest (or percent of shares) of a company's stock. A leveraged buy out is affected with borrowed money.

■ **buy-side analyst**

a financial analyst employed by a non-brokerage firm, typically one of the larger money management firms that purchases securities on its own account.

■ **bylaws**

1. collection of formal, written rules governing the conduct of a corporation's affairs (such as what officers it will have, what their responsibilities are and how they are to be chosen). Bylaws are approved by a corporation's stockholders, if a stock corporation, or other owners, if a non-stock corporation.
2. rules and practices that govern management of an organisation.

■ **cabinet security**

a stock or bond listed on a major exchange with low daily traded volume.

■ **cafeteria benefits**

a system of remuneration provision which offers core benefits, e.g. minimum salary, leaving the balance of benefits to be chosen by the individual from a suitable list within an agreed budget.

■ **cage**

a section of a brokerage firm used for receiving and disbursing funds.

■ **calendar**

list of new issues scheduled to come to market shortly.

■ **calendar effect**

describes the tendency of stocks to perform differently at different times, including performance anomalies like the January effect, month-of-the-year effect, day-of-the-week effect, and holiday effect.

■ **calendar spread**

an option trading strategy that involves buying two calls or two puts on the same underlying, but with different maturity dates. If two call options are used, the spread may be referred to as a calendar call spread. Similarly, if two put options are used, the spread may be described as a calendar put spread.

■ **call**

an option that grants the holder the right to purchase an instrument in the future, at a price established today. The call option gives the holder the right but not the obligation to purchase the underlying instrument.

■ **call an option**

to exercise a call option.

■ **call date**

the date on which a call option may be exercised. The date before the contractual maturity date on which a bond may be redeemed, at the option of its issuer.

■ **call feature**

part of the indenture agreement between the bond issuer and

buyer describing the schedule and price of redemptions prior to maturity.

■ call loan

loan repayable on demand. Also known as demand loan.

■ call money rate

also called the broker loan rate , the interest rate that banks charge brokers to finance margin loans to investors. The broker charges the investor the call money rateplus a service charge.

■ call option

1. a contract or a provision in a contract, that gives its holder the right to buy an underlying security, commodity or currency, before a certain date. The option to purchase is for a predetermined price called the strike price.
2. An option to buy, e.g. shares, at a fixed price on or before a set date in the future.

■ call or calling

making demand for payment in full of a loan, usually a loan that is in default. Often referred to as calling the loan.

■ call premium

premium in price above the par value of a bond or share of preferred stock that must be paid to holders to redeem the bond or share of preferred stock before its scheduled maturity date.

■ call price

the price at which a call option may be exercised. For example, the price that an issuer is required to pay, in order to redeem a bond before its maturity.

■ call protection

a feature of some callable bonds that establishes an initial period when the bonds may not be called.

■ call provision

an embedded option granting a bond issuer the right to buy back all or part of an issue prior to maturity.

■ call risk

the risk that declining interest rates will create an economic incentive for the owner of a call option to exercise that option.

■ call swaption

a swaption in which the buyer has the right to enter into a swap as a fixed-rate payer. The writer therefore becomes the fixed-rate receiver/floating-rate payer.

■ callable

applies mainly to convertible securities. Redeemable by the issuer before the scheduled maturity under specific conditions and at a stated price, which usually begins at a premium to par and declines annually. Bonds are usually called when interest rates fall so significantly that the issuer can save money by issuing new bonds at lower rates.

■ callable bond

a bond that the issuer has the right to redeem prior to maturity. Some callable bonds may be redeemed on a single call date, while others have multiple call dates. Some callable bonds may be redeemed at par, while others can only be redeemed at a premium.

■ callable instrument

bond which accords an issuer the right to redemption before it is due.

■ called away

convertible: Redeemed before maturity.
option: Call or put option exercised against the stockholder.
sale: Delivery required on a short sale.

■ cancel

to void an order to buy or sell from (1) the floor, or (2) the trader/salesperson's scope. In Autex, the indication still remains on record as having once been placed unless it is expunged.

■ cancellation

used in conjunction with unit linked funds, whereby units are cancelled (sold), to pay for certain expenses of the fund or contract.

■ cancellation period

a cooling off period after the purchase of certain investment products. During the period, the purchaser can change his or her mind about going ahead and opt to have any initial payments repaid.

■ cap

an upper limit for a variable, such as the upper limit on the interest rate paid or received in a transaction.

■ cap rate

an interest rate used in the process of capitalisation.

■ capacity

a lending and credit analysis term that describes a borrower's or applicant's ability to meet debt service obligations.

■ capital

1. usually refers to the total of the equity accounts in a firm. For a bank, the equity accounts are common and preferred stock, surplus, and undivided profits. For other corporations, equity accounts are common and preferred stock, surplus, and retained earnings.
2. Sometimes used as a synonym for common stock, as in capital stock.
3. 'Equity' (non-debt) funds made available to invest in a business, at the start and later on.

■ capital account

net result of public and private international investment and lending activities.

■ capital allocation decision

allocation of invested funds between risk-free assets and the risky portfolio.

■ capital allowances

tax allowances which enable the owner of an asset to take into account depreciation on the asset against taxable income.

■ capital asset

a long-term asset, such as land or a building, not purchased or sold in the normal course of business.

■ Capital Asset Pricing Model (CAPM)

an economic theory that describes the relationship between risk and expected return, and serves as a model for the pricing of risky securities. The CAPM asserts that the only risk that is priced by rational investors is systematic risk, because that risk cannot be eliminated by diversification. The CAPM says that the expected return of a security or a portfolio is equal to the rate on a risk-free security plus a risk premium multiplied by the assets systematic risk. Theory was invented by William Sharpe (1964) and John Lintner (1965).

■ capital budget

a firm's planned capital expenditures.

■ capital budgeting

the process of choosing the firm's long-term capital assets.

■ Capital Builder Account (CBA)

a Merrill Lynch brokerage account that allows investors to access the loan value of his or her eligible securities to buy or sell securities. Excess cash in a CBA can be invested in a money market fund or an insured money market deposit account without losing access to the money.

■ capital employed

the value of all resources available to the company, typically comprising share capital, retained profits and reserves, long-term loans and deferred taxation. Viewed from the other side of the balance sheet, capital employed comprises fixed assets, investments and the net investment in working capital (current assets less current liabilities). In other words: the total long-term funds invested in or lent to the business and used by it in carrying out its operations.

■ capital expenditures

expenditures resulting in the acquisition of or addition to fixed assets. Expenditures made for the purpose of acquiring capital assets.

■ capital flight

the transfer of capital abroad in response to fears of political risk.

■ capital formation

expansion of capital or capital goods through savings, which leads to economic growth.

■ capital gain

1. portion of the total gain recognised on the sale or exchange of a non-inventory asset which is not taxed as ordinary income. Capital gains have historically been taxed at a lower rate than ordinary income.

2. The increase in value of an asset or investment.

■ capital gains distribution

a distribution to the shareholders of a mutual fund out of profits from selling stocks or bonds, that is subject to capital gains taxes for the shareholders.

■ capital gains tax

a tax levied on the investment gains of an individual in a tax year, provided, those gains exceed the current exemption. Husband and wife pay the tax separately and have separate allowances.

■ capital gains yield

the price change portion of a stock's return.

■ capital goods

goods used by firms to produce other goods, e.g., office buildings, machinery, equipment.

■ capital international indexes

market indexes maintained by Morgan Stanley that track major stock markets worldwide.

■ capital lease

a lease obligation that has to be capitalised on the balance sheet.

■ capital loss

the difference between the net cost of a security and the net sales price, if the security is sold at a loss.

■ capital market

the market for trading long-term debt instruments (those that mature in more than one year).

■ capital market efficiency

the degree to which the percent asset price accurately reflects current information in the market place.

■ capital market imperfections view

the view that issuing debt is generally valuable, but that the firm's optimal choice of capital structure involves various other views of capital structure (net corporate/personal tax, agency cost, bankruptcy cost, and pecking order), that result from considerations of asymmetric information, asymmetric taxes, and transaction costs.

■ Capital Market Line (CML)

the line defined by every combination of the risk-free asset and the market portfolio. The line represents the risk premium you earn for taking on extra risk. Defined by the capital asset pricing model.

■ capital markets disruptions

a type of systemic liquidity risk. The risk of funding problems arising from problems in the secondary markets for financial instruments.

■ capital markets hedges

hedging done with instruments traded in the capital markets, including but not limited to swaps, options and futures. (These hedge instruments are derivatives.) The term 'capital markets' is slightly broader than 'exchange traded', since some instruments, such as interest rate swaps, are bought and sold outside of the exchanges in Over The Counter (OTC) markets that are still capital markets.

■ capital projects funds

funds used by a not-for-profit organisation, to account for all resources used for the development of a land improvement or building addition or renovation.

■ **capital rationing**

placing limits on the amount of new investment undertaken by a firm, either by using a higher cost of capital, or by setting a maximum on the entire capital budget or parts of it.

■ **capital requirements**

financing required for the operation of a business, composed of long-term and working capital plus fixed assets.

■ **capital shares**

one of two types of shares in a dual-purpose investment company, which entitle the holder to the appreciation or depreciation in the value of a portfolio, as well as the gains from trading in the portfolio. Antithesis of income shares.

■ **capital stock**

ownership shares of a corporation authorised by its articles of incorporation. The money value assigned to a corporation's issued shares. The balance sheet account with the aggregate amount of the par value or stated value of all stock issued by a corporation.

■ **capital structure**

the makeup of the liabilities and stockholders' equity side of the balance sheet, especially the ratio of debt to equity and the mixture of short and long maturities.

■ **capital surplus**

amounts of directly contributed equity capital in excess of the par value.

■ **capital turnover**

calculated by dividing annual sales by average stockholder equity (net worth). The ratio indicates how much a company could grow its current capital investment level. Low capital turnover generally corresponds to high profit margins.

■ **capital-intensive**

used to describe industries that require large investments in capital assets to produce their goods, such as the automobile industry. These firms require large profit margins and/or low costs of borrowing to survive.

■ **capitalisation**

1. the process of imputing a value to an income stream, by dividing the annual net income before income taxes and depreciation by a rate of return expressed as a decimal. This process is used in real estate lending and appraisals.
2. The total of or the mix between a corporation's shareholders' equity and its long-term debt.
3. The process of reflecting a long-term, non-cancelable lease on the lessee's balance sheet.

■ **capitalisation ratio**

a measure of a corporation's reliance on long-term debt. Similar to the debt-to-worth ratio, but not the same. This ratio is calculated by dividing long-term debt by the sum of long-term debt plus equity.

■ **capitalised cost**

expenditure identified with goods or services acquired and measured by the amount of cash paid or the market value of other property, capital stock or services surrendered. Expenditures that are written off during two or more accounting periods.

capitalised interest

1. interest that a lender 'receives' by adding the unpaid interest to the amount of the loan balance to be paid by the borrower.
2. Interest cost incurred during the time necessary to bring an asset to the condition and location for its intended use and included as part of the historical cost of acquiring the asset.

capitalised lease

1. lease obligations that must be capitalised under GAAP. The unpaid future lease payments, due under the terms of the lease, must be shown as a liability on the firm's balance sheet. As a general rule, this requirement applies to most equipment and buildings leased by a business and used in the conduct of the business.
2. Lease recorded as an asset acquisition, accompanied by a corresponding liability by the lessee.

capitalisation

the debt and/or equity mix that funds a firm's assets.

capitalisation method

a method of constructing a replicating portfolio in which the manager purchases a number of the most highly capitalised names in the stock index in proportion to their capitalisation.

capitalisation rate

the rate of interest used to calculate the present value of a number of future payments.

capitalisation ratios

also called financial leverage ratios, these ratios compare debt to total capitalisation and thus reflect the extent to which a corporation is trading on its equity. Capitalisation ratios can be interpreted only in the context of the stability of industry and company earnings and cash flow.

capitalisation table

a table showing the capitalisation of a firm, which typically includes the amount of capital obtained from each source - long-term debt and common equity - and the respective capitalisation ratios.

capitalised

recorded in asset accounts and then depreciated or amortised, as is appropriate for expenditures for items with useful lives longer than one year.

capitalised interest

interest that is not immediately expensed, but rather is considered as an asset and is then amortised through the income statement over time.

caption

an option that grants the holder the right to purchase a cap.

captive finance company

a company, usually a subsidiary that is wholly owned, whose main function is financing consumer purchases from the parent company.

■ **caput**

an exotic option. It represents a call option on a put option. That is, you

■ **car**

a loose quantity term sometimes used to describe the amount of a commodity underlying one commodity contract; e.g., 'a car of bellies'. Derived from the fact that quantities of the product specified in a contract once corresponded closely to the capacity of a railroad car.

■ **carry**

related: Net financing cost.

■ **carrying charge**

the fee a broker charges for carrying securities on credit, such as on a margin account.

■ **carrying costs**

costs that increase with increases in the level of investment in current assets.

■ **carrying value**

1. amount, net or contra account balances, that an asset or liability shows on the balance sheet of a company. Also known as book value.
2. Book value.

■ **carryovers**

provision of tax law that allows current losses or certain tax credits to be utilised in the tax returns of future periods.

■ **cartel**

a group of individuals or businesses that try to profit from a trading situation by fixing prices and/or regulating/restricting the supply of a product.

■ **cash**

the value of assets that can be converted into cash immediately, as reported by a company. Usually includes bank accounts and marketable securities, such as government bonds and banker's acceptances. Cash equivalents on balance sheets include securities that mature within 90 days (e.g., notes).

■ **cash & carry**

applies to derivative products. Combination of a long position in a stock/index/commodity and short position in the underlying futures, which entails a cost of carry on the long position.

■ **cash accounting**

the system of accounting for income and expenditure, as and when cash is received or paid.

■ **cash and equivalents**

the value of assets that can be converted into cash immediately, as reported by a company. Usually includes bank accounts and marketable securities, such as government bonds and Banker's Acceptances. Cash equivalents on balance sheets include securities (e.g., notes) that mature within 90 days.

■ **cash asset ratio**

cash and marketable securities divided by current liabilities.

■ **cash basis**

method of bookkeeping by which revenues and expenditures are recorded when they are received and paid.

■ **cash budget**

a forecasted summary of a firm's expected cash inflows and cash outflows as well as its expected cash and loan balances.

■ **cash commodity**

the actual physical commodity, as distinguished from a futures contract.

■ **cash conversion cycle**

the length of time between a firm's purchase of inventory and the receipt of cash from accounts receivable.

■ **cash cow**

a company that pays out most of its earnings per share to stockholders as dividends. Or, a company or division of a company that generates a steady and significant amount of free cash flow.

■ **cash cycle**

in general, the time between cash disbursement and cash collection. In net working capital management, it can be thought of as the operating cycle less the accounts payable payment period.

■ **cash deficiency agreement**

an agreement to invest cash in a project to the extent required to cover any cash deficiency the project may experience.

■ **cash delivery**

the provision of some futures contracts that requires not delivery of underlying assets but settlement according to the cash value of the asset.

■ **cash discount**

an incentive offered to purchasers of a firm's product for payment within a specified time period, such as ten days.

■ **cash dividend**

a dividend paid in cash to a company's shareholders. The amount is normally based on profitability and is taxable as income. A cash distribution may include capital gains and return of capital in addition to the dividend.

■ **cash earnings**

a firm's cash revenues less cash expenses, which excludes the costs of depreciation.

■ **cash equivalent**

1. the cash equivalent of accrued benefit, under a defined benefit pension scheme, which may be applied as a transfer payment to another approved pension arrangement or to purchase a S32 buy out policy.
2. short-term (generally less than three months), highly liquid investments that are convertible to known amounts of cash.

■ **cash flow**

a finance and accounting term used to describe the net amount of cash generated by a firm's operations. In traditional and oversimplified usage, cash flow is defined as the sum of net income after tax, plus all noncash expenses such as depreciation. More modern and sophisticated usage defines cash flow to include the net difference between all cash outflows and cash inflows.

	Jan	Feb	Mar	Apr
Starting Cash	1,000	1,200	900	(300)
■ In				
– Sales	1,000	1,100	1,200	1,300
Total In	2,000	2,300	2,100	1,000
■ Out				
– Payroll	300	500	600	400
– Purchases	300	400	400	400
– Overhead	200	500	400	300
– Capital Expenses	0	0	1,000	0
Total Out	800	1,400	2,400	1,100
■ Cash Balance	1,200	900	(300)	(100)

(Starting Cash Plus "In" minus "Out")

■ cash flow after interest and taxes

net income plus depreciation.

■ cash flow break-even point

the point below which the firm will need either to obtain additional financing or to liquidate some of its assets to meet its fixed costs.

■ cash flow coverage ratio

the number of times that financial obligations (for interest, principal payments, preferred stock dividends, and rental payments) are covered by earnings before interest, taxes, rental payments, and depreciation.

■ cash flow from operations

a firm's net cash inflow resulting directly from its regular operations (disregarding extraordinary items such as the sale of fixed assets or transaction costs associated with issuing securities), calculated as the sum of net income plus non-cash expenses that are deducted in calculating net income.

■ cash flow gap

the difference between cash inflows and cash outflows in a defined time period. Also called liquidity gap.

■ cash flow matching

also called dedicating a portfolio, this is an alternative to multi-period immunisation that calls for the manager to match the maturity of each element in the liability stream, working backward from the last liability to assure all required cash flows.

■ cash flow per common share

cash flow from operations minus preferred stock dividends, divided by the number of common shares outstanding.

■ cash flow time line

line depicting the operating activities and cash flows for a firm over a particular period.

■ cash forward agreement

a commitment to purchase or sell a security at a future date, that is binding on both the buyer and the seller. Also known as a firm commitment.

■ cash instrument

financial instruments or commodities for which the value is dependent upon the term, coupon rate or other characteristics of the instrument itself.

■ cash letter
items (primarily cheques) along with a letter that specifies amounts and directions. Cash letters are sent to a bank for transmittal to other banks, for the purpose of clearing cheques drawn on other banks.

■ cash management
one or a combination of various techniques for accelerating cash receipts, delaying cash disbursements, effectively utilising banking services, managing or augmenting liquidity, increasing the amount of cash available for investment and/or increasing returns from liquid investments.

■ cash management bill
very short-maturity bills that the Treasury occasionally sells because its cash balances are down and it needs money for a few days.

■ cash market
1. a market for buying or selling financial instruments, commodities or other property for cash settlement and immediate delivery. Also called spot market.
2. A financial instrument or transaction for which the ownership of the financial instrument or commodity is transferred at, or very shortly after, the time of the transaction. Also called spot or spot market transactions.

■ cash offer
often used in risk arbitrage. Proposal, either hostile or friendly, to acquire a target company through the payment of cash for the stock of the target. Compare to exchange offer.

■ Cash on Delivery (COD)
in the context of securities, this refers to the practice of institutional investors paying the full purchase price for securities in cash.

■ cash plus convertible
convertible bond that requires cash payment upon conversion.

■ cash price
applies to derivative products.

■ cash ratio
the proportion of a firm's assets held as cash.

■ cash sale/settlement
1. transaction in which a contract is settled on the same day as the trade date, or the next day if the trade occurs after 2:30 p.m. EST and the parties agree to this procedure. Often occurs because a party is strapped for cash and cannot wait until the regular five-business day settlement.
2. the agreement of a buyer and seller to exchange the security and the payment on the same day as the trade. For money market instruments, cash settlement is the delivery of purchased securities against payment in fed funds, on the same day that the trade is made.

■ cash settlement contracts
futures contracts such as stock index futures that settle for cash and do not involve delivery of the underlying.

■ cash transaction
a transaction in which exchange is immediate in the form of

cash, unlike a forward contract (which calls for future delivery of an asset at an agreed-upon price.)

■ **cashbook**

an accounting book that is composed of cash receipts plus disbursements. This balance is posted to the cash account in the ledger.

■ **cash-equivalent items**

examples include Treasury bills and Banker's Acceptances.

■ **cashflow**

the movement of cash in and out of a business from day-to-day direct trading and other non-trading or indirect effects, such as capital expenditure, tax and dividend payments.

■ **cashflow statement**

one of the three essential reporting and measurement systems for any company. The cashflow statement provides a third perspective alongside the Profit and Loss account and Balance Sheet. The cashflow statement shows the movement and availability of cash through and to the business over a given period, certainly for a trading year, and often also monthly and cumulatively. The availability of cash in a company that is necessary to meet payments to suppliers, staff and other creditors is essential for any business to survive, and so the reliable forecasting and reporting of cash movement and availability is crucial.

■ **cashier's check**

a check drawn directly on a customer's account, making the bank the primary obligor, and assuring firms that the amount will be paid.

■ **cash-on-cash return**

a method used to find the return on investments when there is no active secondary market. The yield is determined by dividing the annual cash income by the total investment.

■ **cashout**

occurs when a firm runs out of cash and cannot readily sell marketable securities.

■ **cash-surrender value**

the amount an insurance company will pay if the policyholder tende4s or cashes in a whole life insurance policy.

■ **casualty loss**

a financial loss caused by damage, destruction, or loss of property as a result of an unexpected or unusual event.

■ **casualty-insurance**

insurance protecting a firm or homeowner against loss of property, damage, and other liabilities.

■ **catastrophe call**

early redemption of a municipal revenue bond because a catastrophe has destroyed the project that provided the revenue source backing the bond.

■ **cats and dogs**

speculative stocks with short histories of sales, earnings, and dividend payments.

■ **caveat**

to enter a caveat means to give legal warning of an interest in a situation.

■ **caveat emptor**

under normal buying/selling contractual arrangements, this is taken to mean 'let the buyer beware' and usually no greater duty of care is due. Because of the greater duty of care required when dealing with investments, however, caveat emptor is not taken as a guiding principle.

■ **caveat emptor, caveat subscriptor**

Latin expressions for 'buyer beware' and 'seller beware', which warn of overly risky, inadequately protected markets.

■ **ceiling**

an upper limit for a variable. For example, an adjustable- rate mortgage may have a ceiling of 10 percent. In this case, the rate can be adjusted, however the loan terms provide without exceeding 10 percent.

■ **central bank**

the main government controlled/influenced bank in a country, which controls the internal and external financial affairs of the country, e.g. setting interest rates, controlling currency and foreign exchange rate.

■ **certainty equivalent**

an amount that would be accepted today (risk free) in lieu of a chance to receive a possibly higher, but uncertain, amount.

■ **certificate**

a formal document used to record a fact and used as proof of the fact, such as stock certificates, that evidence ownership of stock in a corporation.

■ **Certificate of Deposit (CD)**

1. a deposit of funds, in a bank or savings and loan association, for a specified term that earns interest at a specified rate or rate formula. CDs may be secured or unsecured. CDs may be for terms as short as one week or for terms of 10 years or longer. CDs may have fixed or floating rates. CDs may be issued in either non-negotiable or negotiable form and in either physical or book-entry form.

2. Formal instrument issued by a bank upon the deposit of funds which may not be withdrawn for a specified time period. Typically, an early withdrawal will incur a penalty.

MBNA CD Accounts

Minimum Opening Balance $10,000

Terms (months)	Current Interest Rate	Annual Percentage Yields (APYs)
6 to < 9	1.64%	1.65%
9 to < 12	1.79%	1.80%
12 to < 18	2.08%	2.10%
18 to < 24	2.38%	2.40%
24 to < 30	2.57%	2.60%
30 to < 36	2.91%	2.95%
36 to < 48	3.11%	3.15%
48 to < 60	3.54%	3.60%
60	4.02%	4.10%

*CD APYs for the terms shown above are valid for the period from 03/01/04 to 03/07/04 and assume interest remains in the account until maturity. Minimum opening balance is $10,000 for all terms shown above. Withdrawals and fees may reduce earnings on the account. A penalty may be imposed for early withdrawal of CD principal.

■ certificate of good standing

a written form prepared by a state office or officer attesting to the fact that a named corporation is in good standing in that state.

■ certificate of insurance

a document that describes an insurance policy. It is issued for informational purposes only. It is not a legal evidence of insurance and may even describe a policy that has not yet been issued.

■ certificate of origin

a document that specifies the country of origin for goods traded internationally.

■ certificateless municipals

municipal bonds with one certificate, which is valid for the entire issue, and having no individual certificates, easing transactions.

■ Certificates Of Amortised Revolving Debt (CARD)

pass-through securities backed by credit card receivables.

■ Certificates Of Automobile Receivables (CAR)

pass-through securities backed by automobile loan receivables.

■ certified check

a bank guaranteed check for which funds are immediately withdrawn, and for which the bank is legally liable.

■ Certified Financial Planner (CFP)

a person who has passed examinations accredited by the Certified Financial Planner Board of Standards, showing that the person is able to manage a client's banking, estate, insurance, investment, and tax affairs.

■ certified financial statements

financial statements that include an accountant's opinion.

■ Certified Public Accountant (CPA)

accountant who has satisfied the education, experience and examination requirements of his or her jurisdiction necessary to be certified as a public accountant.

■ chair of the board

highest-ranking member of a Board of Directors, who presides over its meetings and who is often the most powerful officer of a corporation.

■ chamber of commerce

an organisation effectively controlled by local businesses to help promote business and commerce for the benefit of the local business community as a whole.

■ **changes in financial position**

sources of funds provided from operations that alter a company's cash flow position: depreciation, deferred taxes, other sources, and capital expenditures.

■ **character**

a term used by lenders and credit analysts to describe an individual's integrity and management ability. The term also may be used to describe the integrity and management ability of individuals managing a corporation. As used by lenders, character does not mean the citizenship or moral rectitude of an individual.

■ **characteristic line**

the market model applied to a single security; a regression of security returns on the benchmark return. The slope of the regression line is a security's beta.

■ **charge**

a creditor's right over a debtor's property, which may be enforced in the event of default.

■ **chargeable event**

chargeable events occur when certain payments are made from packaged life and investment products. They may or may not give rise to a tax charge. Any tax liability which might arise falls within income tax rules.

■ **charge-backs**

the reduction of unpaid invoices owed to a trade creditor due to a dispute, return, offset or any reason other than an account debtor's inability to pay.

■ **charitable remainder trust**

an irrevocable trust that pays income to a designated person or persons until the grantor's death, when the income is passed on to a designated charity. A charitable lead trust by contrast allows the charity to receive income during the grantor's life, and the remaining income to pass to designated family members upon the grantor's death.

■ **Chartered Financial Analyst (CFA)**

an experienced financial analyst who has passed examinations in economics, financial accounting, portfolio management, security analysis, and standards of conduct given by the institute of Chartered Financial Analysts.

■ **charting**

a way of analysing trends, using different types of chart, to forecast future movement, particularly in respect of share movements. A 'chartist' is a person who makes use of such a method.

■ chartists

a technical analyst who charts the patterns of stocks, bonds, and commodities to find trends in patterns of trading used to advise clients. Related: Technical analysts.

■ chasing the market

purchasing a security at a higher price than expected because prices are rapidly climbing, or selling a security at a lower level when prices are quickly falling.

■ chastity bonds

bonds redeemable at par value in the case of a takeover.

■ cheapest to deliver

the cash market instrument that is the least expensive instrument to acquire and deliver into an exchange-traded contract at maturity.

■ cheapest to deliver issue

the acceptable Treasury security with the highest implied repo rate; the rate that a seller of a futures contract can earn by buying an issue and then delivering it at the settlement date.

■ check

a bill of exchange representing a draft on a bank from deposited funds that pays a certain sum of money to a certain person or party.

■ checking the market

searching for bid and offer prices from market makers to find the best deal.

■ cheque

a commercial demand deposit instrument signed by the maker and payable on the presentation to the bank on which it is drawn.

■ cheque truncation

a process whereby deposited cheques are retained by the fist bank (payee's bank), with notification sent to the local bank (payer's bank) that the cheque has been deposited. Cancelled cheques are not returned to the maker. Sometimes called cheque safekeeping.

■ cheque-clearing float

the time between the date a cheque is deposited in a bank and the date it is charged to the drawer. Also called bank float or transit float.

■ Chief Executive Officer (CEO)

a title held often by the Chairperson of the Board, or the president. The person principally responsible for the activities of a company.

■ Chief Financial Officer (CFO)

the officer of a firm is responsible for handling the financial affairs of a company.

■ Chief Operating Officer (COO)

the officer of a firm responsible for day-to-day management, usually the president or an executive vice-president.

■ Chinese hedge

applies mainly to convertible securities. Trading hedge in which one is short the convertible and long the underlying common, in the hope that the convertible's premium will fall. Antithesis of set-up.

■ Chinese wall

communication barrier between financiers at a firm (investment bankers) and traders. This barrier is erected to prevent the sharing of inside information that bankers are likely to have.

■ choice market

applies mainly to international equities. Locked market in London terminology.

■ chose

something belonging to someone.

■ chose in action

a personal right to receive or recover a debt or damages, but only through a lawsuit.

■ churning

1. the process of unnecessary purchases and sales in customers' accounts, for the purpose of generating commissions.
2. The practice of moving investments merely to attract additional commissions.

■ churning

excessive trading of a client's account in order to increase the broker's commissions.

■ circle

underwriters, actual or potential, often seek out and 'circle' investor interest in a new issue before final pricing. The customer circled has basically made a commitment to purchase the issue if it is available at an agreed-upon price. If the actual price is other than that stipulated, the customer supposedly has first offer at the actual price.

■ circuit breakers

measures instituted by exchanges to stop trading temporarily when the market has fallen by a certain percentage in a specified period. They are intended to prevent a market free fall by permitting buy and sell orders to rebalance.

■ citizen bonds

certificate less municipals that can be registered on stock exchanges and are listed in newspapers.

■ city code on takeovers and mergers

see **dawn raid.**

■ claim

generally taken to mean a demand for payment under a policy, whether on surrender, maturity or death.

■ claim dilution

a decrease in the likelihood that one or more of a firm's claimants will be fully repaid, including time value of money considerations.

■ claimant

a party to an explicit or implicit contract.

■ class

in the case of derivative products, options of the same type-put or call-with the same underlying security. In general, refers to a category of assets such as: domestic equity, fixed income, etc.

■ **class a/class b shares**

see **classified stock.**

■ **class action**

a legal complaint filed by a lawyer or group of lawyers for a group of petitioners with an identical grievance, often with an award proportionate to the number of shareholders involved.

■ **class of potential beneficiaries**

under certain types of trust, such as flexible trusts, it is possible to have a general reference to a class of beneficiaries, as well as specific appointments as beneficiary.

■ **classified stock**

the division of stock into more than one class of common stock, usually called Class A and Class B. The specific features of each class, which are set out in the charter and bylaws, usually give certain advantages to the Class A shares, such as increased voting power.

■ **clawback**

money claimed back which has previously been paid out, e.g. life assurance commission may be claimed back if the policy is cancelled within a certain period.

■ **clean**

in the context of general equities, block trade that matches buy or sell orders/interests, sparing the block trader any inventory risk (no net position and hence none available for additional customers). Natural. Antithesis of open.

■ **clean letter of credit**

a letter of credit that can be drawn upon with a simple written request not supported by other documentation. Often used to identify or describe standby letters of credit. This type of letter of credit is often used to enhance the credit quality of securities.

■ **clean opinion**

audit opinion not qualified for any material scope restrictions, nor departures from Generally Accepted Accounting Principles (GAAP). Also known as unqualified opinion.

■ **clean opinion**

an auditor's opinion reflecting an unqualified acceptance of a company's financial statements.

■ **clean price**

bond price excluding accrued interest.

■ **clean up**

in the context of general equities, purchase/sale of all the remaining supply of stock, or the last piece of a block, in a trade-leaving a net zero position.

■ **clear**

1. the collection of funds on which a cheque is drawn and the subsequent payment of these funds to the holder of the cheque. 2. To settle a trade is settled out by the seller delivering securities and the buyer delivering funds in the proper form. A trade that does not clear is said to fail. Comparison of the details of a transaction

between broker/dealers prior to settlement; final exchange of securities for cash on delivery.

■ **clear a position**

to eliminate a long or short position, leaving no ownership or obligation.

■ **clear title**

title to ownership that is untainted by any claims on the property or disputed interests, and therefore available for sale. This is usually checked through a title search by a title company.

■ **clearing**

taken as a banking term, the process of presenting cheques to the drawers bank for payment.

■ **clearing account**

an account used to accumulate total charges or credits, so that they can be distributed later among the accounts to which they are allocable or so that the net differences can be transferred to the proper account.

■ **clearing corporations**

organisations that are affiliated with exchanges and are used to complete securities transactions by taking care of validation, delivery, and settlement.

■ **clearing house**

an organisation set up to arrange settlements of money between a number of parties, e.g. banks or stockmarkets, so that only one balance has to be settled between any two parties at the end of each day or trading period.

■ **Clearing House Interbank Payments System (CHIPS)**

an international wire transfer system for high-value payments operated by a group of major banks.

■ **clearing member**

a member firm of a clearing house. Each clearing member must also be a member of the exchange. Not all members of the exchange, however, are members of the clearing organisation. All trades of a non-clearing member must be registered with, and eventually settled through, a clearing member.

■ **clearinghouse**

an adjunct to a futures exchange through which transactions executed on its floor are settled by a process of matching purchases and sales. A clearing organisation is also charged with the proper conduct of delivery procedures and the adequate financing of the entire operation.

■ **client**

generally taken to mean someone with whom you do business. More specifically, it should be used to refer to someone whom you know and with whom you do business on a regular basis.

■ **client account**

an account held on behalf of clients, which is kept separate from the business finances of a company or partnership.

■ **clientele effect**

describes the tendency of funds or investments to be followed by groups of investors who have a similar preferences that the firm follow a particular financing policy, such as the amount of leverage it uses.

■ clone fund

a new fund set up in a fund family to emulate another successful fund.

■ close

the close is the period at the end of the trading session. Sometimes used to refer to closing price. Related: Opening.

■ close a position

in the context of general equities, eliminate an investment from one's portfolio, by either selling a long position or covering a short position.

■ close company

company controlled by five or fewer individuals and not traded on the stock exchange.

■ close market

an active market in which there is a narrow spread between bid and offer prices, due to a high volume of trading and many competing market makers.

■ closed corporation

a corporation whose shares are owned by just a few people, having no public market.

■ closed fund

a mutual fund that is no longer issuing shares, mainly because it has grown too large.

■ closed out

position that is liquidated when the client does not meet a margin call or cover a short sale.

■ closed-end fund

an investment company that sells shares like any other corporation and usually does not redeem its shares. A publicly traded fund sold on stock exchanges or over the counter that may trade above or below its net asset value. Related: Open-end fund.

■ closed-end management company

an investment company that has only a set number of shares of the mutual fund that it manages, and does not create new shares if demand increases. Antithesis of an open-end management company.

■ closed-end mortgage

mortgage against which no additional debt may be issued.

■ closely held

a corporation whose voting stock is owned by only a few shareholders.

■ closely held company

a company who has a small group of controlling shareholders. In contrast, a widely held firm has many shareholders. It is difficult or impossible to wage a proxy battle for any closely-held firm.

■ closing costs

all the expenses involved in transferring ownership of real estate.

■ closing price

price of the last transaction of a particular stock completed during a day's trading session on an exchange.

■ closing purchase

a transaction in which the purchaser's intention is to reduce or eliminate a short position in a stock, or in a given series of options.

■ closing quote

the last bid and offer prices of a particular stock at the close of a day's trading session on an exchange.

■ closing range

also known as the range. The high and low prices, or bids and offers, recorded during the period designated as the official close. Related: Settlement price.

■ closing sale

a transaction in which the seller's intention is to reduce or eliminate a long position in a stock, or a given series of options.

■ closing tick

the net of the number of stocks whose closing prices are higher than their previous trades (uptick) against the number of stocks whose closing prices were lower than their previous trades (downtick). A positive closing tick indicates 'buying at the close', or a bullish market; a negative closing tick indicates 'selling at the close,' or a bearish market.

■ closing transaction

applies to derivative products. Buy or sell transaction that eliminates an existing position (selling a long option or buying back a short option). Antithesis of opening transaction.

■ cloud on title

any claim or encumbrance, usually discovered in a title search, that may impair the title to a property, and make its validity questionable.

■ cluster analysis

a statistical technique that identifies clusters of stocks whose returns are highly correlated within each cluster and relatively uncorrelated across clusters. Cluster analysis has identified groupings such as growth, cyclical, stable, and energy stocks.

■ clustering

the subdivision of what would otherwise be one large policy into a number of smaller policies. Used for endowments, investment bonds and pension policies. Provides flexibility as allows policyholder to encash/surrender/use part of investment rather than whole.

■ coattail investing

a risky trading practice of making trades similar to those of other successful investors, usually institutional investors.

■ coefficient of determination

a measure of the goodness of fit of the relationship between the dependent and independent variables in a regression analysis; for instance, the percentage of variation in the return of an asset explained by the market portfolio return. Also known as R-square.

■ coincident indicators

economic indicators that give an indication of the status of the economy.

■ coinsurance

a provision in an insurance policy that requires the insured to carry an amount of insurance equal to a certain specified percentage of the value of the insured property. The coinsurance provision or clause provides for full payment of losses, up to the amount of the policy if the amount of insurance carried equals the specified coinsurance percentage. If the amount of insurance carried does not equal the specified coinsurance percentage, the losses are shared between the insurer and the insured, even if the loss is below the amount of the policy.

■ coinsurance effect

refers to the fact that the merger of two firms lessens the probability of default on either firm's debt.

■ cold calling

1. a personal visit or oral communication made without invitation.
2. Calling potential new customers in the hope of selling stocks, bonds or other financial products and receiving commissions.

■ collar

an upper and lower limit on the interest rate on a floating-rate note (FRN) or an adjustable-rate mortgage (ARM).

■ collateral

1. property that a debtor has pledged, mortgaged or assigned to a creditor.
2. Securities exchanges in a repo, reverse repo, buy/sellback or sell/buyback.

■ collateral trust bonds

a type of corporate bond that employs a trustee to hold collateral, other than equipment or real estate, for the bond holders.

■ collateral trust bonds

a bond in which the issuer (often a holding company) grants investors a lien on stocks, notes, bonds, or other financial asset as security. Compare mortgage bond.

■ Collateralised Bond Obligation (CBO)

investment-grade bonds backed by a collection of junk bonds with different levels of risk, called tiers, that are determined by the quality of junk bond involved. CBOs backed by highly risky junk bonds receive higher interest rates than other CBOs.

■ Collateralised mortgage obligation (CMO)

a security backed by a pool of pass-through rates , structured so that there are several classes of bondholders with varying maturities, called tranches. The principal payments from the underlying pool of pass-through securities are used to retire the bonds on a priority basis as specified in the prospectus. Related: mortgage pass-through security.

■ collected balances

collected balances are bank ledger balances minus cheques in the process of collection. Also called available balances, good funds or usable funds.

■ collection

obtaining payment.

■ collection float

the total time period between when a cheque is prepared by the remitter and when the cheque is presented to the remitter's bank. The float also includes the mail float, processing float and transit float, and is considered the disbursement float for the organisation that issues the cheque.

■ collection fractions

the percentage of a given month's sales collected during the month of sale and each month following the month of sale.

■ collection guaranty

a guaranty in which the signer guarantees to pay the bank only if the bank cannot obtain repayment through other means.

■ collection period

see **collection ratio.**

■ collection policy

procedures a firm follows in attempting to collect accounts receivables.

■ collection ratio

the ratio of a company's accounts receivable to its average daily sales, which gives the average number of days it takes the company to convert receivables into cash.

■ collective investment schemes

also known as pooled investments. Refers to unitised schemes where investor's contributions are pooled and they receive units in the fund in exchange for their contribution, e.g. unit trusts.

■ collective wisdom

the combination of all the individual opinions about a stock's or security's value.

■ Continuous On-Line Trading System (COLT)

computerised OTC traders assistance system that provides for trade entry and position monitoring, among other functions.

■ combination

applies to derivative products. Arrangement of options involving two long or two short positions with different expiration dates or strike (exercise) prices.

■ combination bond +

a bond backed by the government unit issuing it as well as by revenue from the project that is to be financed by the bond.

■ combination matching

also called horizon-matching, a variation of multi-period immunisation and cash flow-matching in which a portfolio is created that is always duration-matched and also cash-matched in the first few years.

■ **combination strategy**

a strategy in which a put and call with the same strike price and expiration are either both bought or both sold. Related: Straddle

■ **combined financial statement**

financial statement comprising the accounts of two or more entities.

■ **Combined Loan To Value ratio (CLTV)**

a measure of collateral coverage provided by a consumer borrower's residence. The borrower's total senior and subordinated loan balances divided by the appraised value of the borrower's residence.

■ **come in**

in the context of general equities, a fall in price.

■ **come out of the trade**

in the context of general equities, trader's position in a security that results from executing a trade (or the expectations thereof). Antithesis of going into the trade.

■ **come out**

in the context of general equities, the opening. Antithesis of the close.

■ **comfort letter**

a letter from an independent auditor in securities underwriting agreements to assure that information in the registration statement and prospectus is correctly prepared to the best of the auditor's knowledge.

■ **commercial draft**

demand for payment.

■ **commercial hedgers**

companies that take futures positions in commodities so that they can guarantee prices at which they will buy raw materials or sell their products.

■ **commercial letter of credit**

an obligation issued by a bank, on behalf of a bank customer, to a third party. A commercial or trade letter of credit is a bank promise to pay the third party for the purchase of goods by the bank's customer. If the bank's obligation to pay is not immediate, the transaction can later give rise to a banker's acceptance. Also called trade letter of credit.

■ **commercial loan**

a short-term loan, typically 90 days, used by a company to finance seasonal working capital needs.

■ **commercial mortgage backed securities**

similar to MBS but backed by loans secured with commercial rather than residential property. Commercial property includes multi-family, retail, office, etc., They are not standardised so there are a lot of details associated with structure, credit enhancement, diversification, etc., that need to be understood when valuing these instruments.

■ commercial paper

unsecured, short-term promissory notes issued by corporations for specific amounts and with specific maturity dates. Firms with lower ratings or firms without well-known names usually back their commercial paper with guarantees or bank letters of credit. Commercial paper may be sold on a discount basis or may be interest bearing. Terms can be as short as 1 day and usually do not exceed 270 days.

■ commercial property

real estate that produces some sort of income-producing property.

■ commercial risk

the risk that a foreign debtor will be unable to pay its debts because of business events, such as bankruptcy.

■ commingled funds

money pooled for a common purpose. Often funds pooled for investments.

■ commingled goods

goods that become part of a product or mass of goods. An example is the flour used to bake bread.

■ commingling

in the context of securities, this involves mixing customer-owned securities with brokerage firm-owned securities. This process is referred to as re-hypothecation, which is the use of customers' collateral to secure their loans. This is legal with customer consent, although some securities and collateral must be kept separately.

■ commission

money payable to an agent or third party for services, usually introducing business.

■ commission broker

a broker on the floor of an exchange who acts as agent for a particular brokerage house and buys and sells stocks for the brokerage house on a commission basis.

■ commission house

a firm that buys and sells futures contracts for customer accounts. Related: futures commission merchant, omnibus account.

■ commitment

describes a trader's obligation to accept or make delivery on a futures contract. Related: Open interest.

■ commitment fee

a fee paid to a commercial bank in return for its legal commitment to lend funds that have not yet been advanced. Often used in risk arbitrage.

■ commitment letter

a legally binding letter in which a lender documents the terms, prerequisites and conditions under which it agrees to provide financing to an applicant. Commitment letters may be used in almost any lending transaction but are most common in commercial real estate transactions.

■ Committee On Uniform Securities Identification Procedures (CUSIP)

committee that assigns identifying numbers and codes for all securities. These 'CUSIP' numbers and symbols are used when recording all buy or sell orders.

■ commodities

generally taken to refer to investments involving future pricing of raw materials in foodstuffs and metals.

■ commodity

a commodity is food, metal, or another fixed physical substance that investors buy or sell, usually via futures contracts.

■ commodity futures contract

an agreement to buy a specific amount of a commodity at a specified price on a particular date in the future, allowing a producer to guarantee the price of a product or raw material used in production.

■ commodity indexs

indexs measuring the price and performance of physical commodities, often by the price of futures contracts for the commodities that are listed on commodity exchanges.

■ commodity paper

a loan or advance secured by commodities.

■ commodity-backed bond

a bond with interest payments tied to the price of an underlying commodity.

■ common code

a nine-digit identification code issued jointly by CEDEL and Euroclear. As of January 1991 common codes replaced the earlier separate CEDEL and Euroclear codes.

■ common market

an agreement between two or more countries that permits the free movement of capital and labor as well as goods and services.

■ common shares

in general, a public corporation has two types of shares, common and preferred. The common shares usually entitle the shareholders to vote at shareholders meetings. The common shares have a discretionary dividend.

■ common stock

a type of equity or capital, representing shares of ownership in a corporation. May or may not receive distributions of corporate income in the form of dividends. Receives the lowest priority for repayment, in the event of a corporate liquidation. As opposed to preferred stock, which has a slightly higher claim to corporate funds.

■ common stock equivalent

a convertible security that is traded like an equity issue because the optioned common stock is trading at a high price.

■ common stock fund

a mutual fund investing only in common stock.

■ **common stock market**

the market for trading equities, not including preferred stock.

■ **common stock ratios**

ratios that are designed to measure the relative claims of stockholders to earnings (cash flow per share), and equity (book value per share) of a firm.

■ **common stock/other equity**

value of outstanding common shares at par, plus accumulated retained earnings. Also called shareholders' equity.

■ **common-base-year analysis**

the representing of accounting information over multiple years as percentages of amounts in an initial year.

■ **common-size analysis**

the representing of balance sheet items as percentages of assets and of income statement items as percentages of sales.

■ **common-size statement**

a statement in which all items are expressed as a percentage of a base figure, useful for purposes of analysing trends and changing relationship among financial statement items. For example, all items in each year's income statement could be presented as a percentage of net sales.

■ **commutation**

the option of exchanging pension for cash at retirement at a fixed rate.

■ **companion bonds**

a class of a Collateralised Mortgage Obligation (CMO) whose principal is paid off first when the underlying mortgages are prepaid due to falling interest rates. When interest rates rise, there will be lower prepayments of the principal; companion bonds therefore absorb most of the prepayment risk of a CMO.

■ **company**

a proprietorship, partnership, corporation, or other form of enterprise that engages in business.

■ **company doctor**

an executive, usually appointed from outside, brought in to turn a company around and make it profitable.

■ **company-specific risk**

related: Unsystematic risk

■ **comparative credit analysis**

comparing a firm to others that have a desired target debt rating in order to deduce an appropriate financial ratio target.

■ **comparative financial statement**

financial statement presentation in which the current amounts and the corresponding amounts for previous periods or dates also are shown.

■ **comparative statements**

financial statements for different periods, that all the comparison of figures to illustrate trends in a company's performance.

■ **comparison**

short for 'comparison ticket,' a memorandum between two brokers that confirms the details of a transaction to be carried out.

■ **comparison universe**

a group of money managers of similar investment style used to assess relative performance of a portfolio manager.

■ **compensating balance**

a method of paying the bank for providing services.

1. In lending, compensating balances are minimum balances that the bank requires a borrower to maintain with the bank as partial compensation to the bank for the credit facility.

2. The amount of deposit balances necessary to offset the cost of deposit, cash management or other bank services. Each period, usually monthly, the actual bank service charges applicable for the services used by the depositor are used to determine the level of balances to be left with the bank. Adjustments are made to reduce the deposit total for reserve requirements and float.

■ **compensating balance**

an excess balance that is left in a bank to provide indirect compensation for loans extended or services provided.

■ **compensation package**

the elements of pay and other benefits that go with a particular job.

■ **compensatory balance**

funds that a borrower must keep on deposit as required by a bank.

■ **competence**

sufficient ability or fitness for one's needs. The necessary abilities to be qualified to achieve a certain goal or complete a project.

■ **competition**

intra- or intermarket rivalry between or among businesses trying to obtain a larger piece of the same market share.

■ **competition ahead**

often used in risk arbitrage. Situation whereby another O.T.C. market maker has transacted with investment bank at the stated market level before the bid/offer has been made.

■ **competitive bidding**

a securities offering process in which securities firms submit competing bids to the issuer for the securities the issuer wishes to sell.

■ **competitive offering**

an offering of securities through competitive bidding.

■ **compilation**

presentation of financial statement data without the accountant's assurance as to conformity with Generally Accepted Accounting Principles (GAAP).

■ **compilation statement**

financial statement put together for the client firm by a CPA, that is entirely based upon data submitted to the CPA by the firm with no review, no testing and no opinion expressed by the CPA.

■ complete

in the context of general equities, to fill an order.

■ complete capital market

a market in which there is a distinctive marketable security for each and every possible outcome.

■ complete portfolio

the entire portfolio, including risky and risk-free assets.

■ completion

the end of a transaction, generally used in property purchase transactions to signify the point at which the ownership of property changes hands.

■ completion bonding

insurance that a construction contract will be completed successfully.

■ completion risk

the risk that a project will not be brought into operation successfully.

■ completion undertaking

an undertaking either (1) to complete a project so that it meets certain specified performance criteria on or before a certain specified date, or (2) to repay project debt if the completion test cannot be met.

■ compliance audit

review of financial records to determine whether the entity is complying with specific procedures or rules.

■ compliance department

a department in all organised stock exchanges to ensure that all companies, traders, and brokerage firms comply with Securities and Exchange Commission and exchange rules and regulations.

■ composite

made up of different elements, e.g. a composite insurance company is one which may have a general insurance arm and a life assurance arm.

■ composition

voluntary arrangement to restructure a firm's debt, under which payment is reduced.

■ compound annual return

see **internal rate of return**.

■ compound growth rate

the rate of growth of a figure, compounded over some period of time.

■ compound interest

interest computed by applying the simple rate of interest to calculate interest on principal plus interest on successive increments of interest earned in prior periods.

■ compound option

an option on an option.

■ compounding

the process of accumulating the time value of money forward in time. For example, interest earned in one period earns additional interest during each subsequent time period.

compounding frequency
the number of compounding periods in a year. For example, quarterly compounding has a compounding frequency of 4.

compounding period
the length of the time period that elapses before interest compounds (a quarter in the case of quarterly compounding).

comprehensive due diligence investigation
the investigation of a firm's business in conjunction with a securities offering to determine whether the firm's business and financial situation and its prospects are adequately disclosed in the prospectus for the offering.

comprehensive income
change in equity of a business enterprise, during a period from transactions and other events and circumstances, from sources not shown in the income statement. The period includes all changes in equity except those resulting from investments by owners and distributions to owners.

comptroller
usually taken to mean a senior financial controller or manager.

comptroller of the currency
a government official, appointed by the president, who keeps control over all national banks, and receives reports from the banks at least quarterly, to be published in newspapers.

computerised market timing system
a computer system that compiles large amounts of trading data in search of patterns and trends to make buy and sell recommendations.

concave
property that a curve is below a straight line connecting two end points. If the curve falls above the straight line, it is called convexity.

concentration account
a cash management tool. A single account established by an entity, usually in conjunction with one or more zero balance disbursement accounts. Sometimes, the concentration account is referred to as a parent account, while the associated zero balance accounts are called daughter or subsidiary accounts.

concentration services
movement of cash from different lockbox locations into a single concentration account from which disbursements and investments are made.

concession
the underwriting spread. The difference between the price that an underwriter or underwriting syndicate pays to the issuer and the price that is received from investors who buy the issue. The concession is the income earned by the underwriter.

concession agreement
an understanding between a company and the host government that

specifies the rules under which the company can operate locally.

■ concurrency

term used to describe the ability to be an active member of more than one pension scheme, at the same time, in respect of the same employment.

■ conditional call

applies mainly to convertible securities. Circumstances under which a company can affect an earlier call, usually stated as percentage of a stock's trading price during a particular period, such as 140% of the exercise price during a 40-day trading span.

■ conditional call options

a protective guarantee that, in the event a high yield bond is called, the issuing corporation will replace the bond with a non-callable bond of the same life and terms as the bond that is being called.

■ conditional sales contracts

similar to equipment trust certificates, except that the lender is either the equipment manufacturer or a bank or finance company to which the manufacturer has sold the conditional sales contract.

■ conditions

a term used by lenders and credit analysts to describe the background or underlying economic and industry circumstances affecting a business.

■ condor

applies to derivative products. Option strategy consisting of both puts and calls at different strike prices to capitalise on a narrow range of volatility. The payoff diagram takes the shape of a bird.

■ conduit theory

a theory that because investment companies are merely conduits for capital gains, dividends, and interest, which are in fact passed through to shareholders, the investment company should not be taxed at the corporate level.

■ confidence indicator

a measure of investors' faith in the economy and the securities market. A low or deteriorating level of confidence is considered by many technical analysts as a bearish sign.

■ confidence letter

statement by an investment bank that it is highly confident that the financing for its client/acquirer's takeover can and will be obtained. Often used in risk arbitrage.

■ confidence level

in risk analysis, the degree of assurance that a specified failure rate is not exceeded.

■ confirmation

1. the document used to state in writing, the terms of a trade that were previously agreed to orally by the buyer and the seller.
2. Auditor's receipt of a written or oral response from an independent third party verifying the accuracy of information requested.
3. The written statement that follows any 'trade' in the securities markets. Confirmation is issued

immediately after a trade is executed. It spells out settlement date, terms, commission, etc.

■ **conflict between bondholders and stockholders**

bondholders and stockholders may have interests in a corporation that conflict. Sources of conflict include dividends, distortion of investment, and under investment. Protective covenants in bond documents work to resolve these conflicts.

■ **conformed copy**

a copy of an original document on which the signature, seal and other such authenticating features are typed or otherwise noted.

■ **conforming loans**

mortgage loans that meet the qualifications of Freddie Mac or Fannie Mae, which are bought from lenders and issued as pass-through securities.

■ **conglomerate**

1. widely differing businesses, grouped together as subsidiaries of a 'parent' company.
2. A firm engaged in two or more unrelated businesses.

■ **conglomerate merger**

a merger involving two or more firms that are in unrelated businesses.

■ **consensual lien**

a security interest given to a creditor by a debtor. A consensual lien is granted by the consent of the parties and is the basis for most secured transactions.

■ **consensus ad idem**

an essential element of a valid contract, meaning 'a meeting of minds', of like mind, i.e. both parties to a contract must be in complete agreement.

■ **consensus forecast**

the mean of all financial analysts' forecasts for a company.

■ **conservatism**

an investment strategy aimed at long-term capital appreciation with low risk.

■ **consideration**

1. a legal term used to describe the benefit that a borrower, guarantor or pledgor receives in exchange for agreeing to repay, guarantee or pledge security to the bank. Usually, but not always, the consideration is the proceeds of the loan.
2. Something of value exchanged as part of a contract, an essential of a valid contract. Sometimes used in the sense of 'payment', e.g. premium, or promise to pay a premium.

■ **consignment**

1. goods or inventory that are held by a selling agent, wholesaler or reseller until the goods are either sold or returned to the seller.
2. The physical transfer of goods from a seller/consignor who retains title to a consignee who acts as a selling agent.

■ **consistency**

accounting postulate which stipulates that, except as otherwise noted in the financial statement, the same accounting policies and procedures have been followed, from period to period, by an organisation in the preparation and presentation of its financial statements.

■ **consol**

a government bond with no maturity .

■ **consolidated financial statement**

a financial statement that shows all the assets, liabilities, and operating accounts of a parent company and its subsidiaries.

■ **consolidated financial statements**

combined financial statements of a parent company and one or more of its subsidiaries as one economic unit.

■ **consolidated mortgage bond**

a bond that covers several units of property, sometimes refinancing mortgages on the properties.

■ **consolidated tax return**

a tax return combining the reports of affiliated companies, that are at least 80% owned by a parent company.

■ **consolidating statements**

consolidating financial statements are reports or worksheets that show the financial condition of each entity in a consolidated group of entities, as well as the intercompany eliminations used in the preparation of consolidated reports.

■ **consolidation**

1. business combination of two or more entities that occurs when the entities transfer all of their net assets to a new entity created for that purpose.
2. The combining of financial information from separate accounts, e.g. companies within a group, as though they were a single account.
3. the combining of two or more firms to form an entirely new entity.

■ **consolidation loan**

a loan that is used to combine and finance payments on other loans.

■ **consols**

government bonds which pay interest but which do not have a maturity date.

■ **consortium**

1. independent elements (people or firms) grouped together for a particular purpose, e.g. banks to fund the channel tunnel.
2. A group of companies that cooperate and share resources in order to achieve a common objective.

■ **consortium banks**

a merchant banking subsidiary set up by several banks that may or may not be of the same nationality. Consortium banks are common in the Euro market and are active in loan syndication.

■ **constant dollars**

dollars of a base year used as a general measure of purchasing power.

■ constant ratio plan

maintaining a predetermined ratio between stock and fixed income investments through regular adjustments of distribution of funds into different investments.

■ constant yield method

allocation of annual interest on a zero-coupon security for income tax use.

■ constant-dollar plan

method of purchasing securities by investing a fixed amount of money at set intervals. The investor buys more shares when the price is low and fewer shares when the price is high, thus reducing the overall cost.

■ constant-growth model

also called the Gordon-Shapiro model, an application of the dividend discount model that assumes
1. a fixed growth rate for future dividends, and
2. a single discount rate.

■ construction loan

a short-term loan to finance building costs.

■ constructive receipt

the date a taxpayer receives dividends or other income, for use in the determination of taxes.

■ consumer

domestic and business purchasers of goods and services. Consumables or consumable goods/services are those goods and services purchased by consumers.

■ consumer credit

credit a firm grants to consumers for the purchase of goods or services. Also called retail credit.

■ consumer debenture

an investment note issued directly to the public by a financial institution.

■ consumer durables

consumer products that are expected to last three years or more, such as an automobile or a home appliance.

■ consumer goods

goods used primarily for personal, family or household purposes. Typical examples are jewellery, furniture, automobiles and appliances.

■ consumer interest

interest paid on consumer loans; e.g., interest on credit cards and retail purchases.

■ contagion

excess correlation of equity or bond returns.

■ contango

the fee paid by a buyer of shares, for deferring the purchase of stocks and shares. Also called 'forwardation'.

■ **contingency order**

in the context of general equities, order to buy one security, if the trader can sell another, usually given that certain price limits or conditions reach a certain level. Swap, switch order.

■ **contingent claim**

a claim that can be made only if one or more specified outcomes occur.

■ **Contingent Deferred Sales Charge (CDSC)**

the formal name for the load of a back-end load fund.

■ **contingent immunisation**

an arrangement in which the money manager pursues an active bond portfolio strategy until an adverse investment experience drives the then-available potential return down to the safety net level. When that point is reached, the money manager is obligated to pursue an immunisation strategy to lock in the safety-net level return.

■ **contingent liability**

1. a debt or obligation that becomes a liability only when something else happens. For example, a guarantor becomes liable for his guarantee only if the debt that is guaranteed does not get paid by the debtor.
2. Potential liability arising from a past transaction or a subsequent event.

■ **contingent life policy**

a policy where payment is made on death, only if certain preconditions (contingencies) are met, e.g. death before another person.

■ **continuation**

a form and process by which a secured party extends the priority of its security interest in the public record.

■ **continuation option**

some occupational pension schemes may offer scheme members, upon their leaving the scheme, a chance to continue any life assurance benefit that may have been linked to the scheme. An advantage usually lies in the fact that evidence of health will not be required.

■ **continuing guaranty**

a guaranty in which the guarantor agrees to guarantee all future loans made to that borrower by the bank, not just the loan or loans made as part of the transaction in which the guaranty was obtained.

■ **continuing operations**

portion of a business entity expected to remain active.

■ **continuous compounding**

the process of accumulating the time value of money forward in time on a continuous, or instantaneous, basis. Interest is earned constantly, and at each instant, the interest that accrues immediately begins earning interest on itself.

■ Continuous Net Settlement (CNS)

method of securities clearing and settlement using a clearing house, which matches transactions to securities available, resulting in one net receive or deliver position at the end of the day.

■ continuous random variable

a random value that can take any fractional value within specified ranges, as contrasted with a discrete variable.

■ continuous repo

a repo/reverse repo transaction that does not have a specified term. These transactions are like a series of overnight repos renewed daily. The repo rate, the amount of funds invested and/or the amount of collateral is adjusted each day. Continuing repos are commonly used in conjunction with bank sweep accounts.

■ contra

an amount which offsets another.

■ contra account

1. accounts receivable due from debtors who also have accounts payable due to them from the borrower. 2. account considered to be an offset to another account. Generally established to reduce the other account to amounts that can be realised or collected.

■ contra asset

an asset account that normally has a credit balance. Examples are the allowance for doubtful accounts and accumulated depreciation.

■ contra broker

the broker on the buy side of a sell order or the sell side of a buy order.

■ contra liability

a liability account that normally has a debit balance.

■ contract

an agreement between two parties, usually taken to be enforceable at law.

■ contract hire

a fixed term contract (usually) for the hire of an asset on a set rental.

■ contract month

the month in which futures contracts may be satisfied by making or accepting a delivery.

■ contract note

the confirmation received when shares are bought or sold – proof of the transaction for tax purposes.

■ contractual gap

a crude measure of a financial institution's exposure to adverse consequences resulting from changes in prevailing interest rates. The contractual gap is a gap mismatch measure, calculated using the contractual maturity and repricing dates for all assets and liabilities. It is arguably the least accurate gap methodology.

■ contractual plan

a plan in which fixed dollar amounts of mutual fund shares are purchased through periodic investments, usually featuring some sort of additional incentive for the fixed period payments.

■ contramarket stock

in the context of general equities, stock that tends to go against the trend of the market as a whole, such as a commodities-related stock or one in an industry out of favour with investors in a bull market.

■ contrarian

an investment style that leads one to buy assets that have performed poorly and sell assets that have performed well. There are two possible reasons this strategy might work. The first is a mean-reversion argument; that is, if the asset has deviated from its usual level, it should eventually return to that usual level. The second reason has to do with overreaction. Investors might have overreacted to bad news sending the asset price lower than it should be.

■ contribution

alternative word to premium, usually used in connection with personal payments into a pension scheme or investment based products.

■ contribution margin

the difference between variable revenue and variable cost.

■ control

50% of the outstanding votes plus one vote.

■ control person

see **affiliated person**.

■ control risk

measure of risk that errors exceeding a tolerable amount will not be prevented or detected by an entity's internal controls.

■ control stock

control stock is stock held by a person who directly or indirectly controls the management of the issuing company.

■ controlled disbursement

a service that provides for a single presentation of checks each day (typically in the early part of the day).

■ controlled funding

a method of estimating the size of the pension fund needed to secure the benefits of members of a group pension. It operates on the basis that the scheme is invested only to the extent that its expected liabilities (i.e. scheme withdrawals, retirements, deaths) can be met, plus an allowance for flexibility. Members in the scheme do not have 'earmarked' funds as with PPPs or EPPs, so being a general fund, sums can be taken out as and when needed.

■ controller

the corporate manager responsible for the firm's accounting activities.

■ controlling director

a person who is a company director who owns, or who has control of, 20% or more of the ordinary shares in a company.

■ controls tests

tests directed toward the design or operation of an internal control structure policy or procedure, to assess its effectiveness in preventing or detecting material misstatements in a financial report.

■ convenience yield

the extra advantage that firms derive from holding the commodity rather than a future position.

■ convention statement

an annual statement filed by a life insurance company in each state where it does business in compliance with that state's regulations. The statement and supporting documents show, among other things, the assets, liabilities, and surplus of the reporting company.

■ conventional mortgage

a mortgage loan based solely upon the value of the mortgaged real estate and the creditworthiness of the borrower. A mortgage loan without insurance or guarantees from a government agency.

■ conventional mortgage

a loan based on the credit of the borrower and on the collateral for the mortgage.

■ conventional option

an option contract arranged off the trading floor and not traded regularly.

■ conventional pass-throughs

also called private-label pass-throughs, any mortgage pass-through security not guaranteed by government agencies. Compare agency pass-throughs.

■ conventional project

a project with a negative initial cash flow (cash outflow), which is expected to be followed by one or more future positive cash flows (cash inflows).

■ convergence

the movement of the price of a futures contract toward the price of the underlying cash commodity. At the start, the contract price is higher because of time value. But as the contract nears expiration, and time value decreases, the futures price and the cash price converge.

■ conversion

in the context of securities, refers to the exchange of a convertible security such as a bond into stock. In the context of mutual funds, refers to the free exchange of mutual fund shares from one fund to another in a single family.

■ conversion feature

specification of the right to transform a particular investment to another form of investment, such as switching between mutual funds or converting preferred stock or bonds to common stock.

■ conversion parity/value

applies mainly to convertible securities. Common stock price at which a convertible bond can become exchangeable for common shares of equal value; value of a convertible bond based solely on the market value of the underlying equity. Par value + conversion ratio.

■ conversion premium

a convertible's conversion premium is the amount by which a convertible's market price exceeds its value in stock.

■ conversion price

applies mainly to convertible securities. Dollar value at which convertible bonds, debentures, or preferred stock can be converted into common stock, as specified when the convertible is issued.

■ conversion ratio

the specified number of shares of common stock that will be received for each convertible bond or share of convertible preferred stock, at the time of conversion. This ratio is specified at issuance in the bond indenture agreement. This is often an uneven amount using partial shares.

■ conversion value

for convertibles, the value in stock. Also called the parity value. The conversion value can be determined by multiplying the conversion ratio by the value of the stock at any point in time.

■ convertibility

the ability to exchange a currency without government restrictions or controls.

■ Convertible Adjustable Preferred Stock (CAPS)

the interest rate on caps is adjustable and is pegged to Treasury security rates. They can be exchanged at par value for common stock or cash after the next period's dividend rates are revealed.

■ convertible arbitrage

a practice, usually of buying a convertible bond and shorting a percentage of the equivalent underlying common shares, to create a positive cash flow position (with expected returns above the risk less rate) in a static environment and benefit from capital appreciation should the convertible's premium. This form of investing is far from risk less and requires constant monitoring.

■ convertible bond

a bond that includes a provision allowing the holder to exchange the bond for a quantity of the issuer's common stock, at some fixed exchange ratio. An otherwise normal corporate bond that has a fixed maturity date that pays coupon interest and repays principal at maturity. It is issued with an option to exchange the bond for a fixed number of shares of common stock, at the option of the bondholder, thereby allowing the convertible bond to share in the growth potential of the underlying common stock.

■ convertible eurobond

a eurobond that can be converted into another asset, often through exercise of attached warrants.

■ convertible exchangeable preferred stock

convertible preferred stock that may be exchanged, at the issuer's option, into convertible bonds that have the same conversion features as the convertible preferred stock.

■ convertible preference share

a specific kind of preference share which allows conversion

of an investment into a certain number of ordinary shares at a fixed price and within a specified period of time.

convertible preferred stock

preferred stock that can be converted into common stock at the option of the holder.

convertible price

the contractually specified price per share at which a convertible security can be converted into shares of common stock.

convertible security

a security that can be converted into common stock at the option of the security holder; includes convertible bonds and convertible preferred stock.

convertible stock

stock that may be exchanged for other securities of the issuer.

convex

curved, as in the shape of the outside of a circle. Usually referring to the price/required yield relationship for option-free bonds.

convexity

1. a measure of the sensitivity of duration to changes in yield levels. Convexity is a measure of the stability or instability of the measured duration, over a range of yields. If convexity is low, that is, if the price/yield relationship is close to a straight line, duration is stable. If convexity is high, duration is unstable. The greater an instrument's convexity, the less accurate duration will be.

2. Property that a curve is above a straight line connecting two end points. If the curve falls below the straight line, it is called concave.

conveyance

a document, usually a deed, which transfers an interest in property.

cook the books

to deliberately falsify the financial statements of a company. This is an illegal practice.

cooling-off period

the period of time between the filing of a preliminary prospectus with the Securities and Exchange Commission and the actual public offering of the securities.

cooperative

an organisation owned by its members. Examples are agriculture cooperatives that assist farmers in selling their products more efficiently and apartment buildings owned by the residents who have full control of the property.

copyright

the legal ownership of 'intellectual property', such as written, taped, filmed or computerised material. It gives the basis of legal protection to the owner against copying by others.

core competence

primary area of expertise. Narrowly defined fields or tasks at which a company or business excels. Primary areas of specialty.

■ **core deposits or core funding**

1. a bank's deposits that are the most stable.
2. Deposits that have an indefinite maturity, such as checking accounts, money market deposit accounts and savings accounts.

■ **corner**

control of the supply of a commodity or security, enabling the controller to manipulate its market price.

■ **cornering the market**

purchasing a security or commodity in such volume as to achieve control over its price. An illegal practice.

■ **corporate**

having to do with company affairs.

■ **corporate acquisition**

the acquisition of one firm by another firm.

■ **corporate bonds**

similar to Government Stock (gilts) but with higher risk profile. They are loans to corporate bodies, usually on fixed rate for a fixed period.

■ **corporate bonds**

debt obligations issued by corporations.

■ **corporate charter**

a legal document creating a corporation.

■ **corporate equivalent yield**

a comparison of the after-tax yield of government bonds selling at a discount and corporate bonds selling at par.

■ **corporate finance**

one of the three areas of the discipline of finance. It deals with the operation of the firm (both the investment decision and the financing decision) from the firm's point of view.

■ **corporate financial management**

the application of financial principles within a corporation to create and maintain value through decision-making and proper resource management.

■ **corporate financial planning**

financial planning conducted by a firm that encompasses preparation of both long-and short-term financial plans.

■ **Corporate Income Fund (CIF)**

a unit investment trust featuring a fixed portfolio of high-grade securities and other investments, usually with monthly distribution of income.

■ **corporate processing float**

the time that elapses between receipt of payment from a customer and the deposit of the customer's check in the firm's bank account; the time required to process customer payments.

■ **corporate repurchase**

active buying by a corporation of its own stock in the marketplace. Reasons for repurchase include putting idle cash to use, raising EPS, creating support for a stock price, increasing internal control (shark repellant), or stock for ESOP or pension plans. Repurchase is subject to rules, such as that buying must be on a zero minus or a minus tick, after the opening and before 3:30 p.m.

■ **corporate settlement**

the agreement of a buyer and seller to exchange the security and the payment on the third business day after the trade date.

■ **corporate tax view**

the argument that double (corporate and individual) taxation of equity returns makes debt a cheaper financing method.

■ **corporate taxable equivalent**

rate of return required on a par bond to produce the same after-tax yield to maturity that the quoted premium or discount bond would generate.

■ **corporation**

used in the sense of large scale in local authorities, public or private business.

■ **corporation tax**

tax on companies, levied on trading profits and capital gains. Tax rates applicable for the Financial Year, which is 1/4 to 31/3.

■ **corpus**

see **principal**.

■ **correction**

reverse movement, usually downward, in the price of an individual stock, bond, commodity, or index. If prices have been rising on the market as a whole, and then fall dramatically, this is known as a correction within an upward trend. Antithesis of a technical rally.

■ **correlation**

statistical measure of the degree to which the movements of two variables (stock/option/convertible prices or returns) are related.

■ **correlation coefficient**

a standardised statistical measure of the dependence of two random variables, defined as the covariance divided by the standard deviations of two variables.

■ **correspondent**

a financial organisation that performs services (acts as an intermediary) in a market for another organisation that does not have access to that market.

■ **correspondent bank**

a bank that serves as a depository and provides banking services for another bank.

■ **cosigner, co-maker and co-obligor**

terms used to identify multiple parties who sign as borrowers for a loan.

■ **cost accounting**

1. procedures used for rationally classifying, recording and allocating current or predicted costs that

relate to a certain product or production process.
2. A branch of accounting that provides information to help the management of a firm evaluate production costs and efficiency.

cost basis

the original price of an asset, used to determine capital gains.

cost centre

an activity or function within a business, to which specific costs may be attributed for control purposes.

cost company arrangement

arrangement whereby the shareholders of a project receive output free of charge but agree to pay all operating and financing charges of the project.

cost in excess of billing

an asset created under a type of accrual accounting used when firms such as contractors incur expenses in accounting periods that are repaid in subsequent accounting periods. This account is comprised of money spent by the contractor for things that will be billed to buyer at a future date.

cost of capital

1. the average cost of financing business capital, e.g. loan interest and share dividends. If the average return on investment is less than the cost of financing, the business will be facing problems.
2. The required return for a capital budgeting project.

cost of carry

1. the cost of financing an asset. If the cost of carry is smaller than the interest received from the asset by the investor, the investor has a positive carry. Conversely, if the cost of carry is larger than the interest received from the asset by the investor, the investor has a negative carry.
2. Out-of-pocket costs incurred while an investor has an investment position. Examples include interest on long positions in margin account, dividend lost on short margin positions, and incidental expenses. Related: Net financing cost.

cost of equity

the required rate of return for an investment of 100% equity.

cost of funds

interest rate associated with borrowing money.

cost of goods sold

amount shown on a firm's income statement representing the direct expenses that the firm incurred for sales. Cost of goods sold is always a debit balance and is shown as either a deduction or a negative number.

cost of lease financing

a lease's internal rate of return.

cost of limited partner capital

the discount rate that equates the after-tax inflows with outflows for capital raised from limited partners.

■ Cost Of Sales (COS)

commonly arrived at via the formula: opening stock + stock purchased - closing stock. Cost of sales is the value, at cost, of the goods or services sold during the period in question, usually the financial year, as shown in a Profit and Loss Account (P&L). In all accounts, particularly the P&L (trading account) it's important that costs are attributed reliably to the relevant revenues, or the report is distorted and potentially meaningless. To use simply the total value of stock purchases during the period in question would not produce the correct and relevant figure, as some product sold was already held in stock before the period began, and some product bought during the period remains unsold at the end of it. Some stock held before the period often remains unsold at the end of it too. The formula is the most logical way of calculating the value at cost of all goods sold, irrespective of when the stock was purchased. The value of the stock attributable to the sales in the period (cost of sales) is the total of what we started with in stock (opening stock), and what we purchased (stock purchases), minus what stock we have left over at the end of the period (closing stock).

■ cost records

the records maintained by an investor of the prices at which securities transactions are made, so that capital gains can be computed.

■ cost recovery method

method of revenue recognition which recognises profits after costs are completely recovered. Generally used only when the total amount of collections is highly uncertain. In tax, the accounting method used to depreciate assets.

■ cost-benefit ratio

the net present value of an investment divided by the investment's initial cost. Also called the profitability index.

■ cost-of-carry market

applies to derivative products. Futures contracts trade in a 'cost-of-carry market' where the underlying commodity can be stored, insured, and converted into the future easily and inexpensively. Arbitrageurs, because of the ease of switching from the spot commodity to futures, will keep these markets in line with prevailing interest rates.

■ cost-plus contract

a contract in which the selling price is based on the total cost of production plus a fixed percentage or fixed amount.

■ cost-push inflation

inflation caused by rising prices, usually from increased raw material or labor costs that push up the costs of production. Related: Demand-pull inflation.

■ counter offer

an offer which replaces and supersedes a previous offer.

■ **counter trade**

the exchange of goods for other goods rather than for cash; barter.

■ **countercyclical stocks**

stocks whose price tends to rise when the economy is in recession or the market is bearish, and vice versa.

■ **counterpart items**

in the balance of payments, counterpart items are analogous to unrequited transfers in the current account. They arise through the double-entry system in balance of payments accounting and refer to adjustments in reserves owing to monetisation or demonetisation of gold, allocation or cancellation of SDRs, and revaluation of the various components of total reserves.

■ **counterparties**

the parties to an interest rate swap.

■ **counterparty**

a term used to identify the 'other' party in a two-party transaction. For example, the counterparty of a buyer is the seller to that buyer.

■ **counterparty risk**

the risk that the other party to an agreement will default. In an options contract, the risk to the option buyer that the option writer will not buy or sell the underlying as agreed.

■ **country beta**

covariance of a national economy's rate of return and the rate of return of the world economy divided by the variance of the world economy.

■ **country economic risk**

developments in a national economy that can affect the outcome of an international financial transaction.

■ **country financial risk**

centers around the ability of a national economy to generate enough foreign exchange to meet payments of interest and principal on its foreign debt.

■ **country risk**

general level of political, financial, and economic uncertainty in a country affect which the value of loans or investments in that country.

■ **country selection**

a type of active international management that measures the contribution to performance attributable to investing in the better-performing stock markets of the world.

■ **coupon**

a slip of paper representing a monetary value. Often used with reference to the interest payable on gilts, because the coupon attached to the certificate represents annual interest, and can be encashed.

■ **coupon bond**

a bond featuring coupons that must be presented to the issuer in order to receive interest payments.

■ **coupon equivalent yield**

true interest cost expressed on the basis of a 365-day year.

■ coupon pass

canvassing by the desk of primary dealers to determine the inventory and maturities of their Treasury securities. The desk then decides whether to buy or sell certain issues (coupons) in order to add or withdraw reserves.

■ coupon payments

a bond's interest payments.

■ coupon rate

1. the rate of interest received by the holder of a security. Not necessarily the same as the yield realised by the holder.
2. For pass-through securities, the holder's coupon rate is the gross coupon of the underlying loans, less servicing fees and any agency guarantee fees.

■ coupon rate

in bonds, notes, or other fixed income securities, the stated percentage rate of interest, usually paid twice a year.

■ covariance

a statistical measure of the degree to which random variables move together. A positive covariance implies that one variable is above (below) its mean value when the other variable is above (below) its mean value.

■ covenant

a promise, contained in a deed, to do something.

■ covenants

provisions in a bond indenture or preferred stock agreement that require the bond or preferred stock issuer to take certain specified actions (affirmative covenants) or to refrain from taking certain specified actions (negative covenants).

■ cover

the purchase of a contract to offset a previously established short position.

■ cover note

temporary confirmation of insurance cover, particularly in motor insurance, pending delivery of the policy and/or certificate.

■ coverage initiated

usually refers to the fact that analysts begin following a particular security. This usually happens when there is enough trading in to warrant attention by the investment community.

■ coverage ratios

ratios used to test the adequacy of cash flows generated through earnings for purposes of meeting debt and lease obligations, including the interest coverage ratio and the fixed-charge coverage ratio.

■ covered call

a short call option position in which the writer owns the number of shares of the underlying stock represented by the option contracts. Covered calls generally limit the risk the writer takes because the stock does not have to be bought at the market price, if the holder of that option decides to exercise it.

■ covered call writing strategy

a strategy that involves writing a call option on securities that the investor owns.

■ covered calls

a call option for which the owner of a security grants the buyer of the call option the right to purchase a security owned by the option seller. The opposite of naked calls. In theory, selling covered calls can be a hedging strategy. If investment prices fall, the investor's loss will be offset by the income from the covered call. On the other hand, if prices rise, the seller's gain is limited to the difference between the seller's book value and the option strike price (which in this case is probably less than the market price), but the seller also retains the proceeds of the option sale.

■ covered interest arbitrage

occurs when a portfolio manager invests dollars in an instrument denominated in a foreign currency and hedges the resulting foreign exchange risk by selling the proceeds of the investment forward for dollars.

■ covered option

option position that is offset by an equal and opposite position in the underlying security. Antithesis of naked option.

■ covered or hedge option strategies

strategies that involve a position in an option as well as a position in the underlying stock, designed so that one position will help offset any unfavourable price movement in the other, including covered call writing and protective put buying. Related: Naked strategies

■ covered put

the sale of a put option while holding sufficient cash to buy the underlying.

■ covered writer

an investor who writes options only on stock that he or she owns, so that option positions may be collected.

■ CPI

a measure of inflation.

■ cramdown

the ability of the bankruptcy court to confirm a plan of reorganisation over the objections of some classes of creditors.

■ cram-down deal

a merger in which stockholders are forced to accept undesirable terms, such as junk bonds instead of cash or equity, due to the absence of any better alternatives.

■ crash

dramatic loss in market value.

■ crawling peg

an automatic system for revising the exchange rate. It involves establishing a par value around which the rate can vary up to a given percent. The par value is revised regularly according to a formula determined by the authorities.

■ credible signal

a signal that provides accurate information; a signal that can distinguish among senders.

■ credit

1. a sum of money or equivalent purchasing power available for a person's or business use.
2. A positive balance in a bank account.
3. The practice of making goods or services available before payment.
4. Entries on the right hand side of an account.

■ credit agreement

arrangement in which one party borrows or takes possession in the present, by promising to pay in the future.

■ credit analysis

evaluating information on companies and bond issues in order to estimate the ability of the issuer to live up to its future contractual obligations. Related: Default risk.

■ credit balance

balance remaining after one of a series of bookkeeping entries. This amount represents a liability or income to the entity.

■ credit bureau

an agency that researches the credit history of consumers so that creditors can make decisions about granting of loans.

■ credit derivative

contractual arrangements that allow one party to transfer credit risk of a reference asset, which it may or may not own, to one or more counter-parties. Credit derivatives are contracts for transferring risk - just like foreign exchange, commodity and interest rate risk derivatives. The only difference is the type of risk transferred.

■ credit enhancement

a measure that alters the structure of a security, in a way that reduces its credit risk. Credit enhancement may take the form of a letter of credit issued to back securities.

■ credit enhancement

purchase of the financial guarantee of a large insurance company to raise funds.

■ credit history

a record of how a person has borrowed and repaid debts.

■ credit insurance

insurance against abnormal losses due to unpaid accounts receivable.

■ credit linked security

a type of credit derivative instrument. Credit linked notes are a securitised form of credit derivatives. The protection buyer issues notes. If a specified credit event occurs, the investor who buys the notes has to suffer either a delay in repayment or has to forego interest.

■ credit memos

accounting adjustments that reduce account receivable balances due from account debtors.

■ **credit period**

the length of time for which a firm's customer is granted credit.

■ **credit rating**

an evaluation of an individual's or company's ability to repay obligations or its likelihood of not defaulting.

■ **credit risk**

the risk that an issuer of debt securities or a borrower may default on its obligations, or that the payment may not be made on a negotiable instrument. Related: Default risk.

■ **credit scoring**

a statistical technique that combines several financial characteristics to form a single score to represent a customer's creditworthiness.

■ **credit spread**

applies to derivative products. Difference in the value of two options, when the value of the one sold exceeds the value of the one bought. One sells a 'credit spread.' Antithesis of a debit spread Related: Quality spread.

■ **credit swap**

a type of credit derivative instrument. Swap contracts in which one party makes payments only if a specified credit event occurs. In a credit default swap, the protection seller agrees, for an upfront or periodic fee, to compensate the protection buyer upon the happening of the specified credit event. Credit default swaps are similar to a traditional financial guarantees but more flexible.

■ **credit union**

a not-for-profit institution that is operated as a cooperative and offers financial services such as low-interest loans, to its members.

■ **credit watch**

a warning by a bond rating firm indicating that a company's credit rating may change after the current review is concluded.

■ **crediting rate**

the interest rate offered on an investment type insurance policy.

■ **creditor**

1. a party who is owed money by another party.
2. Party that loans money or other assets to another party.
3. Anyone to whom a business or individual owes money (or services).

■ **creditor**

lender of money.

■ **creditor's committee**

a group representing firms that have claims on a company facing bankruptcy or extreme financial difficulty.

■ **creditworthiness**

a creditor's measure of a consumer's past and future ability and willingness to repay debts.

■ **creditworthiness**

eligibility of an individual or firm to borrow money.

■ **critical illness**

also known as 'dread disease'. Such policies can stand alone or maybe written as an add-on to a variety of other contracts, e.g. whole of life. Critical illness policies pay out a tax-free capital sum, in the event of a qualifying illness being diagnosed, e.g. certain cancers. This is an advance of the sum assured, rather than a surrender of the policy.

■ critical path

a sequence of those tasks (e.g., in payment processing), which must be completed before the next task can be started. Anything not on the critical path is something that can be done later, without delaying an important step.

■ cross

securities transaction in which the same broker acts as agent for both sides of the trade; a legal practice only if the broker first offers the securities publicly at a price higher than the bid.

■ cross collateralisation

extension of the creditor's interest in property of the debtor, so that collateral for one debt also serves as collateral for one or more other debts.

■ cross default

provision in the loan documents in which the debtor agrees that default on one loan will also constitute default on other obligations to the creditor.

■ cross hedge

a hedge transaction in which a cash market instrument is hedged by an option contract for a different underlying instrument. Sometimes called proxy hedge, surrogate hedge or tandem hedge.

■ cross hedging

applies to derivative products. Hedging with a futures contract that is different from the underlying being hedged. Use of a hedging instrument different from the security being hedged. Hedging instruments are usually selected to have the highest price correlation to the underlying.

■ cross option

also called double option or put and call option. A flexible form of buy and sell agreement, whereby, e.g. in the event of the death of a partner, the estate of the deceased has the option to sell and the surviving partners have the option to buy. When one option is exercised, the other must follow.

■ cross rates

the exchange rate between two currencies expressed as the ratio of two foreign exchange rates that are both expressed in terms of a third currency.

■ cross stream guaranty

a phrase sometimes used to describe a guaranty of a loan to a borrowing entity when the borrowing entity is affiliated with the guarantor corporation through common ownership, but is neither a parent nor a subsidiary corporation.

■ cross-border risk

describes the volatility of returns on international investments caused by events associated with a particular country as opposed to events associated solely with a particular economic or financial agent.

■ cross-default

a provision under which default on one debt obligation triggers default on another debt obligation.

■ crossed cheque

a cheque with two lines across to denote that it must be paid into a bank.

■ crossed market

in the context of general equities, happens when the inside market consists of a highest bid price that is higher than the lowest offer price.

■ crossed trade

the prohibited practice of offsetting buy and sell orders without recording the trade on the exchange, thus not allowing other traders to take advantage of a more favourable price.

■ cross-holdings

the holding by one corporation of shares in another firm. One needs to allow for cross-holdings when aggregating capitalisations of firms. Ignoring cross-holdings leads to double-counting.

■ crossing

in banking, 'crossing' a cheque with two perpendicular lines across the face of the cheque means that it must be paid into a bank account.

■ crossover rate

the return at which two alternative projects have the same net present value.

■ cross-sectional approach

a statistical methodology applied to a set of firms at a particular time.

■ cross-share holdings

often used in risk arbitrage. Corporations' or governments' equity share ownership in another corporation's shares.

■ crowd trading

used for listed equity securities. Group of exchange members with a defined area of function tending to congregate around a trading post pending execution of orders. Includes specialists, floor traders, odd-lot dealers, and other brokers as well as smaller groups with specialised functions.

■ crown jewel

a particularly profitable or otherwise particularly valuable corporate unit or asset of a firm. Often used in risk arbitrage. The most desirable entities within a diversified corporation as measured by asset value, earning power, and business prospects; in takeover attempts, these entities typically are the main objective of the acquirer and may be sold by a takeover target to make the rest of the company less attractive.

■ cum div

indicates that a share price includes the right to a company dividend declared but not paid.

■ cum dividend

with dividend; said of a stock whose buyer is eligible to receive a declared dividend. Stocks are usually 'cum dividend' for trades made on or before the fifth trading day preceding the record date, when the register of eligible holders is closed for that dividend period. Antithesis of ex-dividend.

■ cum rights

with rights.

■ Cumulative Abnormal Return (CAR)

sum of the differences between the expected return on a stock (systematic risk multiplied by the realised market return) and the actual return often used to evaluate the impact of news on a stock price.

■ cumulative dividend feature

a requirement that any missed preferred or preference stock dividends be paid in full before any common dividend payment is made.

■ cumulative gap

the net sum obtained by adding all of the interval gaps or mismatches between rate-sensitive assets and rate-sensitive liabilities, beginning with the first bucket in the gap analysis and proceeding to a selected time. For example, the one-year cumulative gap is the sum of the gaps for all of the time intervals prior to and including the gap bucket ending one year from the date that the report was prepared. A crude and highly inexact measure of interest rate risk.

■ cumulative preference share

a type of share bearing the right to receive unpaid dividends on a cumulative basis, taking priority over ordinary share dividend entitlement. Also available as a Redeemable Preference Share.

■ cumulative preferred stock

preferred stock whose dividends accrue, should the issuer not make timely dividend payments. Related: Non-cumulative preferred stock.

■ cumulative probability distribution

a function that shows the probability that the random variable will attain a value less than or equal to each value that the random variable can take on.

■ cumulative redeemable preference share

a redeemable preference share which gives an extra degree of security: if the company misses a dividend payment one year, it is carried forward to the next year and so on until it is eventually paid.

■ Cumulative Translation Adjustment (CTA) Account

an entry in a translated balance sheet in which gains and/or losses from translation have been accumulated over a period of years.

■ cumulative voting

a system of voting for directors of a corporation in which shareholder's total number of votes is equal to the number of shares held times the number of candidates.

■ currency

money.

■ **currency arbitrage**

taking advantage of divergences in exchange rates in different money markets by buying a currency in one market and selling it in another market.

■ **currency basket**

the value of a portfolio of specific amounts of individual currencies, used as the basis for setting the market value of another currency. It is also referred to as a currency cocktail.

■ **currency future**

a financial future contract for the delivery of a specified foreign currency.

■ **currency hedge**

applies mainly to international equities. Hedging technique to guard against foreign exchange fluctuations (i.e., short Euro 100 mm when holding a long position of Euro 100 mm in stocks).

■ **currency in circulation**

paper money, coins, and demand deposits that constitute all the money circulating in the economy.

■ **currency option**

an option to buy or sell a foreign currency.

■ **currency overvaluation**

applies mainly to international equities:
1. consideration that a currency is overvalued if private demand for the currency at the going exchange rate is less than total private supply (i.e., central banks are buying up the difference, supporting the value of the currency through foreign exchange intervention);
2. Currency value exceeding purchasing power parity.

■ **currency risk**

related: Exchange rate risk

■ **currency risk sharing**

an agreement by the parties to a transaction to share the currency risk associated with the transaction. The arrangement involves a customised hedge contract embedded in the underlying transaction.

■ **currency selection**

asset allocation in which the investor chooses among investments denominated in different currencies.

■ **currency swap**

an agreement to swap a series of specified payment obligations denominated in one currency for a series of specified payment obligations denominated in a different currency.

■ **current account**

net flow of goods, services, and unilateral transactions (gifts) between countries.

■ **current asset**

1. asset that one can reasonably expect to convert into cash, sell or consume in operations within a single operating cycle or within a year, if more than one cycle is completed each year.
2. The group of assets considered the most liquid. Usually comprised of cash, accounts receivable, in-

ventory and a few minor items. The subgrouping of assets into current and long-term categories is common for all financial statements, except for firms in the financial industry.

■ **current cost accounting**

accounting method which is based on recording the value of assets and liabilities at their current market value rather than the historical cost.

■ **current coupon**

the term used to refer to all fixed-income securities paying interest at the rate currently required by purchasers for securities of that maturity and quality. Current coupon securities trade at or very near par.

■ **current income**

money that is routinely received from investments in the form of dividends, interest, and other income sources.

■ **current issue**

in Treasury securities, the most recently auctioned issue. Trading is more active in current issues than in off-the-run issues.

■ **current liabilities**

1. the group of liabilities considered to be the shortest term. Usually comprises accounts payable, short-term bank debt, bank overdrafts, other short-term accounts or notes payable, current portion of long-term debt, and a few minor items. The subgrouping of liabilities into current and long-term categories is common for all financial statements, except for firms in the financial industry.
2. Debts due on demand or within a year.
3. Obligation whose liquidation is expected to require the use of existing resources classified as current assets or the creation of other current liabilities.

■ **current market value**

the value of a client's portfolio at today's market price, as listed in a brokerage statement.

■ **current maturity**

current time to maturity on an outstanding debt instrument.

■ **current rate method**

the translation of all foreign currency balance sheet and income statement items at the current exchange rate.

■ **current ratio**

the ratio obtained when total current assets are divided by total current liabilities. A commonly used but not always good proxy for a firm's liquidity.

■ **current value**

1. value of an asset at the present time, as compared with the asset's historical cost.
2. In finance, the amount determined by discounting the future revenue stream of an asset using compound interest principles.
3. The spending power, in today's terms, of a cash sum available at a future date, after allowing for projected inflation.

■ **current yield**

1. for bonds, a measure of the simple interest annual yield for investments with coupon rates and with maturities of one year or more. To calculate the current yield, the annual coupon interest income is simply divided by the amount paid to acquire the investment. It is important to note that the current yield is only accurate for investments purchased at par. The current yield calculation includes just one income cash flow - the annual coupon interest income. It ignores the profit or loss resulting from discounts and premiums.

2. For stocks, the annual dividend income divided by the price per share.

■ **current/noncurrent method**

the translation of all of a foreign subsidiary's current assets and liabilities into home currency at the current exchange rate while noncurrent assets and liabilities are translated at the historical exchange rate; that is, the rate in effect at the time the asset was acquired or the liability incurred.

■ **current-coupon issues**

related: Benchmark issues

■ **cushion**

the minimum period between the time a bond is issued and the time it is called.

■ **cushion bonds**

an informal name for callable bonds with long maturities, that have coupon rates well above current market rates. Because these bonds have such high coupon rates, they trade at prices and yields calculated to the call date, rather than to the maturity date. This makes the cushion bond's price less volatile. If prevailing rates remain the same, fall, or rise to any level not greater than the coupon rate, the bond will offer a competitive return.

■ **cushion bonds**

high-coupon bonds that sell at only at a moderate premium because they are callable at a price below that at which a comparable non-callable bond would sell. Cushion bonds offer considerable downside protection in a falling market.

■ **cushion theory**

the theory that a stock with many short positions taken in it will risc, because these positions must be covered by the stock.

■ **CUSIP number**

unique number given to a security to distinguish it from other stocks and registered bonds.

■ **custodial agreement**

a written contract establishing the responsibilities of a custodian who holds property. In finance, the custodian holds collateral for deposits with financial institutions, investment securities or securities underlying repurchase agreements.

■ **custodial fees**

fees charged by an institution that holds securities in safekeeping for an investor.

■ **custodian bank**

applies mainly to international equities. Bank or other financial institution that keeps custody of stock certificates and other assets of a mutual fund, individual, or corporate client.

■ **customary payout ratios**

a range of payout ratios that is typical according to an analysis of comparable firms.

■ **customer's loan consent**

agreement signed by a margin customer that allows a broker to borrow margined securities up to the level of the customer's debit balance to help cover other customers' short positions.

■ **customised benchmarks**

a benchmark that is designed to meet a client's requirements and long-term objectives.

■ **customs union**

an agreement by two or more countries to erect a common external tariff and to abolish restrictions on trade among members.

■ **cutoff point**

the lowest rate of return acceptable on investments.

■ **cyclical liquidity risk**

a type of systemic liquidity risk. The risk of funding problems arising from national or regional macroeconomic corrections, such as recessions or credit crunches.

■ **cyclical stock**

stock that tends to rise quickly when the economy turns up and fall quickly when the economy turns down. Examples are housing, automobiles, and paper.

■ **dampening**

the phenomenon or the result of a declining volatility trend.

■ **data mining**

obtaining information about customers or groups of customers from a data warehouse, for marketing or other purposes.

■ **data warehouse**

a computerised database composed of data extracted from the data processing and accounting systems used for various bank deposit, loan and other customer products. Typically, data is extracted from the various product systems, balanced, scrubbed and converted into a standardised, readily accessible format.

■ **date of auditors'/accountants' report**

last day the auditors perform fieldwork and the last day of responsibility relating to significant events, subsequent to the financial statement date.

■ **dated billings**

receivables created by invoices that do not require the account party to pay until some date in the future. Sometimes called datings.

■ **dawn raid**

in financial terms, a surprise purchase of a large number of shares in a single company. Generally taken as a forewarning of a takeover bid.

■ days inventory

the level of inventory expressed as its equivalent in days of a portion of cost of goods sold for the year. Calculated by multiplying inventory by 365 and then dividing that product by cost of goods sold.

■ days payables

the level of accounts payable, expressed as its equivalent in days of a portion of cost of goods sold for the year. Calculated by multiplying accounts payable by 365 and then dividing that product by cost of goods sold.

■ days receivables

the level of accounts receivable, expressed as its equivalent in days of a portion of net sales for the year. Calculated by multiplying accounts receivable by 365 and then dividing that product by net sales.

■ de facto

existing as a matter of fact, rather than a right, as in e.g. de facto government, rather than, say, the elected government.

■ de minimis limit

the level below which a funding rate cheque is not required in respect of defined contribution occupational pension schemes.

■ dealer

a firm or an individual who buys and sells for his own account. A dealer has ownership, even if only for an instant, between a purchase from one party and a sale to another party and is thus compensated by the spread between the price paid and the price received. Not the same as a broker, although an individual or firm may act as either a broker or a dealer in separate transactions.

■ dealer paper

retail instalment sales contracts, often for automobiles, that are sold or pledged to a third party, usually a financial institution.

■ dealing

name given to transactions in stocks, shares unit trusts, commodities and other financial instruments.

■ death duties

tax charged on property on the death of the owner.

■ death in service benefits

generally refers to one or more of life assurance, spouses' and dependants' pensions, return of personal contributions, as provided by a pension scheme, on a member's death in service before retirement.

■ debenture

long term loan to a company, usually at a fixed rate of interest and for a specific term. Debenture holders are creditors of the company. In the event of liquidation, debenture holders have a preferential claim on the assets. Debentures are marketable securities.

■ debit

1. entries on the left hand side of an account.

2. A charge against or deduction from an account.

■ debit balance

balance remaining after one or a series of bookkeeping entries. This amount represents an asset or an expense of the entity.

■ debt

1. funds owed by a debtor to a creditor. Outstanding debt obligations are assets for creditors and liabilities for debtors. May or may not be covered by written agreements.
2. General name for money, notes, bonds, goods or services which represent amounts owed.

■ debt security

1. any financial instrument representing a creditor relationship between the issuer (the debtor) and the holder of the instrument (the creditor).
2. Document which is evidence of an obligation or liability.

■ debt service

a term used to refer to the amount of principal and interest payments required by a borrower's loans or securities issued. Also used as a verb to describe making such payments.

■ Debt Service Coverage (DSC)

the margin by which all of a borrower's or bond issuer's required principal payments (not just those for the loan under consideration or just those for loans to one bank) are exceeded by the sum of the firm's cash flow, plus all of the principal repayments and interest expense deducted in the process of calculating that cash flow.

■ debt service coverage ratio

a simple comparison of the cash available to make principal and interest payments to the bank or to bond holders, with the amount of those required principal and interest payments. Debt service coverage is expressed as a ratio, with the annual net income divided by the annual debt service requirement.

■ debt service fund

fund whose principal or interest is set aside and accumulated to retire debt.

■ debt tranche

tranches in a multi-class security that have seniority ranking, for repayment, ahead of equity trances.

■ debtor

1. a party who owes money or other performance to another party.
2. Party owing money or other assets to a creditor.

■ debtor in possession

in some bankruptcy proceedings, the debtor, rather than a trustee, may continue to operate the business. The debtor in possession is the same person or company that controlled the business prior to the bankruptcy, however, the debtor in possession is a different legal entity.

■ debt-to-worth ratio

the simplest way to measure leverage. Calculated by dividing total liabilities by total equity.

decay analysis

statistical analysis of the rate of attrition. Decay analysis is used to analyse historical volatility of core deposit volumes, specifically rates for withdrawals and account closures. Deposit decay rates should be calculated by tracking a representative sample of accounts, over a period of time, that covers at least one interest rate cycle.

decedent

individual who has died.

declaration of trust

written statement to the effect that certain property is to be held in trust. No specific form is required, provided the intention is clear.

declaration page

the page in an insurance policy that contains all or almost all of the policy information specific to that particular insurance policy. The declaration page typically includes the name of the insured, the identification of the insured property, the amount of the insurance coverage, the expiration date of the policy and the name of any lender with an interest in the insured property.

decree

a court order.

deed

a document which is signed, sealed and delivered.

deed in lieu of foreclosure

a deed executed by the mortgagor that transfers ownership in real estate to a lien creditor. This instrument is used when the debtor is unable or unwilling to pay and wishes to avoid foreclosure.

deed of (family) arrangement

a formal document used to override the directions of a will after death.

deed of trust

a three-party document conveying interest in property, almost always real estate, to a trustee. In many states, deeds of trust are used instead of mortgages. In those states, the trustee holds the deed in favour of the lender and then reconveys the title to the borrower when the loan is paid in full. Sometimes called a trust deed.

deep discount

a large discount for a financial instrument. The condition that exists when a financial instrument is trading at a market price that is well below its par value. May also be used to refer to those securities selling at prices well below par.

deep discount bonds

an investment bond issued at a large discount. The bond does not pay interest, but is repaid at par.

deep in the money

a phrase used to describe an option with a high intrinsic value, resulting from the fact that the market value of the underlying instrument is well below (for a call option) or well above (for a put option) the strike price of the option.

default

1. a condition in which a loan or investment is not performing as expected because of the debtor's failure to act or refrain from acting in ways contractually agreed upon. As in 'the loan is in default' or 'an event of default'.
2. A debtor's failure to act or refrain from acting in ways contractually agreed upon in the loan documents. Most often, default is the debtor's failure to pay.
3. Failure to meet any financial obligation. Default triggers a creditor's rights and remedies identified in the agreement and under the law.

default investment option

term used to describe the investment fund into which contributions paid to a stakeholder pension will be placed, if the contributor fails to specify an investment fund.

default notice

a notice served by a creditor on a debtor when the debtor has broken an agreement. The notice must contain details of the breach, what must be done to put the matter right, any compensation due if the matter is not resolved and the period in which the matter must be resolved.

default rate

1. an alternative higher rate of interest or a premium specified in a loan document to be added to the contractual rate of interest that can be charged by the lender if the borrower is in default.
2. The risk arising from the chance that debtors will not make promised payments either on time or in full. Also called credit risk.

defeasance

1. the legal release of a debtor from being the primary obligor under the debt, either by the courts or by the creditor. Also called legal defeasance.
2. Annulment of a contract or deed. A clause within a contract or deed that provides for annulment.

defendant

someone who is accused in a legal action.

deferred annuity

an annuity on which payments will be made at some point in the future – often as a pension.

deferred charge

cost incurred for subsequent periods which are reflected as assets.

deferred income

income received but not earned until all events have occurred. Deferred income is reflected as a liability.

deferred income taxes

assets or liabilities that arise from timing or measurement differences between tax and accounting principles.

deferred interest loan

a type of mortgage which allows you to refer the amount of interest currently due and to pay it at a later date.

■ deferred period

a waiting period.

■ deferred tax asset

an asset reflecting a likely reduction in future income taxes.

■ deferred taxes

a liability account that reflects the accumulated difference between the amount of income tax that the firm shows each year as an expense on its financial statements and the amount of income tax, usually lower, that the firm pays to the government.

■ deficit

1. financial shortage that occurs when liabilities exceed assets.
2. A shortfall in income compared to what needs to be, or has been, spent.

■ defined benefit

pension schemes which base their pension calculation on a defined formula, usually based on salary and service.

■ defined benefit plan

a pension or other employee benefit plan that provides specified amounts of benefits to eligible participants. The specified amounts of benefits are usually determined based upon age, years of service and/or levels of compensation.

■ defined contribution

another term for 'money purchase' pensions. A pension scheme where the final pension will be the result of an agreed contribution input, rather than an agreed formula output, as with a final salary scheme.

■ defined contribution plan

a pension or other employee benefit plan that provides a specified contribution amount for the benefit of eligible employees. The participants ultimately receive amounts that depend on both the accumulated contributions and the investment returns realised from investment of the accumulated contributions.

■ definitive deed

name given to the trust deed which governs an occupational pension scheme. Must be executed within two years of scheme establishment. An interim deed is often used while definitive deed is prepared.

■ de-leveraged bonds

bonds that pay interest to investors according to a formula based on a fraction of the increase or decrease in a specified index. Deleveraged bonds are a type of structured note.

■ delivery and acceptance certificate

a document that evidences the fact that goods have been delivered to a purchaser or lessee and accepted by that purchaser or lessee.

■ delivery float

the time between when a cheque is ready for disbursement and when the vendor or employee actually receives it. For vendors, this may be considered the same as mail float.

■ **Delivery Vs. Payment (DVP)**

the simultaneous exchange of securities and cash. The safest method of settling either the purchase or sale of a security. In a DVP settlement, the funds are wired from the buyer's account and the security is delivered from the seller's account in simultaneous, interdependent wires.

■ **delta**

1. the Greek letter used by mathematicians to refer to change or the quantity of change.
2. The price sensitivity of an option. The change in an option's price divided by the change in the price of the underlying instrument. As an option becomes deeper in the money, its delta gets closer to 1.0. As an option get further out of the money, its delta gets closer to zero.

■ **demand**

term used to describe a creditor's right to request payment, in full, of a debt.

■ **demand deposit**

a deposit account that permits the depositor to withdraw funds on demand.

■ **demand loan**

loan repayable on demand. Also known as a call loan.

■ **demand note**

a promissory note that calls for principal to be payable on demand. In recent years, courts have significantly restricted the circumstances under which a bank could make and enforce a demand for repayment under a demand note.

■ **dematerialised**

a term used to describe a physical certificate representing ownership of a security (a stock certificate or a bond) that is held by a trustee. This is an arrangement through which a physical certificate is held so that all future transactions can be conducted as if the security were issued as a book-entry security. Ownership and liens are recorded in the records of the trustee rather than evidenced by physical possession of the certificate. Also called immobilised. Less often, dematerialised is used to refer to book-entry securities that have never been issued in physical form.

■ **demography**

the statistical study of population.

■ **denomination**

the par value of a bond.

■ **department of trade and industry**

government department dealing with company affairs and operations.

■ **dependant**

someone who is reliant upon others.

■ **dependant's pension**

one of the options with a pension scheme, to provide a pension for a dependant, on the death of the member. Usually pre-determined with a company scheme, but a separate decision with a personal pension.

depletion

1. method of computing a deduction to account for a reduction in value of extractable natural resources.
2. Natural wastage or reduction.

deposit account

an account which pays interest, the interest being determined by reserves and long term investment projections, rather than current investment conditions. Interest may be variable, but once paid is not subject to fluctuations in value, e.g. as with a building society account.

deposit administration

type of investment used by defined benefit schemes. Contributions, net of expense charges, are accumulated in a pool. An agreed amount of interest is added. Additional interest may be declared and added to the fund, retrospectively, for the interest period concerned, e.g. 6% added at beginning of year and additional 2% declared at end of year and backdated. Pensions and other benefits are paid from the fund as they fall due.

deposit method

related to the sales of real estate. Under this method, the seller does not recognise any profits, does not record a note receivable and continues to reflect the property and related debt in the seller's financial statements, recording the buyer's initial investment and subsequent payments as a deposit.

deposit notes

a form of bank obligation that is similar to a deposit. Deposit notes are typically issued with terms from two to five years. Like CDs, deposit notes are issued for specified terms at either specified rates or specified rate formulas. Unlike CDs, deposit notes are sold in a predetermined amount, for a predetermined time period. The deposit note terms are usually described in an offering circular similar to an offering of securities.

depository bank

a bank used as the point of deposit for cash receipts.

depreciation

1. the amount by which a fixed asset's accounting or book value is periodically reduced, to reflect the fact that the economic value of the asset is steadily reduced by a combination of wear and tear from use, age and/or obsolescence. The offsetting entry is depreciation expense.
2. Expense allowance made for wear and tear on an asset over its estimated useful life.

derivatives

1. financial instruments whose value varies with the value of an underlying asset (such as a stock, bond, commodity or currency) or index such as interest rates. Financial instruments whose character-

istics and value depend on the characterisation of an underlying instrument or asset.
2. A form of investment, such as options or futures, which are based, or derived from, ordinary shares or bonds.

■ detection risk

risk that the auditor will not detect a material misstatement.

■ dilution

1. the difference between gross sales and net sales. Dilution is caused by sales that are reversed as a result of returns and/or allowances.
2. The reduction in an existing stockholder's position that results from the issuance of new shares.

■ dilution rate

dilution as a percentage of gross sales.

■ dime

an informal name for 10 basis points.

■ direct costs

costs relating directly to the production of goods or services, such as materials and production labour.

■ direct debit

regular payment system, whereby the supplier of a service instructs their bank to collect the requisite sum from the bank of the purchaser of the service.

■ direct deposit

a system wherein amounts are transferred from a payer's chequing account to the accounts of payees, no matter where they bank. The transfers are made electronically and do not require a paper cheque or draft. The key consideration is that the transaction is accomplished without involving the payee.

■ direct hedges

a form of capital markets or derivatives hedge, in which the cash market instrument being hedged is hedged by an options or futures contract on the same underlying instrument.

■ direct lease

a form of lease financing in which the bank acquires property from a supplier and then leases that property directly to an end user. The bank is the owner and the lessor, and the end user is the lessee.

■ direct tax

a tax levied on capital and sources of income, over which the taxpayer has no discretion.

■ direct verification

the audit procedure of mailing the account debtor a note, requesting the account debtor to confirm the balance owed.

■ directionally correct

an expression used to indicate that a measurement is accurate to the extent that it shows the quantity to be measured to be positive or negative, even though the degree to which the quantity is positive or negative may be measured inaccurately.

■ director

an officer of a company whose actions may bind the company. May be, but need not be, a shareholder.

■ disbursement

payment by cash or cheque.

■ disbursement float

the total time period between when a cheque is prepared by the remitter and when the cheque is presented for payment. This float also includes the delivery float, processing float and transit float. Disbursement float is the float period for the remitter. The collection float for the organisation that will receive the cheque is the same duration as the disbursement float.

■ discharge

1. the action of releasing a lien or the document in which the creditor relinquishes a lien.
2. Relief granted to a debtor by a bankruptcy court. Discharge relieves the debtor from all further responsibility for pre-petition debt covered by the discharge.

■ disclaimer

legal refusal, usually written, to accept responsibility for the action of a third party or an action attributed to the individual concerned.

■ disclaimer of opinion

statement by an auditor indicating inability to express an opinion on the fairness of the financial statements provided and the reason for the inability.

■ disclosure

process of divulging accounting information, so that the content of financial statements is understood.

■ disclosure of information

also referred to as 'utmost good faith' or 'uberrima fides'. A pre-condition of insurance contracts to disclose all relevant facts to the insurer. Disclosure at the point of sale of investment products, the amount of commission earned by the adviser and the extent of expenses incurred by the product provider.

■ discontinued operations

portion of a business that is planned to be or is discontinued.

■ discount

1. the amount by which the price for a security is less than its par or face value. The discount or difference between such a reduced value purchase price and the redemption (par) value comprises all or part of the investor's compensation for owning the security.
2. Reduction from the full amount of a price or debt.

■ discount

a reduction of the full price of goods or services by the provider of those goods or services.

discount house

a business which specialises in buying and selling bills of exchange.

discount rate

1. the percentage rate applied to the redemption value of a security, in order to calculate a reduced value for a purchaser. Some (or all in the case of zero coupon securities) of the investor's return comes from the resulting price discount.
2. The rate of return for short-term securities, for which the investor's entire compensation comes from the discount amount.
3. An interest rate applied to a single cash flow, that will not be paid or received until a future time, in order to calculate the present value of that future cash flow.
4. An interest rate or a series of interest rates applied to every one of the future cash flows of interest and principal expected from a financial instrument, in order to create a single value for that instrument.
5. rate at which interest is deducted in advance of the issuance, purchasing, selling or lending of a financial instrument. Also, the rate used to determine the current value or present value of an asset or income stream.

discounted cash flow

1. a technique or process for valuing a financial instrument by applying a discount rate (or a series of discount rates) to calculate a present value of each future interest and principal cash flow expected from a financial instrument. The sum of the market values of the cash flows is considered to be the value of the instrument.
2. Present value of future cash estimated to be generated.

discretionary service

investment service whereby the adviser makes investment decisions without consulting the client.

discretionary trust

1. arrangement in which the trustee has the authority to make investment decisions and has control over investments, within the framework of the trust instrument.
2. a trust in which the trustees may exercise their discretion, within a class of beneficiary, as to whom should receive benefit.

discretionary will

a will which confers on the executors overriding powers of appointment, in favour of a specified class of beneficiary.

disintermediation

1. the investing of funds that would normally have been placed in a bank or other financial institution (financial intermediaries), directly into investment instruments issued by the ultimate users of the funds. Investors and borrowers transact business directly and thereby bypass banks or other financial intermediaries.
2. The elimination of intermediaries between the first case provides of capital and the ultimate users of capital.

dispersion

the distribution pattern of measurements. The standard deviation is the most common measure of dispersion.

■ **disposal**
sale or distribution of goods.

■ **dissolution**
termination of a corporation.

■ **distribute**
in financial terms, to share out profits as shareholders dividends.

■ **distribution expense**
expense of selling, advertising, and delivery of goods and services.

■ **distributions**
payment by a business entity to its owners of items such as cash assets, stocks or earnings.

■ **diversification**
the spread of risk by investing in a portfolio of securities, each of whose performance is affected by a different set of economic and market conditions.

■ **dividend**
a share in company profits, usually paid annually and related to the number of ordinary shares held. Usually expressed as a value of the shares held.

■ **dividend warrant**
payment of share dividends, which includes details of tax deducted at source shown on tax credit voucher.

■ **dividend yield**
the dividend payment of a share, divided by the current market price of the share and expressed as a percentage.

■ **division**
an unincorporated subunit of a corporation.

■ **documents**
documents are written evidence of title such as bills of lading, warehouse receipts and dock receipts. To be a document of title, it must be issued by or addressed to a third party (called a bailee) and cover goods in the bailee's possession.

■ **documents of title**
paperwork proving ownership or possession or control of goods.

■ **Doing Business As (D.B.A.)**
designation, usually following a name, indicating that a name used by a business is not the legal name of the entity doing business but is an assumed name or trade name instead.

■ **domicile**
the country that a person considers to be, and treats as, a permanent home and which forms the closest ties. An essential element when dealing with legal and taxation matters.

■ **dominion of funds**
a form of receivable lending, in which the bank requires that the borrower give the bank control over the borrower's accounts receivable collections. Dominion is a legal term meaning control. This form of lending is also called ledgering or the detail method financing. Do not confuse with factoring.

■ **double leverage**

leverage in bank holding companies that use borrowed funds to finance the holding company's equity investments in its subsidiaries.

■ **double-entry bookkeeping**

method of recording financial transactions, in which each transaction is entered in two or more accounts and involves two-way, self-balancing posting. Total debits must equal total credits.

■ **downstream funding**

the practice of borrowing funds at the bank holding company level. The funds are then lent by the holding company to a subsidiary.

■ **downstream guaranty**

a guaranty of a loan to a borrowing entity, when the guarantor is a parent company or stockholder of the borrowing entity.

■ **downward sloping yield curve**

a yield curve depicting a situation in which yields for shorter-term maturities are higher than those for longer-term maturities. Downward sloping yield curves are atypical.

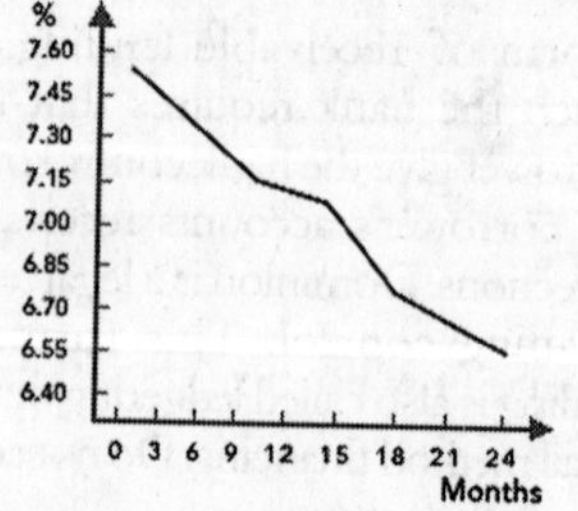

■ **draft**

a written order drawn by one party, called a drawer, that directs a second party (almost always a bank), called a drawee, to pay a sum of money to a third party, called the payee. For example, a cheque. Drafts are used with letters of credit. Drafts may be sight drafts, payable upon receipt or time drafts, payable on some specified future date.

■ **drawee**

the party to whom a check or draft is written. Also called payee.

■ **drawor**

the party who writes a draft or check against funds he or she owns. Also called payor.

■ **dual dating**

dating of the acccountants' or auditors' report when a subsequent event disclosed in the financial statements occurs after completion of the field work but before issuance of the report.

■ **dual index notes**

securities with coupon rates that are determined by the difference between two market indexes. These bonds often have a fixed coupon rate for a brief period, followed by a longer period of variable rates.

■ **due bill**

an instrument evidencing the obligation of a seller to deliver sold securities to the buyer of those securities.

■ **due-on-sale clause**

a provision in a mortgage permitting the lender to demand payment in full when the property is sold.

■ **duration**

a sophisticated measure of the average timing of cash flows from an asset or a liability or from an asset portfolio or a liability portfolio. Essentially, duration is a more accurate measure of maturity because it reflects the timing of cash flows from periodic interest and/or principal payments, in addition to the cash flows represented by the funds transferred at maturity.

■ **duration drift**

a phrase used to describe the slow but inexorable change in duration that occurs with the passage of time. Measurements of duration must be regularly recalculated because of duration drift.

■ **duty**

tax to be paid on certain imported goods.

■ **early amortisation event**

a type of credit enhancement used in asset backed securities. One or more triggers, defined in the asset backed security's documentation, require the termination of revolving periods, controlled amortisation periods and/or accumulation periods. Once triggered, the early amortisation provision requires that the monthly principal payments be distributed to investors as they are received.

■ **early leavers**

generally refers to occupational pension scheme members who leave the scheme before normal retirement age.

■ **earned income**

wages, salaries, professional fees and other amounts received as compensation for services rendered.

■ **Earnings At Risk (EAR)**

the quantity by which net income is projected to decline in the event of an adverse change in prevailing interest rates. One measure of an institution's exposure to adverse consequences from changes in prevailing interest rates.

■ **earnings before..**

there are several 'Earnings Before..' ratios and acronyms: EBT = Earnings Before Taxes; EBIT = Earnings Before Interest and Taxes; EBIAT = Earnings Before Interest after Taxes; EBITD = Earnings Before Interest, Taxes and Depreciation; and EBITDA = Earnings Before Interest, Taxes, Depreciation, and Amortisation. (Earnings = operating and non-operating profits (eg interest, dividends received from other investments). Depreciation is the non-cash charge to the balance sheet which is made in writing off an asset over a period. Amortisation is the payment of a loan in installments.

■ **earnings credit rate**

an interest rate applied to investable account balances, to determine how much expense for bank services used by a depositor is offset by the deposits maintained by that depositor. The same calculation can work in the opposite way by applying the earnings credit rate to the actual service charges, to determine how much deposit balance is needed to pay for the charges. The earnings credit rate is always expressed as an annual rate, even though the calculations are usually done monthly. Also called earnings allowance rate.

■ Earnings Per Share (EPS)

1. measure of performance calculated by dividing the net earnings of a company by the average number of shares outstanding during a period.
2. A ratio calculated as share earnings for the year divided by number of shares in issue.

■ earnings retention rate

the percent of current period earnings retained by the firm, as opposed to being paid out as dividends or partners' withdrawals. The after-tax net income minus dividends, then divided by the after-tax net income. Not to be confused with retained earnings, a name for the quantity on the balance sheet that includes the accumulated total of earnings retained.

■ earnings yield

a company's earnings available for shareholders divided by the current market value of the company's equity capital, or earnings per share dividend by the share price.

■ easement

rights of a landowner exercised over neighbouring land, e.g. a right of way.

■ econometric models

systems of mathematical formulas that attempt to represent the interaction of various macroeconomics variables. Some

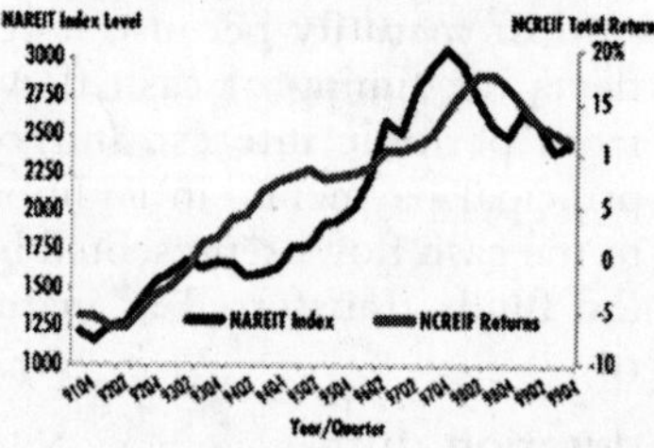

economists use these models to predict the alterations that will result from changes in one or more economic conditions.

■ econometrics

mathematical methods used in analysing economic models or problems.

■ economic

whether something can be produced profitably.

■ Economic Value of Equity (EVE)

one measure of exposure to interest rate risk. The difference between the sum of the present values of all cash flows from assets and the sum of the present values of all cash flows from liabilities. Sometimes called net portfolio value (NPV).

■ economics

the study of an economy (business, or country or trade grouping) and its related financial structures and procedures.

■ effective annual yield

a seldom-used expression to refer to the yield on an investment, expressed on a compound interest basis.

■ effective date

1. the date on which funds will be transferred electronically from or to a customer's account.
2. The date on which cash flows due under a swap contract begin to accrue.

■ effective duration

used to identify those calculations of duration that more accurately include assumptions regarding estimated calls or estimated, non-contractual principal prepayments.

■ effective margin

the effective margin is the average spread over the underlying index that the investor expects to earn over the life of a floating-rate security. For a floating-rate security selling at its par line, the effective margin is identical to the spread between the coupon rate and the underlying index. An advantage of using an effective margin measurement is that it applies equally well to floating-rate securities trading at discounts, at par or at premiums.

■ effective tax rate

total income taxes expressed as a percentage of net income before taxes.

■ effective yield

a measure of the annual return from an investment. The effective yield is calculated by dividing the coupon interest rate by the amount invested, expressed as a percentage of the par value.

■ effectiveness

a measure of achievement in respect of a specific objective.

■ efficiency

a measure of output compared to input.

■ efficient asset or efficient portfolio

an asset or portfolio of assets that earns the maximum possible return for its given level of risk. An asset or a portfolio of assets is considered to be efficient if no other asset or portfolio of assets offers a higher expected return with the same (or lower) risk or offers a lower risk with the same (or higher) expected return.

■ election

an unequivocal choice.

■ electronic chattel paper

a document that includes both monetary obligation and a security agreement, consisting of information stored in an electronic medium.

■ Electronic Funds Transfer (EFT)

an electronically based, rather than paper-based, system of transferring funds to and from accounts. Two main EFT remittance methods are wire transfers and automated clearing house (ACH).

■ eligible accounts

receivables that are acceptable to the lender, for the purpose of making advances to the borrower under a line of credit with an advance formula. The criteria for determining the eligibility of accounts must be set forth in the loan documentation.

■ embargo

instruction which stops or delays something happening - usually relates to a trading situation, but may also relate to release of information, e.g. company announcement.

■ embedded option

a provision in a financial contract or financial instrument, such as a loan or a security, that allows one party to change the timing or amount of one or more cash flows associated with that contract or instrument.

■ embezzlement

a form of theft. The misappropriation of an employer's funds by an employee.

■ emoluments

used as a term for the total earnings package when calculating the potential benefits from an occupational pension scheme and calculating maximum approvable benefit limits.

		2001/2			2000/1		
Name	Age	Emoluments 2001/2	Real increase in pension at at 60	Total accrued pension at 60 at 31 March 2002	Emoluments 2000/1	Real increase in pension at 60	Total accrued pension at 60 at 31 March 2001
		£ '000	£ '000	£ '000	£ '000	£ '000	£ '000
PD Ewins	59	100-105	2.5-5	40-45	95-100	2.5-5	40-45
PJ Mason	56	85-90	0-2.5	35-40	80-85	0-2.5	30-35
CR Flood	58	65-70	0-2.5	25-30	60-65	0-2.5	25-30
SJ Caughey	56	65-70	0-2.5	25-30	60-65	0-2.5	20-25
RD Hunt	53	60-65	0-2.5	20-25	55-60	0-2.5	20-25
S Lawrenson		consent to disclosure withheld			consent to disclosure withheld		
P Mabe	43	85-90	0-2.5	10-15	80-85	0-2.5	5-10
JF Ponting	52	50-55	0-2.5	15-20	50-55	0-2.5	15-20
AJ Thorpe	49	30-35	n/a	20-25	65-70	0-2.5	15-20
M Sands	53	70-75	2.5-5	25-30	65-70	n/a	20-25
S Noyes	42	60-65	0-2.5	15-20	55-60	0-2.5	10-15
A Dickinson	52	55-60	0-2.5	15-20	50-55	n/a	15-20
D Griggs	44	55-60	n/a	10-15	n/a	n/a	n/a
A Douglas	55	55-60	n/a	20-25	n/a	n/a	n/a

■ employee

someone who works under the control and direction of another in return for wages/salary.

■ employee profit sharing scheme

a type of share incentive scheme whereby a special trust is established to purchase company shares which, provided certain conditions are met, will escape income tax on profits on resale.

■ employee share incentive schemes

arrangements which enable employees to purchase the shares of their employing company, some with tax advantages, some without.

■ **employer**

someone who controls and directs the work of another, an employee, in a master/servant sense and who pays that person a wage or salary for work done.

■ **encumbrance**

mortgage or other lien on the entity's assets.

■ **end point analysis**

a determination of the number and value of cheques drawn on each transit routing number.

■ **end user**

a counterparty who intends to own the position. Contrast with a counterparty, such as a dealer who intends to sell the position to an end user.

■ **endorse**

signature on a document, e.g. cheque, to show that ownership has passed, or e.g. a bill, to show that goods have been received. Add additional information to an insurance policy to amend the existing wording.

■ **endorsement**

a written statement on a document, usually on the back of the document, in which the owner assigns his rights to an individual or entity named in the endorsement.

■ **endorser**

technically, an endorser is anyone who signs the back of a financial instrument. In lending, the term is used as functional equivalent of a guarantor. A loan endorser usually signs a guaranty agreement included on the promissory note form, often on the back.

■ **endowment**

funds or property that are donated with either a temporary or permanent restriction as to the use of principal.

■ **endowment assurance**

a medium to long term life assurance/savings contract, incorporating an investment element and a protection element. Policy proceeds normally paid on maturity or earlier death.

■ **endowment mortgage**

an interest on property purchase loan, where the outstanding capital will be repaid at the end of the term, out of the fund accumulated under an endowment policy.

■ **engrossment**

preparation of a legal document in its final form prior to signing.

■ **enterprise fund**

1. a fund established to account for government operations, financed and operated in a manner similar to private business enterprises (e.g., water, gas, electric utilities, airports, parking garages or transit systems). In this case, the governing body intends that costs (i.e., expenses, including depreciation) of providing goods or services to the general public on a continuing basis be refinanced or recovered primarily through user charges.
2. A fund established because the governing body has decided that

periodic determination of revenue earned, expenses incurred and/or net income is appropriate for capital maintenance, public policy, management control, accountability or other purposes.

■ **equalisation of estates**

when a husband and wife divide their assets, so that they save the maximum amount of tax.

■ **equipment**

goods used primarily in the operation of a business. It includes professional equipment and farm equipment. Any personal property that is tangible and is not consumer goods, farm products or inventory.

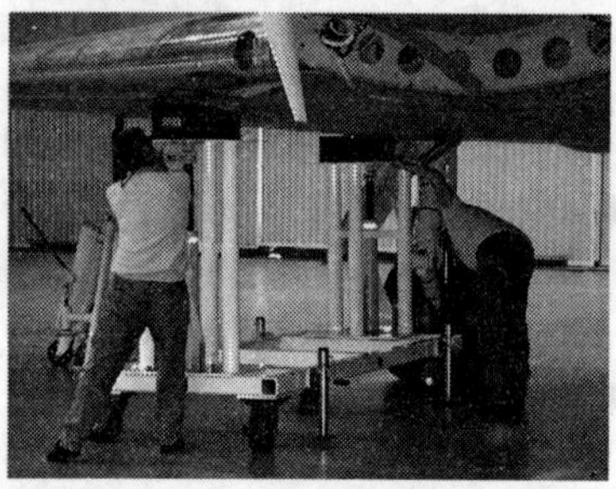

■ **equitable subordination**

a legal term used in bankruptcy, to describe a process in which a bankruptcy judge decides that fairness can only be achieved by giving lower priority (subordinating) the claims of one or more creditors (usually a secured bank), to the claims of other (usually unsecured) creditors.

■ **equities**

common alternative term for ordinary shares.

■ **equity**

residual interest in the assets of an entity that remains after deducting its liabilities. Also, the amount of a business' total assets less total liabilities. Also, the third section of a balance sheet, the other two being assets and liabilities.

■ **equity account**

account in the equity section of the balance sheet. Includes capital stock, additional paid in capital and retained earnings.

equity financing

the sale of an ownership stake in a company represented by stock in the case of a corporation.

■ **equity method**

an accounting method used to reflect an investor's interest in a company. This method is used when the investor owns 20 percent or more of the investee and has significant influence over the investee. Under the equity method, the investment is originally recorded on the books of the investor at its cost. Subsequently, the asset value of that investment on the investor's financial statements is increased or decreased by the investor's proportionate share of the increase or decrease in the investee's net worth.

■ **equity of redemption**

the rights of the mortgagor, i.e. the property owner, over the mortgaged property, i.e. the right to redeem the property.

■ equity securities

capital stock and other securities that represent ownership shares or the legal rights to purchase or acquire capital stock.

■ error

act that departs from what should be done. Imprudent deviation, unintentional mistake or omission.

■ escalation

a term used to describe contracted increases in pensions in payment or in regular contributions.

■ escrow

money or property put into the custody of a third party for delivery to a grantee, only after fulfilment of specified conditions.

■ escrow accounts

cash held in abeyance until an event occurs or does not occur. For example, funds paid monthly by a mortgagor to the mortgagee are held in escrow until they are due to the taxing authority.

■ estate

more properly used in connection with ownership of land. Generally used in a wider context, however, relating to one's personal possessions.

■ estate planning

general phrase relating to personal financial planning, the emphasis being on passing on intact as much of one's estate on death, with as little tax as possible being paid.

■ estate protection

generally a mix of asset reorganisation and use of packaged life products, to reduce tax liability and to pay any tax that does become due.

■ estate tax

tax on the value of a decendent's taxable estate, typically defined as the decedent's assets less liabilities and certain expenses which may include funeral and administrative expenses.

■ estimated tax

amount of tax liability a taxpayer may expect to pay for the current tax period. Usually paid through quarterly instalments.

■ estoppel

a legal term describing the preclusion of a party from alleging in a legal action anything that is contrary to previous actions or admissions of that party.

■ estoppel letter or estoppel certificate

a document used in commercial mortgage transactions where the lender is secured by property that is leased to tenants. Also known as tenant estoppel letters or tenant acceptance letters. Written admissions that are obtained by the lender, prior to funding, to create estoppel. In an estoppel letter, the tenants attest that they believe the lease to be valid and enforceable, that they are making lease payments as agreed, that the landlord is not in default of any lease provisions requiring landlord performance and that no rent has been prepaid.

■ ethical investment

making investments only in companies which are considered acceptable according to a set of criteria concerning the type of product, environmental issues and political issues.

■ evaluation

the act or process of estimating the market value of real estate, when a transaction secured by real estate falls within one or more of the exemptions, set forth to the requirements for obtaining a full appraisal. If a transaction falls under one of three exemptions, an evaluation is required. If the transaction is exempted under one or more exemptions, not including one of the three that require an evaluation, an evaluation may still conducted if the lender considers it prudent. An evaluation may be conducted by independent bank personnel or by an appraiser.

■ event of default

an event described in a promissory note, security agreement or loan agreement that triggers rights of the lender to take remedies set forth in the documents. The most common event of default is the debtor's failure to make required interest and/or principal payments to the bank when they are due.

■ event risk

the risk of an unexpected, future decrease in credit quality, that is a result of events such as a corporate acquisition or material changes in taxes, laws or regulations.

■ evidential matter

underlying accounting data and other corroborating information that support the financial statements.

■ ex gratia

a payment made without obligation.

■ ex officio

latin, 'by virtue of holding an office', i.e. being in one job will involve taking on other jobs.

■ excess clause

a clause in an insurance policy, requiring the policyholder, in the event of a claim, to bear part of the claim.

■ excess servicing or excess spread

a term used in asset backed securities to describe the amount by which the yield from the loan collateral, net of charge-offs, exceeds the sum of the servicing fee and the interest paid to holders of the security.

■ exchange rate

the value of a country's money compared with other currencies.

■ **exchanges**

transfer of money, property or services, in exchange for any combination of these items.

■ **exchange-traded derivative contracts**

some derivatives are traded on organised exchanges. These derivatives usually have margin requirements. Common exchange-traded derivatives include futures and options. Other derivatives, such as swaps, are not exchange traded but are traded in Over-The-Counter (OTC) capital markets.

■ **excise tax**

tax or duty on the manufacture, sale or consumption of commodities.

■ **executor**

person appointed by a will to manage a decendent's estate.

■ **exemplary damages**

damages awarded to punish the defendant, rather than compensate the plaintiff.

■ **exempt income**

investment income which escapes tax, such as National Savings Certificate.

■ **exemption**

amount of a taxpayer's income that is not subject to tax. All individuals, trusts and estates qualify for an exemption, unless they are claimed as a dependent on another individual's tax return. Exemptions also are granted to taxpayers for their dependents.

■ **exercise**

the implementation or use of a contractual right, for example, a call option holder's purchase of the underlying security.

■ **exercise price**

the price at which an option may be used. The price at which the owner of the option has the right to buy or sell whatever the option contract is for. Sometimes called the strike price.

■ **expatriate**

someone who works away from their own country.

■ **expectation gap**

the difference in perception between the public and the CPA, as a result of accounting and audit service.

■ **expectations hypothesis**

the theory that the shape of yield curves is determined by investors' collective expectations of future interest rates.

■ **expected loss or expected risk**

the portion or component of risk or loss that is predicted by statistical analysis.

■ **expenditure**

1. payment, either in cash, by assuming a liability or by surrendering asset.

2. Decreases in net financial resources. Expenditures include current operating expenses requiring the present or future use of net current assets, debt service and

capital outlays, intergovernmental grants, entitlements and shared revenue.

expenses

outflows or other reductions of assets or increases in liabilities (or a combination of both) from delivering or producing goods, rendering services or carrying out other activities that constitute the entity's ongoing major or central operations.

experienced investor

one who regularly invests in their own right and should, therefore, have a clear understanding of the risks and rewards involved.

expiration date

the final date on which an option may be used.

expression of wish

term generally used in relation to the payment of benefit from a group life assurance scheme, whereby to maintain the tax-free status of payments from the scheme, the Trustees have complete discretion on how to pay out the benefit.

extension

time granted by a taxing authority, such as a state or city, which allows the taxpayer to file tax returns later than the original due date.

extension risk

the risk that rising interest rates may slow prepayment speeds and therefore cause an investment in a pass-through to last longer than the investor anticipated. By taking longer to return the investor's principal, the extension prevents the investor from taking advantage of higher rates available from other investments.

external reporting

reporting to stockholders and the public, as opposed to internal reporting for management's benefit.

extinguishment of debt

to get rid of the liability by payment; to bring to an end.

extraordinary items

events and transactions distinguished by their unusual nature and by the infrequency of their occurrence. Extraordinary items are reported separately, less applicable income taxes, in the entity's statement of income or operations.

face value

1. amount due at maturity from a bond or note.
2. The figure shown on a coin, banknote, share certificate, and similar, to confirm its value.

facsimile

an exact copy of something, such as a signature.

fact find

an important stage in the advice cycle, one which enables the adviser to draw out all pertinent information about a potential client and to update information already held concerning an existing client.

■ **factor**

1. an individual or firm that purchases accounts receivable from firms in need of working capital. Usually, a specialised financial firm engaged exclusively or almost exclusively in factoring.
2. An agent holding goods belonging to a principal for the purpose of eventual sale. The agent has implied authority to sell them in his/her own name. May also be called a Mercantile Agent.

■ **factoring**

1. providing working capital to businesses by buying their receivables (usually at a discount), rather than lending against them. Factoring is not lending, it is an outright purchase of the receivable assets, usually on a nonrecourse basis.
2. Selling a receivable at a discounted value to a third party for cash.

■ **fail**

the event of a securities purchase or sale transaction not settling as intended by the parties.

■ **fair market value**

price at which property would change hands between a buyer and a seller without any compulsion to buy or sell, and both having reasonable knowledge of the relevant facts.

■ **family income benefit**

a type of reducing term assurance, under which proceeds in event of a claim are paid as income instalments for remainder of term. Total payments equal the reduced sum assured at the time of claim.

■ **favourable variance**

excess of actual revenue over projected revenue, or actual costs over projected costs.

■ **fed float**

the time lag between when the proceeds of a cheque are available to a bank according to the availability schedule and when the cheque is actually presented for payment (clears against the payer's bank). The fed float represents the difference between available and collected balances.

■ **fee**

the charge imposed for provision of professional services.

■ **fee simple**

the full term is Fee Simple Absolute in Possession, meaning complete and unconditional ownership of land.

■ **fictitious name**

a name used by a proprietorship, partnership or corporation to conduct business that is different from the legal name of the proprietorship, partnership or corporation.

■ **fidelity bond or fidelity insurance**

insurance protecting an employer from losses resulting from the deliberate misappropriation of the firm's assets by one or more of its employees. Fidelity insurance is obtained by most financial institutions.

■ fiduciary

person who is responsible for the administration of property owned by others. Corporate management is a fiduciary, with respect to corporate assets that are beneficially owned by the stockholders and creditors.

■ field audits

any on-site inspection of the bank's collateral may be referred to as a field audit. However, the phrase is most often used to refer to on-site audits of a borrower's records related to sales, accounts receivable, accounts payable, customer records and shipping documents. Field audits are often conducted by specially trained bank employees, but may be done by internal bank auditors, external accounting firms hired by the bank or firms specialising in this service. Written field audit reports contain significant information for secured lenders.

■ field warehousing

a method of financing inventories in which the inventory is held in custody for the lender by an agent of the lender, at the borrower's place of business.

■ final maturity

the maturity date of the single loan in a pool of mortgage loans that has the maturity date furthest in the future. Because mortgage loans tend to be repaid sooner than their contractual maturity dates, the actual final payment is likely to occur earlier than the final maturity date.

■ final salary scheme

a pension scheme providing pension benefit by reference to the scheme member's salary at or near retirement.

■ finance leasing

a lease where the lessor aims to recover capital expenditure and related costs during the lease period.

■ financial accounting

general terms covering preparation of the 'ordinary' business accounts, i.e. balance sheet, profit and loss account and related notes and statements.

■ financial adviser

a person offering financial advice. There are two types of advisers, those who offer advice based on the sale of the products of a single company (tied agents or company representatives), and those who select the most suitable product from those available in the market.

■ financial institution

organisation engaged in any of the many aspects of finance, including commercial banks, thrift institutions, investment banks, securities brokers and dealers, credit unions, investment companies, insurance companies and real estate investment trusts.

■ financial instrument

cash, evidence of ownership in an entity (e.g., stock), a contract that creates a right or obligation to receive or deliver cash (e.g., notes and bonds) or a contract that creates a right or obligation to receive or deliver another financial instrument or commodity (e.g., options and futures).

■ financial intermediary

a party such as a bank or other financial institution that accepts funds from a provider and places those funds with a user. The intermediary's investment from the user is usually for a longer term, usually has less liquidity and usually has more credit risk than the intermediary's liability to the provider.

■ financial statements

1. collective name for historical financial reports of assets, liabilities, capital, income and expense.

2. Presentation of financial data including balance sheets, income statements and statements of cash flow, or any supporting statement that is intended to communicate an entity's financial position at a point in time and its results of operations for a period then ended.

■ financial underwriting

underwriting in general is concerned with assessing the risk that a proposal represents to the insurance company. Part of the assessment involves the health hazard. Equally important is assessing the moral hazard attached to a proposal, part of which requires a question to be asked along the following lines: 'Given the circumstances outlined and the information provided, is the sum assured in question disproportionately high in the light of lifestyle/business requirements', i.c. is there deliberate over insurance, and why.

■ financial year

financial years run 1/4 to 31/3 and are identified by the calendar year in which they commence e.g. financial year 1995 is the year to 31.3.1996.

■ firm

generally used in the context of referring to a business or partnership, not a limited company. Also used in the sense of steady, finalised, e.g. firm offer.

■ first in, first out (FIFO)

accounting method of valuing inventory, under which the costs of the first goods acquired are the first costs charged to expense. Commonly known as FIFO.

■ fiscal

relating to tax, e.g. fiscal year, fiscal policy.

■ fiscal year

period of 12 consecutive months chosen by an entity as its accounting period, which may or may not be a calendar year.

■ fixed asset

an asset (e.g. machinery, plant) used by a company on a long term basis.

■ fixed cost

a cost which does not vary with changing sales or production volumes, e.g. building lease costs, permanent staff wages, rates, depreciation of capital items.

■ fixed rate

unchanging, not subject to movement or fluctuation, usually for a specified term, e.g. fixed rate mortgage, where the rate reverts to the normal variable rate at the end of the fixed period.

■ fixtures

fixtures are items that become attached to real property. Examples are heating and air conditioning systems, wall-mounted shelving and security alarm systems. Lenders must be extremely cautious about what constitutes a fixture.

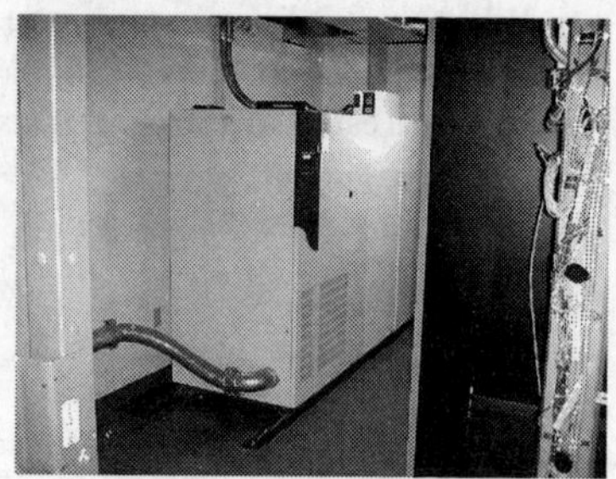

■ flex repo

a term repo/reverse transaction that allows for the investor to sell some of the collateral securities back to the borrower before the final maturity date of the transaction.

■ flexible mortgage account

combined mortgage and current account, whereby the whole of one's salary is paid into the mortgage account using it as an ordinary current account.

■ flexible trust

one under which the settlor may change the beneficiaries to the trust property or the way in which the property is divided.

■ flight to quality

the situation in which many investors sell or reduce purchases of less creditworthy investments and simultaneously buy or increase purchases of the most creditworthy investments. Flights to quality often occur suddenly after a major unexpected default or a major political event.

■ float

in monetary terms, cash used for running expenses.

■ float analysis

an analysis of an organisation's disbursements to determine the approximate number of days between issuance of a cheque and presentation of the cheque for payment at the organisation's bank.

■ floater

an informal name for a security with a variable coupon rate.

■ floating lien

the name for and the nature of a creditor's interest in a debtor's accounts receivable and inventory. In the natural operation of any business, the specific receivables and inventory owned at one point in time are replaced over time by new receivables and new inventory. Thus, a creditor's security interest in accounts receivable and inventory floats from the specific accounts and inventory held today to that held next week, next month and thereafter.

■ flood insurance

insurance protection against damage caused by floods. For applicable parcels of real estate, lenders with a security interest in that real estate are required by law to either require that borrowers obtain flood insurance or to obtain flood insurance for their borrowers.

■ floor

1. a lower limit for a variable, such as the lower limit on an interest rate paid or received in a transaction. For example, an adjustable-rate loan may have a floor of 5 percent. In that example, the rate can adjust however loan terms provide, but it can never fall below 5 percent.

2. Term used when discussing inventories. Inventory cannot be valued lower than the 'floor', which is the net realisable value of the inventory, less an allowance for a normal profit margin.

■ floor planning

a form of inventory financing involving loans or advances for specific items of inventory.

■ floortion

an option that grants the holder the right to purchase a floor.

■ flotation

the open sale of shares in a company 'going public', rather than the issuing of shares in a private company start-up.

■ flow chart

a visual explanation of an activity using diagrams. Each action is represented by a shape which leads on to the next related action or actions, each shape attached to the next by a line to denote the flow of the activity.

■ forbearance agreement

an agreement between a creditor and a debtor. A forbearance agreement is utilised when a debtor has defaulted or is likely to default. Under the terms of the forbearance agreement, the debtor is given more time to make loan payments, a reduction in the amount of loan payments due each month or both. Typically, the lender agrees not to exercise rights to foreclose or accelerate during the forbearance period. In return, the debtor agrees not to contest any actions taken by the creditor, to collect the debt in the event that the debtor fails to comply with the payment schedule or other terms specified in the forbearance agreement.

■ **force majeure**

events outside the control of the parties to a contract, which may have effect on the contract. Some contracts may contain a specific clause allowing for such events and which determine what should happen in such circumstances.

■ **forecast**

prospective financial statements that are an entity's expected financial position, results of operations and cash flows.

■ **foreclose**

to acquire the security for a loan if the loan cannot be serviced or repaid.

■ **foreclosure**

seizure of collateral by a creditor when default under a loan agreement occurs.

■ **forfaiting**

rather like factoring for exporters, in that a third party, the agent or forfaiter, purchases a bill of exchange at a discount and collects payment in full from the customer.

■ **forward delivery**

the transfer of commodities or foreign exchange at a specified date, subsequent to the date of the contract that provides for the transfer.

■ **forward market**

the informal (nonexchange) trading of foreign exchange or commodities to be delivered at a future date. Contracts for forward delivery are not standardised. Instead, the delivery time and amount are negotiated by the parties.

■ **forward pricing**

price quoted for units where the manager arranges the underlying assets after the investor applies for the units. The price reflects the future or rearranged asset valuation.

■ **forward rate**

the interest rate for a specified maturity of a fixed-income security for a future date. For example, the forward rate for six-month Treasury bills one month from today.

■ **Forward Rate Agreement (FRA)**

a customised agreement between two parties specifying the rate to be paid at some future date.

■ **forward roll**

the sale of an investment position when the sale proceeds are used to acquire a new position that is very similar to the one that was sold.

forwards

contracts for the sale/purchase of a specified quantity of a financial instrument, currency or commodity at an agreed-upon price on a given future date. Unlike an option, a forward contract obligates both parties to consummate the transaction. Forwards are very similar to futures - the principal difference is that futures are almost always exchange traded while forwards are traded over the counter.

Four Ps

conventional approach to marketing, namely: Product, Price, Place, Promotion.

franchise

legal arrangement whereby the owner of a trade name, franchisor, contracts with a party that wants to use the name on a non-cxclusive basis to sell goods or services, franchisee.

franked investment income

dividend income received by corporate investors which, because corporation tax has already been paid on it by the distributing company, will not attract additional tax in the hands of the investing company.

fraud

wilful misrepresentation by one person of a fact, inflicting damage on another person.

fraudulent conveyance/ fraudulent transfer

a transfer of an interest of the debtor made within one year prior to the filing of bankruptcy, that is either made by the debtor with the intent to defraud its creditors or for which the debtor receives less than reasonable consideration.

free cash flow

cash flow from operations minus capital expenditures and dividends. Cash flow from operations is reduced by those adjustments, to generate a measure of cash available to meet other corporate purposes. While the above definition is commonly used by equity investors, bank credit analysts create similar measures of free cash flow that may involve more or different adjustments to cash flow from operations.

free cover

usually relates to group employee benefit schemes (life assurance) where an element of protection is offered without the need for medical evidence.

freehold

complete ownership of land, held in 'fee simple absolute in possession', i.e. not likely to end on death or after a time (fee simple), unconditional (absolute), the owners rights are immediate (in possession).

freight forwarder

person or business who arranges documentation and travel facilities for companies despatching goods to customers.

friendly society

a mutual benefit organisation having the main aim of providing maintenance and relief to members during sickness and retirement. Their tax advantages enable them to offer tax effective policies, but for limited premium levels only.

■ fringe benefits

extra benefits, available to some or all employees, on top of salary, e.g. staff restaurant, pension scheme. Also termed 'Perks', which is a shortened form of perquisite.

■ front end loading

one of the reasons for heavy penalties if a life or investment policy is cancelled in its early years, is that often the expense of selling and setting up the policy is recouped by the insurance company in the first year or two of the policy. This method of expense allocation is called front end loading.

■ full faith and credit

a pledge of the general taxing power for the payment of debt obligations. Bonds carrying such pledges are referred to as general obligation bonds or full-faith-and-credit bonds.

■ full payout

a phrase used to describe personal property leases that are structured such that the bank/lessor receives its total repayment from one customer/lessee and that the total repayment comes from the proceeds of rents, tax advantages and the residual value assumption.

■ fund

a fiscal and accounting entity with a self-balancing set of accounts in which cash and other financial resources, all related liabilities and residual equities, or balances, and charges therein, are recorded and segregated, to carry on specific activities or attain certain objectives in accordance with special regulations, restrictions or limitations.

■ fund accounting

method of accounting and presentation, whereby assets and liabilities are grouped according to the purpose for which they are to be used. Generally used by government entities and not-for-profits.

■ funded status

a term used to describe either the excess or shortfall of pension assets in relation to pension liabilities. When pension liabilities exceed the assets, the funded status is a shortfall. When a plan liquidation or termination is being analysed, the funded status is calculated using the accumulated benefit obligation (ABO) as the liability value.

■ funding liquidity risk or funding risk

the potential that an institution will be unable to meet its obligations as they come due because of an inability to liquidate a sufficient quantity of assets or to obtain a sufficient quantity of new liabilities.

■ Funds Transfer Pricing (FTP)

an internal cost accounting system or methodology that transfers a cost of funds expense to profit centres that generate assets and a credit for funds to profit centres that provide funding. Most funds transfer pricing systems are matched maturity systems that attempt to reflect the term structure of interest rates in their transfer rates.

■ fungible

1. a security which can be exchanged for another of a similar, or the same, type. A fungible asset is one which is so similar to another as to be indistinguishable. 2. Property that is indistinguishable from other property of the same type. Fungibles are completely substitutable or interchangeable. Two examples of fungibles are pork bellies and dollar bills.

■ future advance clauses

provisions in mortgages or security agreements that attempt to extend the secured party's interest in the collateral, to cover future extensions of credit made by that creditor to the debtor.

■ future contract

transferable agreement to deliver or receive, during a specific future month, a standardised amount of a commodity.

■ future value

the value at which a sum of money invested now will grow, when invested at a given rate or rates of interest during the period.

■ futures

contracts for the sale/purchase of a specified quantity of a financial instrument, currency or commodity at an agreed-upon price on a given future date.

■ futures and options fund

an authorised unit trust which can invest a limited amount of its fund in derivatives.

■ G & A expense

a shorthand expression used by many bankers to refer to general and administrative expenses. These are a subgrouping of a firm's operating expenses. In most banks, the term refers to all operating expenses excluding interest, depreciation and amortisation.

■ gain

excess of revenues received over costs relating to a specific transaction.

■ gains trading

the practice of purchasing securities and then selling those that subsequently appreciate in value, while retaining as investment portfolio assets those that cannot be sold at a profit. Accounting and banking regulators have repeatedly and strongly criticised this practice.

■ gamma

the rate of change of an option's delta, for a small change in the price of the option's underlying.

■ gapping

mismatching assets and liabilities, usually by borrowing short and lending long.

■ garage

to transfer assets to another company to reduce tax liability.

■ garnishee order

a court order preventing a person owing money to another person from paying it, until that second person has satisfied other claims outstanding against him or her.

■ gazumping

accepting an offer which is later rejected in favour of a higher offer when selling a house.

■ gearing

1. the ratio of ordinary share capital and reserves to borrowings.
2. The ratio of debt to equity, usually the relationship between long-term borrowings and shareholders' funds.

■ general fund

in fund accounting, the fund used to account for all financial resources, except those required to be accounted for in another fund. Often used as and referred to as the operating fund.

■ general intangibles

a catch-all term for intangibles other than accounts such as copyrights, trademarks, patent rights, franchise rights, good will, tax refunds, relocation claims, operating rights and legal claims.

■ general ledger

collection of all asset, liability, owners equity, revenue and expense accounts.

■ General Obligation (GO)

a municipal obligation that is supported by the full faith and credit — the full taxing authority — of the municipality (as opposed to support from only the revenues from specific user fees.)

■ general partnership

1. a partnership in which every partner is fully liable to the full extent of his, her or its net worth for all the obligations of the partnership.
2. Partnership with no limited partners.

■ geographic liquidity risk

a type of systemic risk where deterioration in regional economic conditions triggers liquidity crisis. Usually, such a crisis is triggered by credit loss. See **systemic liquidity risk.**

■ gift with reservation

a transfer of value in which the donor retains an interest, e.g. the donor gives a house to a friend, on condition the donor continues to live in the house.

■ gilt strip

where each interest payment and the redemption value become investments in their own right, which can be bought and sold.

■ give as you earn

a system of donating to charity direct from one's salary, which attracts tax relief at the highest tax rate payable.

■ going concern

assumption that a business can remain in operation long enough for all of its current plans to be carried out.

■ **going public**

activities that relate to offering a private company's shares to the general investing public.

■ **good delivery**

delivery of a security, from a seller to a buyer, that complies with all terms of the contract of sale.

■ **good faith estimate**

a document that lenders are required by regulation to provide all applicants for covered real estate loans. This document discloses the anticipated expenses that the applicant(s) will have to pay if the covered transaction is approved and closed.

■ **goods**

a category of personal property. Sometimes called tangible goods. Further divided into consumer goods, equipment, farm products and inventory.

■ **goodwill**

premium paid in the acquisition of an entity, over the fair value of its identifiable tangible and intangible assets less liabilities assumed.

■ **Graduated Payment Mortgage (GPM)**

a mortgage in which the monthly payment of principal and interest begins at a low amount and progressively increases to a predetermined higher amount. Thereafter, the amount of the monthly payment remains constant for the remaining life of the loan. The interest rate is fixed for the entire period.

■ **grantee**

person to whom property is transferred.

■ **grantor**

a person, partnership or corporation that gives or conveys an interest in property. Often used to identify the creator of a trust.

■ **gratuity**

usually taken to mean a cash gift or tip for services rendered. Also a cash sum paid to service personnel on leaving the service.

■ **greenmail**

almost blackmail, in that the exercise involves buying enough shares in a company to threaten a takeover bid and all the expenses that exercise involves, but then selling the shares back to the company at a higher price than was made.

■ **gross**

the sum total, without deduction.

■ **Gross Domestic Product (GDP)**

the total value of finished goods and services produced within an economy over a specific period, normally one year.

■ **gross national product**

GDP plus net property income and profits from abroad.

■ **gross profit**

a subtotal on a firm's statement of income, that is net sales minus cost of goods sold. Sometimes called gross profit on sales.

■ **gross sales**

the total value of all revenue derived by the firm from the principal operations of its business, during the period covered by the income statement report.

■ **gross-bonded debt**

the total amount of direct debt of an issuer, represented by outstanding bonds before deduction of any assets available and earmarked for their retirement.

■ **grossing up**

converting a net amount into its corresponding gross amount, e.g. calculating a rate of return, anticipating a tax deduction on a gift or will bequest.

■ **group life**

a life assurance scheme operated by an employer for his employees. May be stand-alone or running alongside an occupational pension scheme. Will pay out, tax free, a maximum of 4 times qualifying salary, (final remuneration), plus spouses/'dependants' pensions.

■ **group pension**

generally operated by an employer for a group of employees and may be a 'conventional' scheme where the employer helps fund the arrangement or may be a group personal pension scheme, where the grouping is merely for administrative convenience. Alternative name for occupational pension scheme.

■ **group sort**

a service enabling a collecting bank to deposit cheques drawn on a limited preselected group of payer institutions.

■ **guaranteed annuity option**

some pension policies may have a 'safety net' guarantee as a safeguard against heavy market fluctuations.

■ **guaranteed bonds**

a type of corporate bond for which a corporation other than the issuing corporation guarantees the repayment of a bond issue. Usually, the guarantee is provided by the parent firm of the issuing corporation.

■ **guaranty**

legal arrangement involving a promise by one person, to perform the obligations of a second person, to a third person, in the event the second person fails to perform.

■ **guidance line of credit**

a line of credit approved by the bank, but not disclosed to the borrower until some specific event, est rate risk. For example, holding equal amounts of assets and liabilities of the same duration.

implied waiver

a legal name for a situation in which a lender is deemed to have lost the right to enforce a provision in the loan documents, as a result of the lender's failure to enforce the same provision when it was previously violated.

improvement

expenditure directed to a particular asset, to improve its performance or useful life.

imputation system

the system of dividend taxation, where the company pays Advance Corporation Tax (ACT) on dividends and the dividends are assumed to be paid net of basic rate tax. The shareholder receives a tax credit with the dividend cheque as proof of tax paid.

imputed costs

estimated costing of what a company gives up by not selling or leasing an asset, rather than continuing to use it in production.

in re

latin, 'in the matter of', sometimes abbreviated to 're'. Used to head some law reports, followed by the name of the person or subject the case concerns.

in the money

the situation in which an option has value because of the relationship between the option's strike price and the current market price for the underlying instrument, the spot price. A call option is in the money when the strike price is below the spot price. A put option is in the money when the strike price is above the spot price.

■ **income**

1. inflow of revenue during a period of time.
2. money received from employment (earned income) or investments (unearned).

■ **income statement**

summary of the effect of revenues and expenses over a period of time.

■ **income tax**

direct tax levied on income, whether earned or unearned.

■ **income tax basis**

1. for tax purposes, the concept of basis determines the proper amount of gain to report when an asset is sold. Basis is generally the cost paid for an asset, plus the amounts paid to improve the asset, less deductions taken against the asset, such as depreciation and amortisation.
2. For accounting purposes, a consistent basis of accounting that uses income tax accounting rules.

■ **incorporation**

the act of turning a business into a limited liability company.

■ **increment**

regular, automatic increase.

■ **incumbency certificate**

a list of the names of the individuals holding various corporate offices within a corporation.

usually a request for funding from the borrower. Also called an unadvised line.

■ **haggle**

verbal negotiations regarding the price of goods or services, during which the seller will try to keep the price high and the buyer will try to bring the price down.

■ **haircut**

a lender's informal expression for a collateral margin. Commonly used with repurchase and reverse repurchase agreements informally called repos and reverses.

■ **handle**

an informal name for the portion of a security's price that is comprised of the numbers to the left of the decimal point, colon or dash. For example, if a bond's price is 103.25, its handle is 103. Sometimes brokers and dealers only quote the numbers to the right of the decimal point and assume that the handle is understood.

■ **hard call protection**

for convertible bonds, one of two types of call protection. Hard call protection prohibits an issuer from calling an issue within a certain period of time. For convertible bonds, hard call protection is most often set at three years, but can range from two to five years.

■ **hazard insurance**

insurance covering losses incurred by an insured, as a result of damage, destruction or loss of property. Mainly, but not entirely, insurance against fire and lightning damage. Insurance other than life or liability insurance.

■ **hedge**

1. to reduce risk or behaviour that reduces risk from future price movements.
2. A transaction undertaken to reduce risk by offsetting the risk in another transaction. The risk in one position is hedged by counterbalancing it with the risk in another transaction. The values of each position must change inversely and with a high degree of correlation. Hedges may be cash to cash, in which a position in a cash instrument, such as a loan or investment, reduces or offsets the risk in another cash position such as a deposit.
3. Action taken against the possibility of loss caused by a change in prices e.g. by buying raw materials in advance of having to supply the finished goods.

■ **hedge ratio**

the relationship between the size of a position needed in a hedge instrument and the size of the position being hedged. The hedge ratio is determined by the delta.

■ **hidden option**

an option feature in an instrument in which the option feature is only a minor feature of that product. Sometimes called an embedded option. They are hidden because they are not separate, detachable features that issuers or holders can add or subtract to customise individual transactions. Instead, they are one part of a number of features embedded in the product.

■ higher rate tax

any rate of income tax in excess of basic rate tax.

■ high-yield securities

a formal name for junk bonds.

■ hire

short term use of an asset in return for a fee.

■ hire purchase

a method of buying goods by paying regular sums over an agreed period. The sums involved will usually cover the cost of the item and an element of interest. At the end of the hire period, the asset will legally pass to the hirer on payment of a nominal sum.

■ historic pricing

price quoted for units, based on existing valuation of underlying fund assets.

■ historical cost

original cost of an asset to an entity.

Shares of different regions in USDIA in 2000 on historical cost basis and in fresh USDIA made in 2000 (in percentages)

Region/Country USDIA	Share in USDIA in 2000 on historical cost basis (%)	Share in fresh made in 2000 (%)
Asia & Pacific	16.04	15.56
Africa	1.27	0.82
Latin America & other Western Hemisphere	19.23	16.41
Middle East	0.95	1.17
Canada	10.16	13 50
Europe	52 12	53.04

■ hive off

generally taken to mean separating a small, autonomous part of a business, so that it becomes a separate, subsidiary business in its own right.

■ hold-harmless agreement

a contract under which the liability of one party for damages is assumed by another.

■ holding company

'Parent' company with controlling interest in subsidiary company. A company which often exists only to hold shares in a group of subsidiary companies and which holds over 50% of the ordinary shares of those companies.

■ holistic

when used in conjunction with financial planning, refers to the consideration of all aspects of a persons financial involvements.

■ home banking

the use of a computer and special terminal connection to conduct basic banking transactions, such as paying bills, transferring sums from account to account.

■ home income plan

a plan to use one's home to generate extra income. The basic idea is to borrow money (using the home as security) to buy an annuity. Part of the annuity pays the loan repayments or loan interest, the balance representing the extra income.

■ home service

in insurance terms, insurance that is transacted by collecting agents calling at policyholders homes for premiums due. Both premium and sum assured levels are of low value.

■ honorarium

money paid out for services rendered voluntarily, i.e. when a fee has not been requested.

■ horizon analysis

a less-common name for total return analysis. The term 'horizon analysis' derives from the fact that total return analysis requires the user to select an ending date for the investment being analysed. That ending date is sometimes called the investor's horizon.

■ horse trading

haggling, hard bargaining.

■ hospital cash plan

an insurance which pays out cash sums of varying amounts, depending on the reason for a hospital stay and determined by the length of the stay.

■ hospital report

this may be requested during the underwriting of a life assurance, when relevant information relating to hospital treatment may not be available from the GP.

■ hot money

an informal term used to describe funds provided by the most price-sensitive and credit quality-sensitive sources. The bank liabilities that are likely to be lost most quickly in the event of a loss of confidence or competitiveness.

■ hybrid or hybrid security

a package or combination of financial instruments. Hybrid structures range from sin
complex.

■ hybrid schemes

occupational pens
which combine mo
and final salary bene
to describe self a
schemes marketed
companies, where so
invested in insuranc
funds.

■ hypothecation

1. an archaic term
that did not involve e
sion or title transfer.
2. Any pledge of an
lateral for a debt.
3. The pledge of ma
curities or deposits to
— particularly the ple
ketable securities
owned by someone o
borrower.

■ illustration

figures or graphs showi
costs and/or returns f
packaged products, i
determined by the reg

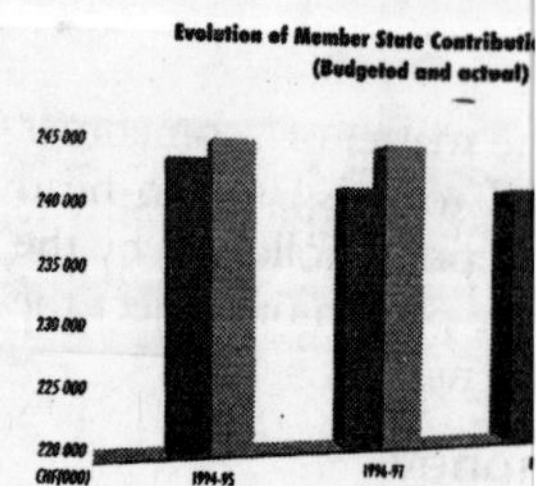

■ immunisation

establishing and mainta
and offsetting exposur

■ indemnification agreement

an agreement in which the borrower promises to protect the bank or reimburse the bank for any damages, claims, costs, penalties or liabilities that may arise from some problem. For example, the bank may obtain an indemnification agreement to protect itself from costs, penalties or liabilities arising from environmental contamination or from violations of environmental regulations.

■ indemnify

to provide an indemnity.

■ indemnity

guarantee payment or compensation following a financial loss.

■ indeterminate maturity

an unspecified maturity date for a financial instrument. For example, the maturity date of a savings account.

■ index

1. a benchmark upon which the payment rate or accrual rate for an adjustable-rate loan or investment is based. For example, a business loan may pay interest at the prime rate plus 1 percent. In that example, the prime rate is the index.
2. List of items in performance or alphabetical order.

■ indexation

price adjustment which allows capital or income to take account of, or benefit from, inflation.

■ indexed

also Index-linked. Growth in income or capital which follows one of the many growth or performance indices, e.g. Retail Prices Index, Average Earnings Index.

■ indirect costs

costs which cannot be related directly to the production of specific goods or services, such as rent, overheads and selling costs.

■ industrywide scheme

scheme set up by employers in the same industry, having the advantage of offering continuous accrual of benefit, if moving from one employer to another within the industry, i.e. obviates potential reduced benefit through transfers.

■ inflation

in simple terms, when production costs increase for the same level of output, the result is often an increase in the product price. This in turn results in a reduction in purchasing power because more is needed to buy the same goods. This leads to higher wage demands, which leads to higher production costs, and so on. The results of this cycle is price inflation, which is what is generally meant by the term inflation.

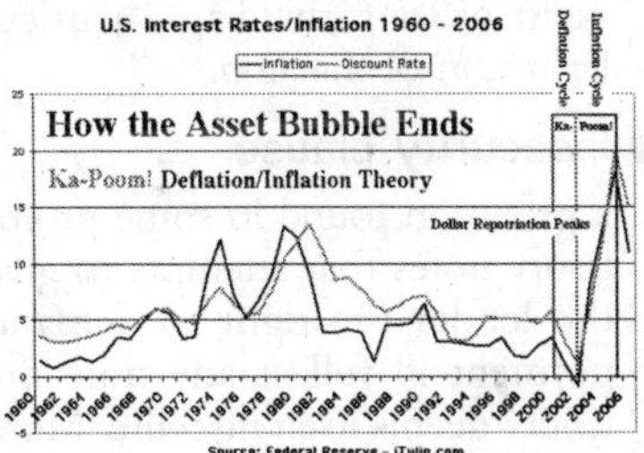

■ inflation accounting

a system of accounting, such as current cost accounting, that seeks to compensate for the deficiencies in conventional historic cost accounting, in taking into account the variable cost of money during an inflationary period.

■ inherit

to receive something from the estate of someone who has died.

■ inheritance tax

tax payable on certain gifts and transfers during lifetime. Also payable on estate at death, if its value exceeds the inheritance tax threshold figure.

■ initial public offering (IPO)

when a private company goes public for the first time.

■ initial units

with some unit linked products, management expenses are recouped by having two types of unit. Initial or capital units are purchased by new contributions for one or two years, then accumulation units are purchased thereafter. The initial units have a higher charge to help offset expenses.

■ injunction

court order forbidding a particular action or inaction.

■ insecurity clause

a provision found in some promissory notes that attempts to give the lender the right to demand payment in full at any time the lender deems itself insecure. More often than not, such a clause is unenforceable, except when other material defaults are also involved.

■ insider trading

the buying/selling of shares on a recognised stock exchange by someone employed (currently or within the last six months) by the company concerned and who is in possession of restricted information not generally available on the market.

■ insiders

a legal term used in bankruptcy to describe parties that have a special relationship to the bankrupt debtor. Creditors who are officers, directors or stockholders are obvious examples of insiders. In some cases, the bank may be deemed to be an insider. The main consequence of being deemed an insider is that insiders are subject to a one-year preference period, while other creditors are only subject to a 90-day preference period.

■ insolvency

1. the lack of adequate capital. The condition that exists when the amount of losses exceeds the amount of capital.
2. The inability of a business to meet its liabilities.

■ insolvent

when an entity's liabilities exceed its assets.

■ inspector

in insurance terms, an 'inspector of agents', i.e. someone representing an insurance company, who calls upon intermediaries who hold an agency with the company. The role is generally seen as a new business generating one.

■ **instalment**

partial payment.

■ **instalment method**

tax accounting method of reporting gain on the sale of an asset exchanged for a receivable. In general, the gain is reported as the note is paid off.

■ **instalment note**

in consumer lending, name used to describe a promissory note that calls for mostly regular, periodic payments of principal.

■ **instrument**

a legal document, generally relating to a financial transaction.

■ **instrument-specific liquidity risk**

a type of systemic or capital markets liquidity risk. The risk that the failure of a market for a financial instrument, such as the commercial paper market, might trigger a bank funding crisis.

■ **insurable interest**

a basic requirement of insurance in order for the contract to be valid. There must be present the possibility for monetary loss in the event, say, of the death of the life assured.

■ **insurance**

in return for agreed payments, the recipient agrees to recompense the payer in the event of certain events, e.g. loss, damage, injury, death. Encapsulated in the phrase 'You pay the small cheques, we pay the big ones'.

■ **insurance broker**

somebody who derives an in

come from arranging insurance policies.

■ **insure**

to protect something of value by means of risk transfer, i.e. payment of small regular sums to a specialist company (insurance company), so that in the event of loss or damage, the company will pay monetary compensation.

■ **insurers**

general term for insurance companies.

■ **intangible**

property or belongings which cannot be touched or seen, but which have value, e.g. goodwill in a business.

■ intangible asset

asset having no physical existence such as trademarks and patents.

■ intercompany accounts

accounts receivable or payable from or to affiliated companies.

■ intercompany eliminations

accounting entries made on consolidating statements, in the process of generating consolidated financial statements. Intercompany eliminations cancel the accounting effects of transactions between firms in the consolidated group, so that the final consolidated numbers exclude all transactions between entities in the group.

■ interest

1. payment for the use or forbearance of money.
2. Money received as income from investments.
3. Money paid for the use of borrowed money.
4. Part ownership of something, e.g. an interest in possession or controlling interest.

■ interest in possession

an entitlement to the income from trust property.

■ interim

occurring during a company's financial year rather than at its end. Interim results are often accompanied by interim dividends, whereas the year end accounts may give rise to final dividends.

■ interim deed

a temporary measure whilst waiting for the full and final version to be engrossed. Often used when establishing group pension arrangements.

■ interim financial statements

financial statements that report the operations of an entity for less than one year.

■ intermediaries

generic term referring to anyone who assists two other parties to do business.

■ internal audit

audit performed within an entity by its staff rather than an independent certified public accountant.

■ internal control

process designed to provide reasonable assurance regarding achievement of various management objectives, such as the reliability of financial reports.

■ internal float

elapsed time for processing cheques. Also called administrative float or processing float.

■ Internal Rate of Return (IRR)

method that determines the discount rate at which the present value of the future cash flows will exactly equal the investment outlay.

■ intestacy

the result of having died intestate, i.e. without a valid will.

■ **intestate**

without a valid will.

■ **intrinsic**

inherent and essential to the object concerned, e.g. intrinsic value may have no relationship to the real value, the intrinsic value being, say, sentimental.

■ **intrinsic value**

that portion of an option's value that derives from the fact that the option is in the money. The difference between exercise price of the option and the price of the underlying. The other primary component of an option's price is its time value.

■ **introducers agreement**

an agreement used where a non-registered individual introduces a potential client to an authorised financial adviser. Necessary where the introduction is to a tied agent, as the inference of the introduction is that not only is the adviser being recommended, but also the adviser's limited range of products.

■ **inventory**

1. tangible property held for sale or materials used in a production process to make a product.
2. a list of stock or contents.

■ **invest**

to put money into trading ventures, existing contracts or organisations (e.g. shares or building societies), with a view to producing income and/or increases in capital value.

■ **investment**

1. expenditure used to purchase goods or services that could produce a return to the investor.
2. The use and management of money with the aim of increasing its value by means of generating income and/or capital growth.

■ **investment bond**

a single premium unit linked life policy, containing a nominal amount of life cover. A non-income producing investment. Any partial or full encashment proceeds are subject to special tax rules.

■ **investment premium (for convertible bonds)**

the amount by which the convertible bond's market price exceeds its value as a bond only, expressed as a percentage. The calculation is done by subtracting the investment value from the market value and dividing the difference by the investment value.

■ **investment property**

an informal term for real estate owned for investment rather than the owner's use.

■ **investment trust**

a public limited company which invests in shares of other companies. Its shares are traded on Stock market. They are not true trusts and can borrow money to buy additional investments.

■ **investment value (for convertible bonds)**

the value of a convertible bond calculated as a straight bond, without giving any value to the conversion feature. Although this is done according to normal bond calculations, the rate used to discount the bond is that for similar, nonconvertible debt. The discount rate is likely to be two to five percentage points higher than the convertible's coupon rate. Also called the bond value.

■ **investor**

person or organisation who invests money or time.

■ **invisible**

invisible assets - assets which have value but cannot be seen, such as patents.

■ **invisible earnings**

foreign currency earned by providing services, rather than goods, abroad, e.g. insurance.

■ **invitation to treat**

a pre- offer and acceptance stage which may lead to formulation of a contract, e.g. goods displayed in a window are deemed an invitation to treat, not an offer for sale.

■ **invoice**

a formal request for payment for goods and/or services previously supplied.

■ **irredeemable**

certain government bonds are irredeemable (e.g. war loans), which means that whilst they pay interest they have no maturity date and so will be repaid only at the discretion of the government.

■ **irrevocable**

cannot be rescinded or changed. An irrevocable trust is a necessity for exempt approval of a group pension scheme.

■ **issue date**

the date on which interest for a new security issue begins accruing. For mortgage-backed bonds, the issue date of the pool is not the same as the origination date of the underlying mortgages. A pool may be assembled from new loans or from older loans.

■ **issued capital**

the amount of the authorised capital of a limited company that has actually been allocated i.e. not necessarily 100%.

■ **issuer**

a party or entity that sells a security representing a claim on its assets (an equity security) or its contractual obligation to pay the holder at a future date (a debt security).

■ **joint and several**

a legal expression used to indicate that two or more parties, each are fully liable rather than together fully liable. For example, if two individuals execute joint and several guaranties, either one can be asked to repay the entire amount of the guaranteed debt.

■ joint life

a life policy option where life assurance is taken out by two (or more) individuals, the payout coming with either the first or final death.

■ joint tenancy

where a property is in the names of two owners, on the death of the first owner, the property passes in its entirety to the survivor.

■ joint venture

when two or more persons or organisations gather capital to provide a product or service. Often carried out as a partnership.

■ journal

any book containing original entries of daily financial transactions.

■ judgement

a sum due for payment or collection as a result of a court order.

■ judgement clause

a provision in bank promissory notes or guaranties. In this clause, the borrowers or guarantors authorise the bank to create a judgement lien at any time after the documents have been executed. The bank only has to take the documents to a court.

■ judicial lien

an interest in property acquired from a judicial or court proceeding. A judicial lien is usually the result of a judgement that a winning party of a lawsuit receives in the form of a court order.

■ junior debt

obligations of an issuer for which repayment has contractually been given a priority that is lower than the repayment priority of other debts of the same obligor. This arrangement may arise from either a specific subordination agreement or a public issuance of subordinated debt instruments.

■ junk bonds

debt securities issued by companies with higher than normal credit risk. Considered 'non-investment grade' bonds, these securities ordinarily yield a higher rate of interest, to compensate for the additional risk.

■ jurisdiction

strictly speaking, the legal power of a court, but often taken generally to mean within a particular sphere of influence.

■ key employee

an individual who makes a significant profit contribution to the business activity and profitability of a company, and whose loss would have an effect on the continued profitability of the business.

■ key features document

a document that will contain key information, such as: details of what the policy might be worth in future years, details and explanation of the charges made on the policy, and an explanation of the purpose, type and risk level of the policy.

■ **key person insurance**
business-owned life insurance contract typically on the lives of principal officers that normally provides for guaranteed death benefits to the company and the accumulation of a cash surrender value.

■ **kiting**
writing cheques against a bank account with insufficient funds to cover them, hoping that the bank will receive deposits before the cheques arrive for clearance.

■ **know your client**
legal obligation on financial salespeople to record all aspects of a client's personal financial situation and to ensure that all advice takes this into account.

■ **last in, first out (LIFO)**
accounting method of valuing inventory under which the costs of the last goods acquired are the first costs charged to expense.

■ **last survivor**
term used in joint life policies where the policy proceeds are paid out only on the last death.

■ **launder**
to 'clean up' 'dirty money' earned through illegal means by easing it into the normal monetary systems, so that all traces of its origins are removed or 'washed out'.

■ **lease**
conveyance of land, buildings, equipment or other assets from one person (lessor) to another (lessee) for a specific period of time for monetary or other consideration, usually in the form of rent.

■ **leasehold**
property interest a lessee owns in the leased property.

■ **leasehold property**
property held under lease.

■ **ledger**
book in which accounts are kept.

■ **legacy**
property inherited on the death of someone.

■ **legal tender**
the form of currency in which someone has the legal right to pay a debt and which a creditor must accept.

■ **legatee**
someone who receives a legacy.

■ **lending multiple**
money borrowed to help with a house purchase is usually calculated with reference to a ceiling multiple of income(s).

■ **lending panel**
generally used in relation to a group of lending organisations, e.g. building societies, used by a life company to provide advances for house purchase.

■ **lessee**
person or entity that has the right to use property under the terms of a lease.

■ lessor

owner of property, the temporary use of which is transferred to another (lessee) under the terms of a lease.

■ let

to make available living or office accommodation in return for rent.

■ letter of credit

conditional bank commitment issued on behalf of a customer to pay a third party, in accordance with certain terms and conditions. The two primary types are commercial letters of credit and standby letters of credit.

■ letters of administration

authority granted by the court to an individual permitting that person to administer the estate of someone who died intestate.

■ letters of credit

these mechanisms are used by exporters and importers, and usually provided by the importing company's bank to the exporter to safeguard the contractual expectations and particularly financial exposure of the exporter of the goods or services. (Also called 'export letters of credit, and 'import letters of credit'.) When an exporter agrees to supply a customer in another country, the exporter needs to know that the goods will be paid for. The common system, which has been in use for many years, is for the customer's bank to issue a 'letter of credit' at the request of the buyer, to the seller. The letter of credit essentially guarantees that the bank will pay the seller's invoice (using the customer's money of course) provided the goods or services are supplied in accordance with the terms stipulated in the letter, which should obviously reflect the agreement between the seller and buyer. This gives the supplier an assurance that their invoice will be paid, beyond any other assurances or contracts made with the customer. Letters of credit are often complex documents that require careful drafting to protect the interests of buyer and seller. The customer's bank charges a fee to issue a letter of credit, and the customer pays this cost. The seller should also approve the wording of the buyer's letter of credit, and often should seek professional advice and guarantees to this effect from their own financial services provider. In short, a letter of credit is a guarantee from the issuing bank's to the seller that if compliant documents are presented by the seller to the buyer's bank, then the buyer's bank will pay the seller the amount due. The 'compliance' of the seller's documentation covers not only the goods or services supplied, but also the timescales involved, method for, format of and place at which the documents are presented. It is common for exporters to experience delays in obtaining payment against letters of credit because they have either failed to understand the terms within the letter of credit, failed to meet the terms, or both. It is important therefore for sellers to understand all aspects of letters of credit and to ensure letters of credit are properly drafted, checked, approved and their conditions met. It is also important for sellers to use appropriate professional services to validate the authenticity of any unknown bank issuing a letter of credit.

■ letters of exchange

a method of creating a trust for a one-person pension arrangement. The method works simply by the employer writing to the employee setting out the scheme details the employee replies accepting.

■ letters of guarantee

there are many types of letters of guarantee. These types of letters of guarantee are concerned with providing safeguards to buyers that suppliers will meet their obligations or vice-versa, and are issued by the supplier's or customer's bank depending on which party seeks the guarantee. While a letter of credit essentially guarantees payment to the exporter, a letter of guarantee provides safeguard that other aspects of the supplier's or customer's obligations will be met. The supplier's or customer's bank is effectively giving a direct guarantee on behalf of the supplier or customer that the supplier's or customer's obligations will be met, and in the event of the supplier's or customer's failure to meet obligations to the other party then the bank undertakes the responsibility for those obligations.

Typical obligations covered by letters of guarantee are concerned with:

Tender Guarantees (Bid Bonds) - whereby the bank assures the buyer that the supplier will not refuse a contract if awarded.

Performance Guarantee - This guarantees that the goods or services are delivered in accordance with contract terms and timescales.

Advance Payment Guarantee - This guarantees that any advance payment received by the supplier will be used by the supplier in accordance with the terms of contract between seller and buyer.

There are other types of letters of guarantee, including obligations concerning customs and tax, etc, and as with letters of credit, these are complex documents with extremely serious implications. For this reasons suppliers and customers alike must check and obtain necessary validation of any issued letters of guarantee.

■ leveraged buy out

acquisition of a controlling interest in a company, in a transaction financed by the issuance of debt instruments by the acquired entity.

■ leveraged lease

transaction under which the lessor borrows funds to acquire property, which is leased to a third party. The property and lease rentals are security for the lessor's indebtedness.

■ leveraged lease

where the lessor obtains the funds to purchase the leased asset from a third party on a non-recourse basis.

■ **levy**

a tax duty or fine imposed by a government or other organisation, often on a per capita basis.

■ **liabilities**

general term for what the business owes. Liabilities are long-term loans of the type used to finance the business and short-term debts or money owing as a result of trading activities to date.

Long term liabilities, along with Share Capital and Reserves make up one side of the balance sheet equation showing where the money came from. The other side of the balance sheet will show Current Liabilities along with various Assets, showing where the money is now.

■ **liability**

debts or obligations owed by one entity (debtor) to another entity (creditor) payable in money, goods or services.

■ **licence**

officially authorised paperwork, effectively a permit to do something, e.g. import or export licence.

■ **licensed deposit taker**

business which is licensed to take money on deposit and pay interest on it, e.g. building society or friendly society.

■ **lien**

a charge or claim over an asset, often for security as a loan.

■ **life assurance**

a general term covering a variety of types of personal protection policy. The one thing they all have in common is that a payout on death is the main purpose for the contract.

■ **life assured**

the person on whose life the life assurance policy is based.

■ **life business**

general term which can be applied specifically to life assurance, but often is applied to all life, pensions, savings and investment business.

■ **life insurance**

same as life assurance. Although life insurance is probably the more correct term, life assurance has become generally accepted as the generic term for the market.

■ **life interest trust**

a trust which controls property which may be held only as life tenant.

■ **life of another**

means of writing a policy on the life of another person. Policyholder receives policy proceeds on the death of the life assured. Insurable interest must exist when policy established. Often used as security against death of spouse or business partners.

■ **life offices**

generally taken to refer to those companies which sell life assurance, pensions and related packaged products.

■ **life tenant**

person with an interest in property for their life only, e.g. income from investments. At death, the interest ceases and cannot be passed on by the life tenant's will.

■ **limited liability**

a form of business which limits liability to the assets of the company and does not extend to the personal assets of the shareholders or offices of the company.

■ **limited liability corporation**

a new form of organisation under which income and losses are passed through to owners but which, like a corporation, frees the owners from liability for debts of the business.

■ **limited partnership**

partnership in which one or more partners, but not all, have limited liability to creditors of the partnership.

■ **liquid assets**

assets that are easily converted to cash.

■ **liquid assets cash**

cash equivalents and marketable securities.

■ **liquidation**

winding up an activity by distributing its assets to the appropriate parties and settling its debts.

■ **liquidator**

person appointed to wind up a company and to distribute company assets or their value to creditors and shareholders.

■ **liquidity**

cash and readily convertible (to cash) assets. The liquidity of a business is its ability to meet outstanding debts.

■ **liquidity ratio**

indicates the company's ability to pay its short term debts, by measuring the relationship between current assets (i.e. those which can be turned into cash) against the short-term debt value. (current assets/current liabilities) Also referred to as the Current Ratio.

■ **liquidity ratios**

it should be realised that ratio's are static, rather like the balance sheet, and should only be used to discern trends. The various ratios are: 1. Current (working capital) ratio is a guide to financial safety in that it shows how many times current assets will cover current liabilities. It is expressed as Current assets divided by current liabilities.
2. Acid Test ratio reveals the capability of a business to repay current obligations immediately and is calculated as: Cash and marketable securities and debtors divided by current liabilities. In some cash based businesses, the cash ratio may be a better guide. This is practically the same as above, but excludes debtors.

■ **listed company**

a company that satisfies the listings rules of the Stock Exchange, and whose shares are quoted and traded on the Exchange.

■ **listed security**

a share which is quoted on a stock exchange.

■ **loan fee**

the fee charged by a lender for making a loan. It's designed to recover costs of processing the loan.

■ **loan stock**

a security paying a fixed rate of interest, which returns capital at the end of a stipulated period of time. Secured by the company's assets.

■ **longs**

government stock maturing in 15 years or more.

■ **long-term debt**

debt with a maturity of more than one year from the current date.

■ **loophole**

an admissible interpretation of law or regulation which leads to a legal way of avoiding the law.

■ **loss**

excess of expenditures over revenue for a period or activity. Also, for tax purposes, an excess of basis over the amount realised in a transaction.

■ **low start endowment**

endowment policy designed for use with mortgages where premiums increase at a fixed rate over a period of years.

■ **lower rate tax**

the rate of tax paid on the first band of income which exceeds the personal allowance.

■ **macro**

prefix meaning large, covering a wide area, often used in connection with economics.

■ **macro hedging**

hedging the net risk exposure of an entity's entire portfolio or balance sheet. As opposed to micro hedging a single instrument. In interest rate risk management, macro hedging involves hedging the net mismatch or the net duration for the entire entity.

■ **management accounting**

1. reporting designed to assist management in decision-making, planning and control. Also known as Managerial Accounting.
2. This describes the analysis of historical and current accounts of revenue and expenses to assist managers in their decision making.

■ **management buyout**

when the senior management of a company, usually with institutional funding, take control of the company by buying its shares.

■ **management charge**

an annual charge on investment funds to pay for their management, usually expressed as a percentage of fund value.

■ **mandate**

instruction, order, permission to allow or permit something to happen. Usually written, e.g. bank mandate, as in a standing order to pay sums to another account.

■ **margin**

the difference between one thing and another. In financial terms, usually relates to percentage differences between costs and prices.

In general terms, allowable flexibility between, say, safety and danger.

■ marginal
near the limit of acceptability.

■ marginal cost
the change in cost resulting from production of a single additional unit of production.

■ marginal costing
the assignment of variable costs only to production costs, excluding fixed/overhead costs.

■ marginal rate/marginal return
the incremental rate or return realised by making just one change, adding a single additional unit or deleting a single unit. For example, if one more new loan is added to an existing portfolio and the yield on that loan is 10%, the marginal yield for the portfolio is 10%. Not the same as the average.

■ marginal tax rate
the highest tax rate an individual pays, usually taken to mean less basic rate tax.

■ market capitalisation
the value of a company on the market, computed by multiplying the number of shares by the current market price.

■ market counterparty
a category of investor identified under financial services legislation. Person who, in course of own profession, transacts the same type of business as he transacts on his own behalf via an adviser. Deemed to have full understanding of nature and risks of the investment transaction, e.g. stockbroker purchasing shares.

■ market depth
a term used to describe the characteristic of a secondary market for a financial instrument evidenced by more than a minimal amount of active daily trading. One of the requirements for readily marketable assets.

■ market level indicator
an index comparing the values of fixed interest securities and shares, used in determining state scheme premiums.

■ market liquidity risk
the potential that an institution cannot easily unwind or offset specific exposures, such as investments held as liquidity reserves, without incurring a loss because of inadequate market depth or market disruptions. One of the three primary components of liquidity risk, along with mismatch liquidity risk and liquidity contingency risk.

■ market maker
an individual or entity that stands ready to buy or sell financial instruments at all times. Market makers quote both a bid and an offer price to the market. Market makers provide liquidity to markets. They profit from the spread between bid and offer prices, as well as from changes in market prices. Market makers adjust their

bid or offer prices, depending upon positions that they hold and/or upon their outlook for changes in prices.

■ mark-to-market

method of valuing assets that results in adjustment of an asset's carrying amount to its market value.

■ master agreement

a written contract covering all future transactions between the parties to repurchase/reverse repurchase agreements and establishing each party's rights in the transactions. A master agreement often will specify, among other things, the right of the buyer-lender to liquidate the underlying securities, in the event of default by the seller-borrower.

■ match fund or matching

an entity is said to match fund a loan or investment when it acquires a liability in equal amount for the same maturity. However, it is not perfectly match funded unless all of the interest and principal cash flows and any prepayment options are also the same for the asset as they are for the liability.

■ matched bargain

where the purchase and sale of the same stock are matched, quantity for quantity, at a price agreed by buyer and seller, rather than on the open market.

■ matched trade

a trade that is mirrored by an equal and offsetting trade with a different counterparty. In a matched trade, the interest rate, market and price risks are offset but not the credit risk. The trading entity incurs credit risk for the counterparties on each side of the trade.

■ matching principle

a fundamental rule of basic accounting. In any one given accounting period, you should try to match the revenue you are reporting with the expenses it took.

■ material fact

information relevant to the discussion or situation, e.g. information to be provided on a life assurance proposal form.

■ materiality

magnitude of an omission or misstatements of accounting information that, in the light of surrounding circumstances, makes it probable that the judgement of a reasonable person relying on the information would change or be influenced.

■ materialman's lien

a lien against real property, created under state laws, that give a person who supplies materials used to repair or improve real estate the right to place a lien against the property if that person is not paid.

■ maturity

in financial planning terms, the date at which a financial document or insurance policy becomes payable.

■ maturity date

the date a financial instrument's contractual term expires. The date on which the principal or last principal payment on a debt is due and payable.

■ **maturity transformation**

the term economists use to describe the activity of a financial intermediary that accepts deposits or investments of one term (usually short) and places those funds with a debtor in another term (usually intermediate or long term).

■ **memorandum of association**

in conjunction with the Articles, the Memorandum forms the official documentation of the limited company. Where the general purpose of the Articles is to govern the internal operation of the company, the Memorandum governs the companies external operations and business relationships.

■ **mercantile**

relating to business, commercial activity.

■ **merchant banks**

a bank which deals in corporate finance rather than domestic bank accounting.

■ **merchantable quality**

to be fit (in respect of goods purchased) for the purpose for which they are bought.

■ **merger**

1. business combination that occurs when one entity directly acquires the assets and liabilities of one or more entities and no new corporation or entity is created.

2. The union of two or more companies. Distinct from a takeover where one company purchases another.

■ **meta data**

data about data. A term used in database management and data warehousing.

■ **metes and bounds**

a name for a type of property description used to identify parcels of land for which the legal identification is expressed in surveying terms. 'Metes' means measurements and 'bounds' means boundaries. A metes and bounds description gives the length and direction of the boundaries of a property.

■ **mezzanine finance**

business finance following the start-up phase of a business. Less risky, in general, than start up finance.

■ **mezzanine financing**

financing wherein the junior debt in a leveraged buyout comes from a lender willing to take a subordinate position.

■ **micro**

prefix meaning very small.

■ **micro hedging**

hedging the interest rate risk exposure of a single asset or liability.

■ **middle band earnings**

earnings between the lower earnings limit and upper earnings limit.

mitigate
to alleviate, make less onerous.

model risk
the risk that incorrect or sub-optimal interest rate risk management decisions will be made because of errors in the model used to measure risk exposure. Errors may arise from inaccurate data input into the model, from inaccurate assumptions used in the simulation and/or from errors in model logic or programming.

modelling
using numerical methods and relationships to represent real life situations as a basis for business projections.

moral hazard
the potential for the attitudes, lifestyle and conduct of individuals to affect the level of risk attaching to a proposal for life assurance.

moral obligation bond
revenue bonds issued by state agencies, government commissions or other special purpose municipal entities, that purport to have the added backing of a moral obligation of the city or state government. Since there is no legal obligation for the state or city to back the principal or interest due on these bonds, the moral obligation provides limited, if not dubious, support.

moratorium
a temporary halt.

morbidity
the incidence of sickness and disability.

mortality risk
the risk of the life assured dying during the term of the policy.

mortality table
a statistical table showing the likelihood of death at any particular age.

mortgage
1. a legal instrument that creates a lien upon real estate for the purpose of securing a debt. The instrument is executed by a lender and a borrower or guarantor as collateral for the payment of a debt that creates a lien on real estate owned by the borrower or guarantor.
2. The borrower or guarantor is called the mortgagor and the lender is called the mortgagee. The action of granting a lien to pledge real property as security for the repayment of a debt.

mortgagee
a secured party to whom insurance proceeds are paid as stipulated in a mortgagee payee clause of an insurance policy obtained by a debtor and covering property owned by a debtor and pledged to the secured party. Generally applies to real property.

mortgagor
someone who offers security to be able to borrow money.

■ municipal bond
bond issued by a government or public body, the interest on which is typically exempt from taxation.

■ municipal derivatives
synthetic securities created from municipal securities. Variable-rate, short-term securities are, for example, created from long-term, taxable municipals when remarketing agents add a series of put options, the backing of a letter of credit and an agreement to pay interest at rates that vary weekly, monthly, quarterly or semi-annually.

■ mutual
relating to two or more involved parties.

■ mutual fund
investment company which generally offers its shares to the general public and invests the proceeds in a diversified portfolio of securities.

■ mutual life office
a company without shareholders and effectively owned by the with-profits policyholders, who are entitled to a share of any surplus funds at valuation. These 'surplus' distributions are termed bonuses.

■ national insurance contributions
an additional form of tax paid by most employers, employees, self employed (and some unemployed) people. For the employed, it is deducted from income by the employer, on a scale related to income levels. The employed pay part flat rate, part income related. The self employed and the unemployed may pay a flat rate voluntary contribution to keep their benefits entitlement up to date.

■ national savings
a 'branch' of the treasury, selling investment, savings and deposit products over the counter at post offices, with the aim of raising money for the government and providing medium to long term financial planning products for customers.

■ national savings stock register
register of gilts which may be purchased through the Post Office.

■ natural hedges
balance sheet hedge activity done by altering asset and/or liability repricing characteristics or volumes, to reduce the entity's interest rate risk exposure, without purchasing derivative hedge instruments, such as interest rate swaps or futures.

■ needs analysis
the breaking down of a situation to determine whether there are areas of risk or weakness that should be protected.

■ negative amortisation
the increase in a loan balance, resulting from a situation in which the payments due from the borrower are not sufficient to cover the full amount of the interest due. The amount of interest due, that

is not covered by the amount of the payment, is added to the unpaid principal balance of the loan. Negative amortisation typically occurs during periods of high interest rates for loans with floating interest rates but fixed monthly payments.

■ **negative assurance**

report issued by an accountant, based on limited procedures that states that nothing has come to the accountant's attention to indicate that the financial information is not fairly presented.

■ **negligence**

the omission to do something which a reasonable man, guided by those ordinary considerations which ordinarily regulate human affairs, would do, or the doing of something which a reasonable and prudent man would not do. Negligence is the failure to use such care as a reasonably prudent and careful person would use under similar circumstances. It is the doing of some act which a person of ordinary prudence would not have done under similar circumstances or failure to do what a person of ordinary prudence would have done under similar circumstances. The term refers only to that legal delinquency which results whenever a man fails to exhibit the care which he ought to exhibit, whether it be slight, ordinary or great.

■ **negotiable**

open to discussion and bargaining. Something in which the title can easily be transferred to another person.

■ **nest egg**

supply of 'emergency' or 'future use only' money, usually saved over a period of time.

■ **Net Asset Value (NAV)**

a mutual fund's share value. It is calculated by subtracting total liabilities from total assets, to determine net worth or equity. The equity value is then divided by the number of outstanding shares. The NAV is calculated once each day at the close of business.

■ **net assets**

excess of the value of securities owned, cash, receivables and other assets over the liabilities of the company.

■ **net book value**

the written down value (after allowing for depreciation) of an asset.

■ **net current assets**

current assets less current liabilities.

■ **net income**

excess or deficit of total revenues and gains, compared with total expenses and losses for an accounting period.

■ **net profit**

profit after all deductions, except tax and dividends.

■ **net sales**

term used to describe a firm's revenue after the amount of returns.

allowances and discounts is deducted from gross revenue from the firm's principal operations.

■ **net worth**

assets minus liabilities of a business. It's the owners' share of the business after creditors' interests are accounted for.

■ **nominal**

small payment or value.

■ **nominal capital**

total face value of authorised issuable capital.

■ **nominal ledger**

the account book showing expenditure on nominal accounts, i.e. named business accounts such as postage, printing, etc.

■ **nominal value**

the par or face value of something, e.g. a share issue.

■ **nomination**

the naming of a person to receive an award or benefit, e.g. similar to an expression of wish under a group life assurance scheme.

■ **non-notification**

receivable lending in which the borrower's account debtors are not notified of the bank's lien. (The bank may use non-notification lending but still have a provision in the loan document that allows the bank to switch to notification-based financing in the event of a default.) Under non-notification financing arrangements, payments may be sent directly to the bank by the account debtors.

■ **non-profit**

a policy where the value of the policy at maturity is guaranteed at outset.

■ **non-qualifying policy**

one which does not satisfy all of the qualifying rules.

■ **non-recourse**

where finance is raised to purchase a leased asset, the lender will have recourse to the assets held by the lessee in case of default, but not to the lessor/borrower.

■ **nonsubstitution clause**

a provision in some municipal leases. This lease provision stipulates that if the municipal lessee terminates the lease under a non-appropriation clause, the lessee will not use any other property performing a similar function to that performed by the property covered by the lease, for the period of time covered by the lease. The non-substitution clause is intended to be a deterrent to termination of the lease contract under a non-appropriation clause.

■ **no-par stock**

stock authorised to be issued but for which no par value is set in the articles of incorporation. A stated value is set by the board of directors on the issuance of this type of stock.

■ **no-par value**

stock or bond that does not have a specific value indicated.

■ **normal retirement age**

the expected retirement age, usually for pension purposes, as defined in the scheme rules.

■ **normal retirement date**

refers to the expected or usual retirement date, assumed when setting up a pension scheme, e.g. end of the month following 60th birthday.

■ **notary public**

lawyer with authority to witness written documents and verbal statements, thus making them official. Someone who attests to the validity of deeds and other documents for official use.

■ **notice of adverse action**

in many cases, lenders are required by law to provide applicants with timely notice of adverse action, such as denial of credit applications.

■ **notification**

receivable lending, with the requirement that the borrower's account debtors must be notified of the bank's lien. The payments on the accounts are then usually sent directly to the lender by the account debtors. Sometimes called notification plan.

■ **notional**

value assigned to assets or liabilities that is not based on cost or market (e.g., the value of a service not yet rendered).

■ **novation**

1. the substitution of an existing debt with a newer debt.

2. An agreement to substitute an existing party to a contract with a new party. All of the original parties to the contract must agree to the substitution.

■ **objectivity**

emphasising or expressing the nature of reality as it is, apart from personal reflection or feelings, independence of mind.

■ **obligations**

any amount which may require payment by an entity at a future time.

■ **obligor**

any party with an obligation to discharge; usually used to refer to a borrower.

■ **off the shelf company**

a company which has already been registered but which has not started to trade, so is available for sale at nominal cost if someone wants a new company quickly.

■ **off-balance sheet**

a term used to describe contingent liabilities, contingent assets and commitments that are legally binding but are not assets or liabilities shown on the balance sheet. Examples include loan commitments and letters of credit.

■ **offer and acceptance**

two of the necessary stages in a viable contract.

■ **offer or offered price**

the trading price proposed by the prospective seller of securities. Also called the asked or asking price.

■ offer to bid

compares the original purchase cost or offer price – usually of a unit trust – with its bid price, the price you receive if you sell.

■ offer to offer

compares the original purchase cost or offer price – usually of a unit trust – with its current offer price.

■ office of fair trading

government body charged with ensuring a 'level playing field' for competition in all sectors of the economy.

■ officer

someone with an official position in an organisation.

■ offset

to balance one item with another.

■ operating agreement

agreement, usually a written document, that sets out the rules by which a limited liability company (LLC) is to be operated. It is the LLC equivalent of corporate by-laws or a partnership agreement.

■ operating cycle

period of time between the acquisition of goods and services involved in the manufacturing process and the final cash realisation resulting from sales and subsequent collections.

■ operating expense ratio

a ratio used in real estate lending analysis. The ratio is the total operating expenses divided by the effective gross income.

■ operating income

an income statement subtotal that is variously called operating income or operating profit. Gross profit minus operating expenses. A credit balance here, shown as a positive number, indicates that the firm makes money on its principal operations. A debit balance, shown as a negative number, indicates that the firm loses money on its principal operations.

■ operating profit

the figure which remains after deducting all operating costs (except capital expenses) from sales revenue.

■ operational efficiency

a term used to describe the characteristic of a secondary market for a financial instrument evidenced by low transaction costs and smooth execution of trades. The spread between bid and offered prices, brokerage commissions and taxes are the three main types of transaction costs. One of the requirements for readily marketable assets.

■ operational risk

the risk to the bank that errors made in the course of conducting its business will result in losses.

■ opinion letter

letter issued by a certified public accountant to accompany financial statements. Accountant's opinions are categorised as unqualified, qualified, disclaimer or adverse, depending upon the nature of the comments in the letter.

■ **opportunity cost**

the cost of pursuing one course of action measured in terms of the foregone return that could have been earned on an alternative course of action that was not undertaken.

■ **option**

right to buy or sell something at a specified price during a specified time period.

■ **Over The Counter (OTC)**

purchases and sales of financial instruments that do not take place in organised exchanges such as the New York Stock Exchange or the Chicago Board of Trade are termed over the counter. The phrase may be used as a noun to describe capital markets other than organised exchanges. The phrase may also be used as an adjective to describe instruments not traded on an organised exchange, such as over-the-counter derivatives.

■ **overdraft**

in banking terms, drawing out more money from an account than there are available funds.

■ **overhead**

an expense that cannot be attributed to any one single part of the company's activities.

■ **overheads**

everyday costs of running a business.

■ **overtrading**

shortage of liquidity, caused by not having enough working capital to support the level of sales and production. Taking on business which cannot be funded by cash flow.

■ **p/e ratio (price per earnings)**

the P/E ratio is an important indicator as to how the investing market views the health, performance, prospects and investment risk of a public company listed on a stock exchange (a listed company). The P/E ratio is also a highly complex concept - it's a guide to use alongside other indicators, not an absolute measure to rely on by itself. The P/E ratio is arrived at by dividing the stock or share price by the earnings per share (profit after tax and interest divided by the number of ordinary shares in issue). As earnings per share are a yearly total, the P/E ratio is also an expression of how many years it will take for earnings to cover the stock price investment. P/E ratios are best viewed over time so that they can be seen as a trend. A steadily increasing P/E ratio is seen by the investors as increasingly speculative (high risk) because it takes longer for earnings to cover the stock price. Obviously whenever the stock price changes, so does the P/E ratio. More meaningful P/E analysis is conducted by looking at earnings over a period of several years. P/E ratios should also be compared over time, with other company's P/E ratios in the same market sector, and with the market as a whole. Step by step, to calculate the P/E ratio:

Establish total profit after tax and interest for the past year.
Divide this by the number of shares issued.
This gives you the earnings per share.
Divide the price of the stock or share by the earnings per share.
This gives the Price/Earnings or P/E ratio.

■ **paid in capital**

portion of the stockholders' equity which was paid in by the stockholders, as opposed to capital arising from profitable operations.

■ **paid up**

it is possible, with certain policies having an investment content e.g. endowment, to cease paying premiums and retain a paid-up policy which will pay out on eventual claim. Also another name for 'preserved' pensions.

■ **paper**

documents such as bills of exchange which represent money, e.g. share certificates, banknotes.

■ **par**

1. the principal or maturity value of a non-amortising, debt security.
2. The current face of a mortgage-backed security.
3. The price at which the face value of a debt security equals its selling price or 100.
4. For stocks, the face or nominal amount of a share.

■ **par line**

the parity price at which the yield of a mortgage-backed bond equals its net coupon rate. Because of the delay days, the par line is not 100 but instead is somewhat lower. Par line is not constant for different coupon rates at different delay days. However, it is not a function of prepayment speeds.

■ **par value**

amount per share set in the articles of incorporation of a corporation to be entered in the capital stocks account, where it is left permanently and signifies a cushion of equity capital for the protection of creditors.

■ **partner**

in a legal sense, someone with whom you carry on a business.

■ **partnership**

relationship between two or more persons based on a written, oral or implied agreement, whereby they agree to carry on a trade or business for profit and share the resulting profits. Unlike a corporation's shareholders, the partnership's general partners are liable for the debts of the partnership.

■ **partnership agreement**

a written agreement defining the rights, duties and responsibilities of the partners in a partnership.

■ **payback period**

the length of time taken for the net cash inflow from a new project to cover the initial investment of the project.

■ **payee processing float**

time between when a payment is received and when the funds are deposited. When employees hold their paycheques over a weekend and when vendors process receipts only once a week, the payor benefits from the extra time its investments earn interest. These beneficial payee processing delays are limited to payments by cheque. Electronic payments produce no processing delay at all.

■ **paying agent**

an entity responsible for paying bond principal and interest on behalf of the debtor.

■ **pension**

an annual income, usually associated with the post-retirement period of one's life, but not necessarily so.

■ **personal guarantee**

a promise that the signer personally will repay a loan in the event the business cannot.

■ **personal property**

movable property that is not affixed to the land (real property). Personal property includes tangible items, such as cash, cars and computers, as well as intangible items, such as royalties, patents and copyrights.

■ **personal representative**

person who deals with the estate of a deceased person, under the terms of a will or the rules of intestacy. Duties and responsibilities end when the estate has been dispersed and all taxes and debts paid.

■ **personalty**

personal property.

■ **plaintiff**

someone who starts a legal action against another person

■ **pledge**

an item retained by a pawnbroker in exchange for cash and held until the cash is repaid. Essentially, a form of security.

■ **pledged asset**

asset placed in a trust and used as collateral for a debt.

■ **plenary**

complete. A 'plenary session' is a meeting attended by all.

■ **plus**

an informal term for 1/64. Half of 1/32, the smallest increment commonly used to quote the price of an agency security.

■ **power of attorney**

appointment of an agent to act on one's behalf.

■ **preference period**

a legal term used in bankruptcy to describe a transaction deemed to have occurred under circumstances favoura-ble to the creditor, that benefited from the transaction. This provision is intended to protect unsecured creditors.

■ **preference shares**

usually non-voting shares which pay out dividend before ordinary shareholders and which will pay out first if the company goes into liquidation.

preferred stock

a type of equity or capital representing shares of ownership in a corporation. May or may not receive distributions of corporate income in the form of dividends. Has a higher priority claim to corporate earnings or assets than common stock but lower priority than corporate debt. A corporation may issue more than one class of preferred stock with differing priority status, such as first or second preferred. Often, preferred stock issues have a defined dividend payment rate as long as there are sufficient corporate earnings to distribute.

premium

(1) the amount by which the price for a security is greater than its par amount.

prepaid expense

cost incurred to acquire economically useful goods or services that are expected to be consumed in the revenue-earning process within the operating cycle.

prepaids

expenses that are capitalised as assets on a firm's financial statements because they will be charged against activities in the near future, rather than past activities. Also called prepaid expenses, prepaid assets or prepaid items. For example, if insurance premiums for the next six months are paid today, the amount paid may be shown as a pre- paid asset. The asset in that example would then be reduced to zero over the following six months by recognising one-sixth of the amount as an expense in each of next six months. Insurance, taxes and subscriptions are common prepaid expenses.

present value

the cash sum you would need to put on deposit at a compound rate of interest to grow to a given figure at a future given date.

presentment

a process by which a cheque is presented for payment at the drawee's bank.

principal

1. face amount of a security, exclusive of any premium or interest. The basis for interest computations.
2. The initial cash sum invested, excluding interest earned or to be earned.

privilege

a right or immunity granted as a peculiar benefit advantage.

privity

an interest in a transaction, contract or legal action to which one is not a party, arising out of a relationship to one of the parties.

privity of contract

legal concept whereby only those party to a contract may sue or be sued on the contract.

pro forma

presentation of financial information that gives effect to an assumed event (e.g. merger).

■ **pro forma statement**

a financial statement that assumes future events a merger of two businesses, for example in order to project the financial conditions of a company as a result of those events.

■ **pro rata**

distribution of an expense, fund or dividend proportionate with ownership.

■ **products**

generic term for life assurance, pensions, savings and investment policies.

■ **profession**

an occupation or vocation needing skills and experience learned over a period of time, the practitioners of which are governed by an organised system of rules and ethics.

■ **profit**

the difference between the cost of goods and services, and their sale price.

■ **profit and loss account (P&L)**

one of the three principal business reporting and measuring tools (along with the balance sheet and cashflow statement). The P&L is essentially a trading account for a period, usually a year, but also can be monthly and cumulative. It shows profit performance, which often has little to do with cash, stocks and assets (which must be viewed from a separate perspective using balance sheet and cashflow statement). The P&L typically shows sales revenues, cost of sales/cost of goods sold, generally a gross profit margin (sometimes called 'contribution'), fixed overheads and or operating expenses, and then a profit before tax figure (PBT). A fully detailed P&L can be highly complex, but only because of all the weird and wonderful policies and conventions that the company employs. Basically the P&L shows how well the company has performed in its trading activities.

■ **promissory note**

evidence of a debt with specific amount due and interest rate. The note may specify a maturity date or it may be payable on demand. The promissory note may or may not accompany other instruments, such as a mortgage, providing security for the payment thereof.

■ **proposal**

a formal application, perhaps for insurance or business.

■ **proposer**

the person applying to an insurance company for a policy.

■ **proprietorship**

business owned by an individual without the limited liability protection of a corporation or a limited liability company (LLC). Also known as sole proprietorship.

■ **prospectus**

a document that describes the details and financial support for a new bond or stock issue offering. A prospectus is required by the

Securities and Exchange Commission.

■ proxy

a document authorising a third party to act on behalf of someone. May also be used as a term for the authorised person.

■ prudential liquidity

liquidity held for liquidity contingency risk or as a safety cushion. Also called standby liquidity.

■ pyramid selling

an illegal form of 'hierarchical' selling, whereby franchise agreements are sold to operators, along with stocks of the goods in question. These goods are then sold on down a distribution and sales chain. The system is viewed as illegal because the distributors tend to make the most money, leaving the final stage of salespeople in a situation where commissions earned are unlikely to pay back the payments made for the stock.

■ qualified opinion

audit opinion that states, except for the effect of a matter to which a qualification relates, the financial statements are fairly presented in accordance with Generally Accepted Accounting Principles (GAAP).

■ quantify

illustrate the effect of something in terms of figures.

■ quick ratio

ratio of liquid assets to current liabilities, taken as a measure of liquidity.

■ quit claim deed

a document by which title to real estate is conveyed from one party, the grantor, to another party, the grantee. The distinguishing characteristic of a quit claim deed is that it transfers only such interest, title or right that the grantor has at the time of conveyance to the grantee. A quit claim deed is common in divorce or other situations such as equitable interests, in which the grantor's interest is not clearly defined.

■ ratio

the value of one thing compared to something else.

■ ratio analysis

comparison of actual or projected data for a particular company to other data for that company or industry, in order to analyse trends or relationships.

■ real property

land and improvements, including buildings and personal property, that is permanently attached to the land or customarily transferred with the land.

■ rebasing

to ensure that capital gains tax is not paid on any inflation linked increase in the value of an asset, the purchase price is index linked from date of purchase to date of disposal. Where the asset was acquired before 31.02.1982, the purchase price is taken to be the market value as at that date, this is the rebasing - rebasing for indexation purposes.

■ rebate

either a reduction in price or a return of an overpayment.

■ receivables

amounts of money duc from customers or other debtors.

■ receiver

someone appointed by the court, or under statute, to protect and preserve property, or to receive income from property and apply it as directed.

■ recession

fall or reduction in trading volume.

■ redeemable

an investment where one's initial investment is repayable at some future date or event.

■ redemption date

the date on which a loan is to be repaid.

■ release

a document or a process in which a secured party gives up its collateral interest in the property of the debtor. Releases may be for all of the property of the debtor or may be partial. For example, if a real estate developer has pledged 10 lots as collateral for a loan, a partial release may be used for each lot as it is sold.

■ remuneration

in pension planning terms, generally taken to mean the full and total earnings package, i.e. salary and benefits in kind.

■ renewable

generally used in connection with a type of term assurance, which runs for an initial period of years. At expiry, the policyholder has the option to 'renew' the policy, at premium rates current at the time, but without need for further underwriting.

■ rent

payment by a tenant to a landlord for the use of property.

■ repo

an informal name for a repurchase agreement.

■ rescission

cancellation of a contract without penalty.

■ research and development (R&D)

research is a planned activity aimed at discovery of new knowledge, with the hope of developing new or improved products and services. Development is the translation of research findings into a plan or design of new or improved products and services.

■ reserve

account used to earmark a portion of equity or fund balance to indicate that it is not available for expenditure.

■ reserve account

a type of credit enhancement used in some asset backed securities. The reserve account may be created by an initial deposit from the seller and may be augmented over time by the application of funds from excess servicing income. Credit is enhanced because withdrawals from the reserve account are made to reimburse investors when excess servicing is insufficient to cover charge -offs. Until needed, funds in a reserve account are invested.

■ reserves

the accumulated and retained difference between profits and losses year on year since the company's formation.

■ reset cap

the maximum amount by which an adjustable-rate security's coupon rate can change in any given period of time. Also called the periodic cap.

■ residual value

the value of property or assets remaining after, e.g. repayment of a loan, or at the end of a lease agreement.

■ restricted assets

cash or other assets whose use in whole or in part is restricted for specific purposes bound by virtue of contracted agreements.

■ restricted cash

cash held subject to limitations on how or when it may be used. For example, refundable customer deposits, cash in escrow accounts and debt sinking funds.

■ restricted fund

fund established to account for assets whose income must be used for purposes established by donors or grantors of such assets.

■ restricted stock

restricted stock is stock purchased from the issuer or from a person in a controlled relationship to the issuer in a nonpublic or private transaction.

■ restructuring

reorganisation within an entity. Restructuring may occur in the form of changing the components of capital, renegotiating the terms of debt agreements, etc.

■ retained earnings

earnings of a corporation from the current as well as prior years, that have neither been distributed to the shareholders as dividends nor transferred to the surplus account. Corporate earnings accumulated over time. One of a corporation's equity or capital accounts.

■ Return On Assets (ROA)

a percentage calculated by dividing net income after tax by total assets. Annual income is usually used in the numerator, however, the annualised income for a month, quarter or half year can be used. Period-end assets is often used in this calculation, however, average assets for the period is more accurate. This ratio is a measurement of how profitably assets are used in an enterprise. Firms in different industries usually have quite different returns on assets. This ratio is best used to compare firms in the same industry.

■ return on capital

profit before tax and interest, expressed as a percentage of capital employed.

■ Return On Capital Employed (ROCE)

a fundamental financial performance measure. A percentage figure representing profit before interest against the money that is invested in the business. (Profit before interest and tax/capital employed x 100)

■ Return On Equity (ROE)

a measure of the return realised by the owners of an enterprise. Calculated by dividing an enterprise's annualised net income by its average capital for the period. Alternatively, it can be calculated by multiplying the enterprise's ROA by its leverage/equity multiplier. ROE indicates how effectively the enterprise is using its capital to produce income.

■ return on investment (ROI)

another fundamental financial and business performance measure. This term means different things to different people (often depending on perspective and what is actually being judged) so it's important to clarify understanding if interpretation has serious implications. Many business managers and owners use the term in a general sense as a means of assessing the merit of an investment or business decision. 'Return' generally means profit before tax, but clarify this with the person using the term - profit depends on various circumstances, not least the accounting conventions used in the business. In this sense most CEO's and business owners regard ROI as the ultimate measure of any business or any business proposition, after all it's what most business is aimed at producing - maximum return on investment, otherwise you might as well put your money in a bank savings account. Strictly speaking Return On Investment is defined as:

Profits derived as a proportion of and directly attributable to cost or 'book value' of an asset, liability or activity, net of depreciation.

In simple terms this the profit made from an investment. The 'investment' could be the value of a whole business (in which case the value is generally regarded as the company's total assets minus intangible assets, such as goodwill, trademarks, etc and liabilities, such as debt. N.B. A company's book value might be higher or lower than its market value); or the investment could relate to a part of a business, a new product, a new factory, a new piece of plant, or any activity or asset with a cost attached to it.

The main point is that the term seeks to define the profit made from a business investment or business decision. Bear in mind that costs and profits can be ongoing and accumulating for several years, which needs to be taken into account when arriving at the correct figures.

■ returns

reductions to gross sales that occur when customers are given credit for sold goods that are returned to the firm.

■ revaluation

a means of increasing a figure from a base date in line with inflation, e.g. pensionable salary, accrued pension deferred, pension in payment or capital gains.

■ revenue anticipation note (RAN)

a short-term note sold by a public entity that will be repaid from the proceeds of anticipated nontax income.

■ revenue maxima

revenue imposed ceilings on benefits and contributions when calculating maximum approvable benefits.

■ revenue obligation

a bond or note for which the payments of principal and interest made to the investors by the issuer are payable exclusively from the earnings of the underlying project.

■ revenue recognition

method of determining whether or not income has met the conditions of being earned and realised or is realisable.

■ risk

1. the possibility of loss.
2. The uncertainty of whether events, expected or otherwise, will have an adverse impact. In this context, the adverse impact is usually a quantity of return (income) or value at risk.
3. The compound estimate of the probability of, and the severity of, an adverse event. The amount of risk is the product of the probability of the adverse consequence and the potential severity of that adverse consequence.
4. To incur the possibility of loss, to create or accept the possibility of uncertain returns, or to create or accept volatility.

■ risk aversion

the degree to which a client is unwilling to take on a risk.

■ risk management

process of identifying and monitoring business risks in a manner that offers a risk/return relationship that is acceptable to an entity's operating philosophy.

■ risk-based capital

rules for establishing minimum required levels of book capital for financial institutions. Capital is allocated to types of bank assets based upon weightings assigned to those assets.

■ S corporation

a private corporation of 35 or fewer stockholders that pays no income taxes. Instead, the corporation's net income or losses are included in individual shareholders' tax returns.

■ salvage value

selling price assigned to retired fixed assets or merchandise unsalable through usual channels.

■ save as you earn

a method of saving regularly from salary, by employer deduction. There are various schemes to accommodate this, some tax efficient, others merely savings administration.

■ seasoned loans
loans for which a year or more has passed since periodic payments began.

■ secondary market
markets for the purchase and sale of any previously issued financial instrument. The first sale of a financial instrument by the original issuer is said to be made on a primary market. All subsequent trades are said to be secondary market.

■ secured party
a creditor that has been granted a collateral interest in property. The collateral interest is usually given to the creditor by the debtor but may be given by a guarantor or another third party.

■ securitisation
the process of making a loan into a tradeable security by issuing a negotiable document encompassing the loan and selling it on.

■ security
any kind of transferable certificate of ownership, including equity securities and debt securities.

■ security interest
legal interest of one person in the property of another, to assure performance of a second person under a contract.

■ settlement
1. the standard number of days between the date that a purchase or sale is agreed upon (the trade date) and the date that the security and the payment actually change hands (the settlement date).
2. The process of exchanging a security delivered by a seller for the payment delivered by a buyer.

■ settlement date
the agreed-upon date for transferring funds to complete a transaction. For example, the date of both the delivery of and the payment for a security.

■ settlement method
method of accounting for securities, whereby transactions are recorded on the date the securities settle by the delivery or receipt of securities and the receipt or payment of cash.

■ settler
a person who establishes a trust.

■ share capital
the money paid (subscribed) for ordinary and preference shares in a limited company. Authorised share capital means the total amount of shares available to be issued. Issued share capital relates to the total amount of shares actually subscribed for.

■ share option
an offer by a company, usually to its employees and directors, to buy its shares at a given price before a specified date. With a growing company this can be a valuable employee incentive.

■ shareholders' funds
a measure of the shareholders' total interest in the company rep-

resented by the total share capital plus reserves.

■ **short-term**

current, ordinarily due within one year.

■ **sight bill**

a bill of exchange payable when presented.

■ **sight draft**

a draft that is payable upon presentation to the drawee.

■ **simultaneous deaths**

where husband and wife die 'together', say, in an accident, and there is no evidence as to which of them died first, the elder is deemed to have died first.

■ **Single Monthly Mortality Rate (SMM)**

a measure of the amount of monthly principal reduction in excess of the scheduled monthly principal payment. The SMM is simply the amount of prepaid principal in a given month, expressed as a percentage of the principal balance at the beginning of the month. It is not commonly quoted, however, an annualised SMM, called the constant prepayment rate or CPR, is commonly quoted.

■ **sinking fund**

cash set aside under restricted conditions as required by the terms of certain types of debt.

■ **small companies rate**

rate of corporation tax below the standard and marginal rates.

■ **smoothing**

also called yield curve smoothing. The name for a set of alternative techniques for creating continuous yield curves by connecting the dots between observed. If, for example, we have observed rates for 1, 2, 3, 5 and 10 year maturities, smoothing is the technique used to infer rates for all maturities between those known points. The known points are called 'knot points'. The simplest smoothing technique is 'linear smoothing'. The most commonly used technique is 'cubic splines'. For forward rates, the most accurate method is called 'maximum forward rate smoothing'.

■ **sole proprietor**

sole owner of a business, usually referring to a self employed person not in partnership.

■ **solvency**

1. the condition of having sufficient funds to cover losses. In the short term, solvency is a manifestation of liquidity. Fundamentally, however, solvency is a function of capital adequacy.
2. The state of being able to pay outstanding debts on their due date.

■ **sort code**

in banking, the three pairs of figures usually found at the top right hand corner of cheques. Each branch has a unique identifying number to facilitate payments and receipts.

■ **spread**

difference between two prices, usually a buying and selling price.

statement of cash flows

a statement of cash flows is one of the basic financial statements that is required as part of a complete set of financial statements prepared in conformity with generally accepted accounting principles. It categorises net cash provided or used during a period as operating, investing and financing activities and reconciles beginning and ending cash and cash equivalents.

statement of financial condition

basic financial statement, usually accompanied by appropriate disclosures that describe the basis of accounting used in its preparation and presentation as of a specified date, the entity's assets, liabilities and the equity of its owners. Also known as balance sheet.

statutory

relating to law contained in statute.

statutory lien

a lien created by either state legislatures or through court rulings. For example, a lien that banks are given against a borrower's deposits.

statutory sick pay

payable to employed persons by their employer after 3 days sickness for up to 28 weeks.

stock exchange

a market where stocks and shares are bought and sold.

straight-line depreciation

accounting method that reflects an equal amount of wear and tear during each period of an asset's useful life.

structural liquidity

a term used to refer to the liquidity available to a financial institution from its current positions - principally its unpledged marketable assets and its holdings of term liabilities with long remaining lives.

structured finance

a general term used to describe either the practice or the result of creating securities by repackaging cash flows from financial contracts.

subrogation

recovery of an indemnity granted to an insured from the third party liable for the loss incurred.

subsidiary

a separate corporation that is owned by another corporation.

sunrise industries

new, high-tech, electronics based industries which are replacing 'sunset industry', or old style heavy industries, as the source of major employment and capital investment.

surety

generally the same as guarantor.

surrender value

the amount paid to a policyholder who stops paying premiums into a policy before the expected date. The amount depends on the period the policy had run and expenses still to be recouped by the insurance company.

■ swap

financial contract in which two parties agree to exchange net streams of payments over a specified period. The payments are usually determined by applying different indices (e.g., interest rates, foreign exchange rates, equity indices) to a notional amount. The term notional is used because swap contracts generally do not involve exchanges of principal.

■ swap curve

the yield curve of interest rate swap rates from 1 week to 30 years.

Chart 16: The interest rate swap curve (June 2002)

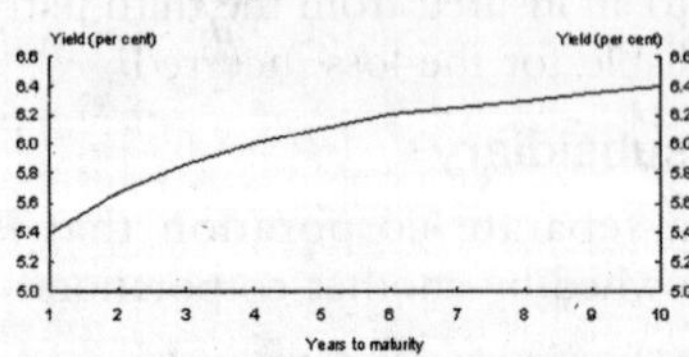

■ sweep account

a deposit account, usually at a bank, that periodically removes a portion of the customer's funds into a higher yielding instrument. Bank sweep accounts are often sold as cash management tools. With a bank sweep account, idle funds are swept each night from a transaction account into a higher-yielding, overnight investment. Some banks offer sweep accounts that only remove excess balances weekly. Brokerage firms offer sweep accounts as well with weekly or monthly sweep frequencies.

■ SWOT analysis

a list and examination of the Strengths, Weaknesses, Opportunities and Threats inherent in any situation and course of action.

■ symmetric

behaviour exhibited by financial instruments whose rates or values move linearly with respect to changes in market rates.

■ tangible asset

assets having a physical existence, such as cash, land, buildings, machinery, or claims on property, investments or goods in process.

■ tangible equity or tangible net worth

terms used to describe the amount of owners' or stockholders' equity after deduction of intangible assets. Total assets minus intangible assets minus total liabilities.

■ tax

charge levied by a governmental unit on income, consumption, wealth or other basis.

■ tax allowance

an allowance creates reduction in taxable income, unlike a tax relief, which arises when an expense is incurred.

■ Tax and Revenue Anticipation Notes (TRAN)

short-term notes sold by a public entity that will be repaid from the proceeds of anticipated tax and/or fee collections.

■ tax avoidance

making full use of reliefs and exemptions to ensure as little tax as possible is paid.

■ tax break investment

used to describe an investment which offers a method of tax avoidance – legally reducing the amount of tax normally paid.

■ tax code

a code that tells your employer how much tax to deduct from your salary.

■ tax evasion

a criminal offence, generally involving fraud in escaping tax liability.

■ tax free cash

both occupational and personal pensions permit a certain account of cash to be taken in lieu of pension from the pension fund at retirement.

■ tax haven

a country which legally enables individuals and companies from other countries to avoid or pay lower rates of tax, by allowing them to live or base their operations there.

■ tax lien

encumbrance placed on property as security for unpaid taxes.

■ tax relief

the system of exemptions and deductions on income and expenditure whereby the Tax Inspector can identify taxable income.

■ tax schedules

the different categories under which different sources of income and capital accrual are taxed.

■ tax shelter

arrangement in which allowable tax deductions or exclusions result in the deferral of tax on income that would otherwise be payable currently.

■ tax voucher

statement that an amount of money has been paid in tax, for example, when tax is deducted from a share dividend. No-taxpayers use the tax voucher to reclaim the tax.

■ tax year

the 12 month period from 6th April to 5th April the following year.

■ Taxable Equivalent Yield (TEY)

the yield that a tax-free investment would provide to an investor if the tax-free yield was 'grossed up' by the amount of taxes not paid. This is the most common way of comparing yields on taxable and tax-free investments. Instead of reducing a taxable yield by the amount of applicable taxes to compare it with a tax-free yield, the tax-free yield is increased by a hypothetical amount of income tax.

■ taxable income

total income minus any tax free allowances.

■ **tenancy**

agreement to occupy a property and can refer to both the agreement and the period of occupation.

■ **tenant**

a person or business who is granted a lease or tenancy.

■ **tender**

a proposal to carry out a particular job or project.

■ **term assurance**

a life assurance policy without investment content, which lasts for a specified period, provides a guaranteed sum assured in the event of death within that period and terminates at the agreed date.

■ **term insurance**

a form of life insurance that has no built-in savings feature and does not accumulate any cash surrender value.

■ **term loan**

loan for a specified time period.

■ **term note**

1. a name used to describe a promissory note used for any closed-end loan granted for a predetermined amount of time (e.g., short-term, medium-term or long-term).
2. A name used in business or commercial lending to describe a promissory note that calls for mostly regular, periodic payments of principal and interest.

■ **time deposit**

a deposit with a specific maturity. Usually, but not always, a certificate of deposit.

■ **time draft**

a draft that is payable on a future date.

■ **time value**

the portion of an option's value imputed to the possibility that the price of the underlying will move in the option holder's favour, during the time remaining before the option expires.

■ **title**

right of ownership over property.

■ **title deeds**

documents showing evidence of ownership over land.

■ **title insurance**

an insurance policy that insures that the ownership of a parcel or parcels of real property and the lien priority of secured creditors with an interest in that property is as the title insurance policy states. The insured party protected by the title insurance policy may be the property owner, in which case the policy is called a owner's policy or the lender, in which case the policy is called a lender's policy.

■ **title insurance commitment**

a preliminary report prepared by a title insurance company and submitted to a potential secured party prior to a loan closing. The commitment shows the information and conditions that will appear on the final title insurance policy, unless changes are made in the chain of title or in the outstanding liens prior to the issuance of the final policy.

title opinion

a document prepared by an attorney that states ownership and a brief report of lien priority for a designated parcel of real property. The opinion is usually given in a letter written on the attorney's letterhead stationary. It includes the date and time of the record investigation. Also called attorney's certificate of title or certificate of title.

title search

a report prepared by a title insurance company that indicates the ownership and outstanding liens for a designated parcel or parcels of real property. Even though a title search is prepared by a title insurance company, it does not offer any insurance protection. Also called ownership and encumbrance reports.

tort

a wrongful act or omission, other than a breach of contract, for which civil damages may be claimed.

total gain

excess of the proceeds realised on the sale of either inventory or non-inventory goods.

trade date

the day on which a buyer and seller agree upon a transaction.

trade letter of credit

an obligation issued by a bank, on behalf of a bank customer to a third party. A commercial or trade letter of credit is a bank promise to pay the third party for the purchase of goods by the bank's customer. If the bank's obligation to pay is not immediate, the transaction can later give rise to a banker's acceptance.

trade name

name used by a proprietorship, partnership or corporation to conduct business that is different from the legal name of the proprietorship, partnership or corporation.

trade receivables

also known as accounts receivable - trade. Amounts due from the sale of goods or service on credit that are not evidenced by promissory notes.

traded option

the right to buy or sell certain shares at a fixed price over the life of the option. The writer of the option receives the premium paid in return for the liability of being called upon to buy or sell shares at the fixed price. If the option is not exercised, it expires worthless.

trading

the activity of buying and selling financial instruments or commodities for profit. Individuals or entities may engage in trading either strictly on their own behalf or for current or future transactions with customers. Trading profits may come from market price changes but may also come from the spreads between bid and asked prices or from customer markups. Trading is distinct from investing, although trading activities are not always easy to distinguish from investing activities. In trading, the profit goal is almost always short term. Unlike trading, investing is generally longer term and may even include the intent to hold the instrument to maturity.

■ **trading period**

generally a period of 12 months over which the accounts of a business are prepared

■ **tranche**

an instalment, one of a series.

■ **transit item**

a cheque deposited and processed for collection that is drawn on another bank.

■ **transit routing number**

a nine-digit number contained in the MICR line of each cheque. The routing number identifies the paying bank.

■ **treasury bills**

a short term bill of exchange, depending on discount to give it value, as it does not pay interest.

■ **treasury bond**

long-term obligation that matures more than five years from issuance and bears interest.

■ **treasury note**

intermediate-term obligation that matures one to five years from issuance and bears interest.

■ **treasury stock**

the name for shares of a corporation's stock that were issued and then subsequently repurchased by the corporation.

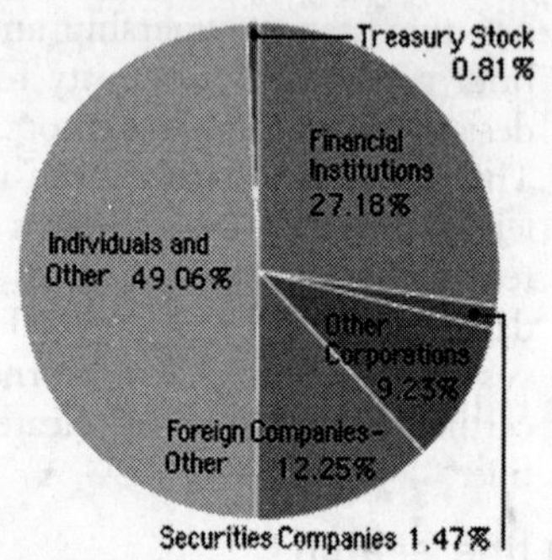

■ **trial balance**

a list of debits and credits from which the profit and loss account is prepared.

■ **troubled debt restructuring**

agreement between debtor and creditor which amends the terms of a debt that has little chance of being paid in accordance with its contractual terms. The agreement may involve the transfer of assets in full or partial satisfaction of the debt.

■ **true lease**

a legal term for a transaction that is intended by the parties to be an actual lease of personal property, rather than a conditional sale.

■ **true yield**

a seldom-used term meaning the simple interest yield for an investment maturing in one year or less. In calculating true yield, the actual number of days in the year (365) is divided by the actual number of days that the investment income is earned.

trust
ancient legal practice where one person (the grantor) transfers the legal title to an asset, called the principle or corpus, to another person (the trustee), with specific instructions about how the corpus is to be managed and disposed.

trustee
individual or corporate body who looks after the assets of a trust and manages the trust in accordance with terms and conditions agreed verbally or in writing.

turnover
effectively, the sales record during the trading year.

turnover or turns
terms used to describe the number of operating cycles in a defined period of time or the length of each specific operating cycle. Typical turnover cycles are: the rate at which accounts receivable converts to cash, the rate at which inventory converts to receivables or cash, the rate at which accounts payable are paid, and the number of times in a year inventory can be said to be sold and replaced. For example, if a firm's average inventory level is equivalent to one quarter of its annual sales, it can be said that inventory turns four times a year. While turnover concepts are most often applied to elements of the working capital conversion cycle, there are other applications. For example, asset turnover is the ratio of net sales divided by total assets.

uberimae fidei
the principle of utmost good faith, or disclosure, in completing a life insurance proposal form.

ultra vires
action outside the agreed powers of a particular body. Such an action would be void.

umbrella fund
an offshore fund offering a variety of sub-funds, allowing an investor to switch between them, e.g. different currencies, different stockmarkets.

unadvised line
a line of credit that is approved by the bank but not disclosed to the borrower until some specific event, usually a request for funding from the borrower.

unaudited financial statements
financial statements which have not undergone a detailed audit examination by an independent Certified Public Accountant (CPA).

uncertificated
legal term used as an adjective, to describe stocks, bonds, other investments and certificates of deposit held in nonmaterial form as electronic computer entries. Ownership of these instruments is usually evidenced by a receipt or confirmation.

underfunded
generally refers to the valuation of an occupational pension fund

where the actuary perceives that there are insufficient funds to support liabilities within the investment review period.

■ underlying or underlier

an option or a future is a right or a commitment to buy or sell something at a future date. The underlying is the financial instrument that may or must be bought or sold in each option or futures contract.

■ underwriter

1. the investment bank, commercial bank or brokerage firm that works with an issuer to sell a new issue. Issuers may select underwriters by obtaining bids or on a negotiated basis. Potential underwriters may form groups called underwriting syndicates to bid collectively.
2. The name used to describe the process of analysing and structuring a proposed loan. Good underwriting is the most important aspect of secured lending. Outside of banking, the term primarily refers to the purchase of risk.
3. Taking up shares not purchased by the public, for commission. Review and analysis of relevant factors affecting an insurance proposal.

■ undivided profits

bank term for retained earnings. Bank profits from current as well as prior years that have neither been distributed to shareholders as dividends nor transferred to surplus. Corporate earnings accumulated over time. One of a corporation's equity or capital accounts.

■ unearned income

payments received for services which have not yet been performed.

■ unexpected loss or unexpected risk

the portion or component of risk or loss that exceeds the predicted amount.

■ unit linked

a life assurance, investment or savings policy, under which the policyholder invests premiums into units in a unit trust-type investment. Performance, therefore, is dependent directly on current investment market conditions.

■ unit trust

a collective investment which invests in a range of assets, e.g. equities, fixed interest and cash. Can either be general fund or more specialist investing particular type of asset, e.g. property or geographical area, e.g. Far East.

■ units

when investing in a unit linked contract, the individual's contribution is used to buy units of equal value. These units will fall or rise in line with the underlying investments.

■ universal life insurance

a form of life insurance that combines term insurance protection with a savings feature. The portion of the funds allocated to the savings feature is invested in a tax-deferred account that typically earns interest at rates comparable to prevailing money market interest rates. A universal insurance policy offers the policy holder the flexibility to change the amount of insurance coverage, the amount of the premium payment and/or the portion of the premium payment allocated to the savings feature.

■ unlimited guaranty

a guaranty agreement that does not include any provisions restricting the amount of debt guaranteed.

■ unplatted land

land that is not platted. Land for which the property description takes the form of a metes and bounds description rather than a lot identification.

■ unqualified opinion

audit opinion not qualified for any material scope restrictions.

■ unrecognised initial net gain

the current unamortised balance, as of the financial statement date, of the off-balance sheet asset for the initial transition asset in a defined benefit pension plan.

■ unrecognised initial net loss

the current unamortised balance, as of the financial statement date, of the off-balance sheet liability for the initial transition obligation in a defined benefit pension plan.

■ upward sloping yield curve

a yield curve depicting a situation in which yields for shorter-term maturities are lower than yields for longer-term maturities. Upward sloping yield curves are common.

■ valuation allowance

method of lowering or raising an object's current value, by adjusting its acquisition cost to reflect its market value by use of a contra account.

■ value added tax

an indirect tax levied on each stage of the production of most goods and services.

■ variable cost

a cost which varies with sales or operational volumes, e.g. materials, fuel, commission payments.

■ variable costs

costs that vary in line with trading activity, e.g. postage, stationery.

■ variance

statistical term that quantifies the dispersion of data, such as rates or prices around the mean. For example, highly volatile rates are rates that are sometimes high above the mean and sometimes way below the mean. Less volatile rates are dispersed closer to the mean and therefore have smaller variances. Similar to, but not the same as, the average amount by which data deviates from the mean for that data.

■ venture capital

investment company whose primary objective is capital growth. New assets invested largely in companies that are developing new ideas, products or processes.

■ void

something which has no legal force from the start.

■ voidable

something which, though it may continue to be valid, may be put aside and be made void, in certain circumstances.

■ waiting period

particularly used in connection with a specified period before joining a pension scheme or becoming eligible for some other employee benefit.

■ waive

to give up a right to something.

■ waiver

the agreement of a lender to overlook a borrower's failure to meet one or more conditions attached to the granting of a credit — conditions that would, in the absence of a waiver, give the lender the right to declare the loan to be in default.

■ warehouse financing

a form of inventory financing in which goods are held in trust as collateral for the loan. Warehouse financing may involve the use of public warehouses in which the goods are held in locations owned by third parties. Alternatively, warehouse financing may involve the use of field warehouses in which the goods are located on the borrower's premises but are controlled by an independent third party.

■ warrant

option to purchase additional securities from the issuer.

■ whole loans

a phrase used to describe mortgage loans when the owner of the debt also owns the servicing rights. In other words, mortgage loans that have not had the servicing separated.

■ whole of life

essentially, a protection policy with investment content that remains in force until death, at which point it pays out. As the contract is capable of acquiring value, it is possible to surrender the policy.

■ wholesale banking

banking business conducted exclusively or almost exclusively with large corporations, governments, financial institutions, trusts, etc.

■ winding up

the termination of a pension scheme, where assets are used to purchase the accrued liabilities of the pension scheme, either by purchasing immediate and deferred annuities, or transfer to another pension scheme.

■ withdrawals

1. any reduction in funds maintained in a deposit account or mutual fund.

2. Funds of a proprietorship or a partnership that are directly removed from the firm by the proprietor or partners. These are distributions distinct from salary,

commission, bonus or rent payments paid to proprietors or partners.

■ withholding

amount withheld or deducted from employee salaries by the employer and paid by the employer, for the employee, to the proper authority.

■ withholding tax

tax deducted by many countries from income payments such as dividends, interest and royalties. May be offset, reduced or negated by Double Taxation Relief.

■ without recourse

a lending expression that means loans or leases that have been acquired from an original lender with no guaranty from the originator.

■ work in progress

inventory account consisting of partially completed goods awaiting completion and transfer to finished inventory.

■ working capital

in accounting and finance, used to describe the amount, if any, by which a business's current assets exceed its current liabilities. Also used more loosely to describe the funds a firm has available to run its day-to-day business affairs.

■ working capital conversion cycle

an accounting and financial phrase used to describe the dynamics of short-term cash flows that occur during the normal operations of a business. The working capital conversion cycle is the circular process of borrowing money first to purchase inventory, then to carry that inventory and finally to carry the resulting accounts receivable that are the proceeds of the inventory. When the receivables are paid, the firm can then use the proceeds to either repay the borrowing or to start the cycle all over again by purchasing new inventory.

■ writ

court order instructing someone either to do or not to do something.

■ writer

the party that sells an option contract. Also called the option grantor or maker.

■ yield

the annual return on an investment expressed as a percentage on an annual basis. For interest-bearing securities, the yield is a function of the rate, the purchase price, the income that can be earned from the reinvestment of income received prior to maturity, cal, or sale and the time from purchase to maturity, call, or sale. Different formulas or methods are used to calculate yields.

■ yield curve slope

yield curves also describe the amount of difference between short-term and long-term rates. A yield curve that depicts the customary situation of long-term rates higher than short-term rates is called an upward sloping or positively sloped yield curve. A yield curve depicting the less common occurrence of short-term rates higher than long-term rates is called a downward sloping, negatively sloped or inverted yield curve. When long-term rates are much higher than short-term rates, the yield curve is steep. When long-term rates are virtually the same as short-term rates, the yield curve is flat.

■ **yield-to-maturity (YTM)**

the annual percentage yield of a security, calculated in a specific manner. The yield-to-maturity is the single discount rate that, when applied to all future interest and principal payments, produces a net present value equal to the purchase price of the security.

■ **zero cost collar**

the purchase of a floor (or cap) option with the proceeds realised from simultaneous sale of a cap (or floor) option. The levels of the floor and cap are selected so that the proceeds from the option sold exactly offset the cost of the option purchased, resulting in a net transaction cost of zero.

■ **zero coupon bond**

a type of debt security that does not pay periodic interest. Zero coupon securities are bought and sold at prices that are less than the par value of the securities. The discount, or difference between the principal paid to purchase the security and the principal returned at maturity, constitutes the investor's return.

■ **zero dividend preference shares**

a share with a predetermined growth rate, but which does not pay dividends.

■ **zero rated**

goods (such as food, books and periodicals) taxed at the lowest, nil, band of VAT. A supplier can reclaim VAT paid in the course of production. All exports are zero rated.

■ **Zero-Balance Account (ZBA)**

a cash management service offered by banks. A bank checking account that can accept deposits and/or make disbursements but that is always maintained at a zero balance. The zero balance is maintained by transferring just enough funds from or to a concentration account to offset each day's activity. The concentration account is sometimes called the parent account and the zero-balance account is sometimes called the daughter or subsidiary account.

■ **zero-coupon bond**

bond on which the holder receives only one payment at maturity which includes both principal and interest from issuance to maturity.

■ **zoning**

a designation given to a particular geographic area by the local government, to regulate the type of use and the density of development permitted for properties in that area. For example, areas may be zoned to allow only residential development.